Issues for
Community College Leaders
in a New Era

George B. Vaughan
and Associates

Foreword by Arthur M. Cohen

Issues for Community College Leaders in a New Era

 Jossey-Bass Publishers
San Francisco • Washington • London • 1983

ISSUES FOR COMMUNITY COLLEGE LEADERS IN A NEW ERA
by George B. Vaughan and Associates

Copyright © 1983 by: Jossey-Bass Inc., Publishers
433 California Street
San Francisco, California 94104
&
Jossey-Bass Limited
28 Banner Street
London EC1Y 8QE

Library of Congress Cataloging in Publication Data
Main entry under title:

Issues for community college leaders in a new era.

Bibliography: p. 249
Includes index.
1. Community colleges—United States—Administration—
Addresses, essays, lectures. I. Vaughan, George B.
√LB2328.I87   1983   378'.052   83-48167
ISBN 0-87589-586-7

Manufactured in the United States of America

The paper in this book meets the guidelines for
permanence and durability of the Committee on
Production Guidelines for Book Longevity of the
Council on Library Resources.

JACKET DESIGN BY WILLI BAUM

Published in cooperation with
ERIC Clearinghouse
for Junior Colleges

FIRST EDITION

Code 8333

EDUCATIONAL RESOURCES INFORMATION CENTER
ERIC Clearinghouse For Junior Colleges
UNIVERSITY OF CALIFORNIA, LOS ANGELES

The Jossey-Bass
Higher Education Series

Foreword

Leaders of public agencies always seem to be facing crises: complaints from the clients they are supposed to serve; dissension among their staff; competition from other public agencies; not enough money to operate the enterprise. Community college leaders suffer notably from these problems. Things are never quite right. Some group of students complains that they are not being treated properly. Proprietary trade schools and universities compete for clients. The faculty are unhappy and the administrators are disloyal. The funds never reach desired levels and the money that is allocated is so earmarked that the leader's discretion is hampered.

Leaders respond to the problems in different ways. Some try to ignore them, knowing with a wisdom derived from experience that the concerns will resolve themselves or soon be superseded by other problems seemingly more urgent. Others shift the burden by organizing committees, task forces, and similarly structured groups to debate and define the issues. Some leaders are masters at political accommodation, shifting the reasons for the problem and the burden that it brings to one

or another group within or outside the college. Some speak
often with their fellows in other institutions, asking how they
have dealt with similar problems. Some keep their staff agitated
by convening crisis-of-the-day meetings, while others play a role
as statesmen, rising above the quotidian wrangling over short-
term issues.

     This book is for community college leaders of any persua-
sion. It calls attention to today's issues and, by putting those
issues in historical perspective, shows how they can be either resolved or turned to advantage. The authors of this book consider
the problems and opportunities presented by changing student
types, policies affecting women, the nagging issues of transfer
and dropout, the never-ending quest for ways of presenting general education. They examine the complexities of developmental education and the issues surrounding the concept and operation of student services. They discuss the importance of literacy
in the community college and how to keep the college from becoming an institution for the middle class. They show how federal policies affect institutional growth and how governance affects leadership. Through it all they point to ways that the
leaders can concern themselves with issues in order to effect
positive change.

     One of the book's more useful functions is pointing out
that the problems are not new, that they have always existed in
greater or lesser form. The only thing that changes is the urgency with which they are brought to the leaders' attention.
Fiscal problems are not new; they merely have changed complexion. In the 1960s it was necessary to find money to build
new colleges, hence the acquisition of capital funds was the issue. In the 1970s contracts negotiated through collective bargaining led to sizable salary increases for the staff, and funds
had to be found to provide for that. The limitations put on enrollments in the 1980s have led to shifting priorities within the
institutions, and the trend toward states bearing a higher proportion of the budget has changed internal patterns of fund allocation.

     Many leaders seek the ready answer, the immediate solu-
tion. Only by facing the reality that there are no instant answers

to complex and continuing problems can we derive the perspective that true leaders must maintain. Fiscal problems, client complaints, staff unrest, agency competition, program generation and termination—each is part of a web of related problems and each affects all the others. And each response must be placed in that context.

Contemporary leaders often state that community colleges have never before been faced with declining enrollments of eighteen-year-old full-time students. However, at the beginning of World War II an entire cohort of potential students was taken away to serve in the nation's armed forces. Some college leaders tend to believe that external agencies, whose managers do not understand the unique mission of the community college, are responsible for imposing policies that limit the services colleges can provide. However, the generation of community college leaders before this one seemed to take the position, "Send up the dollars, don't ask the results. We serve all segments of the community equally well and growth is our sine qua non." Certainly the community colleges were within their rights when they advertised, recruited vigorously, offered classes everywhere, developed a seemingly endless array of new programs for new clients—but this made them fair game for the budget cutters. Their successors discovered that an agency that refuses to evaluate itself, to set priorities for programs and people to be served, to limit its own enrollments to numbers and cohorts that it can teach well sets itself up for limitations imposed by its funding agencies.

One issue that cuts across most of the problems noted by the authors in this volume is the question of whether the community college shall develop further as an adult education center or as a full participant in the stream of graded education that reaches from kindergarten to the doctorate or professional degree. The leaders who believe that their institutions can do both with equal facility engage in harmful self-deception. Half a century ago the universities recognized that the two functions were so different that they had best be kept apart. They organized extension centers and adult education divisions functioning separately from the academic degree programs. Such a separation may have to be faced by community college leaders today. Whether or not they do so, they will still be forced to shift more of the costs of lifelong learning or community service programs to the participants. And whether or not the colleges tend more to put themselves in a position to screen students through to program completion and/or transfer to senior institutions, they will find themselves engaged more in testing and sorting students, enforcing prerequisites, and assessing program effects. In summary, as the funding guidelines become more stringent, program priorities will inevitably be brought to the fore.

Leadership is an essential dimension in any agency. The educational leaders in community colleges must have a sense of history and context into which they can place the issues that come to their attention daily. It is not sufficient for them to shift the burden, to shirk the responsibility. Their institutions deserve leaders who can sustain consistent directions and articulate internal policies that match external realities. And leaders do make a difference; if they did not, all colleges that operate under the same sets of directives in a single state would look alike.

George Vaughan is an educational leader. His making the effort to put together this volume is only one indication of his concern for the dimensions and responsibilities of community college leadership. Those of us who are committed to these institutions as significant forces in American education owe him a debt of gratitude.

Los Angeles, California   Arthur M. Cohen
August 1983

Preface

The community college emerged as a major force in higher education after World War II and grew steadily for the next quarter century. At one time during this period, community colleges were opening at the rate of almost one a week—a source of amazement and pride for those Americans who advocated that two years of postsecondary education be available to virtually all Americans.

Support for the community college during its boom period was more than rhetoric: community after community put up money for "its" college; more important in the long run, state legislators across the country appropriated funds, creating—in fact if not in name—state systems of community colleges. For old-time junior and community college leaders and for new graduates of the amply funded W. K. Kellogg Foundation programs, it seemed as if the millennium had arrived. The community college appeared to be supported and loved by all.

Moving from the affluence of the 1960s and 1970s into the more austere 1980s, the community college appears to have reached a watershed in its development. Leadership has changed at the national level as well as at many leading community colleges and graduate schools. Funds, while by no means disappearing, are becoming more difficult to obtain as federal, state, and local legislators face other priorities. Teaching styles once espoused as innovations are being abandoned as mere fads. Governance has not fostered the collegial model some leaders hoped for, and enrollment caps are now a reality in many states. In addition, new emphasis is being placed on age-old questions such as what constitutes a quality education and what portion of the cost of education should be paid for by the student and what part by society.

Today, the community college is in a rare, perhaps even unique, position to be critically examined, for many of its leaders were directly involved in leading it through its evolution and are still active in the community college scene. University professors and college administrators have also been able to observe the community college during its development.

In spite of the community college's entry into what appears to be a new era in its development, much of the literature dealing with it remains "promotional" rather than analytical. The time is right for a major statement on the community college—its successes, its failures, and its potential. I believe this volume makes that statement, that it will be useful in understanding the community college at this critical point in its development, and that it will provide sound perspectives that will serve those leaders well who will move their institutions into the next era of community college development.

This book began taking shape in my mind approximately three years ago. At that time, I had just edited and contributed to a volume in the *New Directions for Community Colleges* series entitled *Questioning the Community College Role*. While I feel that that volume makes a significant statement on the role of the community college, its primary purpose was to raise questions rather than to provide answers. It is, furthermore, heavily oriented toward the views of the social critics. The need still existed, I felt, for a perspective that would help administrators deal with current issues and plan for the future. The void could be filled, in part, by a book written from the vantage point of leaders who are familiar with the community college, yet who have not accepted its role blindly.

A central theme of the book is that the community college has failed to achieve its full potential in a number of areas, and that in order to reach that potential leaders need to rekindle the enthusiasm and spirit of adventure that marked the community college during the 1960s and 1970s. If the people in leadership positions are to lead, they must understand those forces in society that shape the community college's role. As the community college continues to evolve, as the populations it serves expand and change, we who are committed to the success of the community college need to reexamine and clarify its mission—and pursue it with new energy. The authors of this volume are all acutely aware of these needs and illuminate them in terms of specific issues developed in three main topic areas: student populations and their needs, the special functions of the community college, and management issues community college leaders must face.

Following a brief historical perspective, the authors of Part One discuss the problems and challenges of the community college's complex role as provider of vocational, collegiate, and adult education to the students who come to it from virtually all segments of society; the threat of the community college becoming exclusively a middle-class college; and the reality of community college efforts to serve women adequately. In Part Two, chapter authors look closely at developmental education and the challenge to this essential function posed by new demands for accountability; the need to reformulate and bolster general education programs—and some guidelines for doing just that; ways of strengthening the ongoing transfer function, which links the community college with the larger system of higher education; and ways of adjusting to the drastically changing roles of student services. Part Three focuses on forces and trends affecting leadership decisions. The need for leaders to recognize and respond to broad national trends is considered a course that may allow leaders to realize ideas that are frequently only imagined. Ways governance can be used as a basis for renewing the institution by strengthening faculty commitment and staff development are considered in detail. The need for college leaders to take a hand in shaping governmental policies that evolve in response to major forces affecting higher education—such as population trends and the need for diversity—is clearly stated. The potential benefits of making creative and constructive alliances with business and industry are discussed— along with some important caveats. Finally, the assets that have served the community college well up to now are evaluated in terms of the crucial contribution the community college makes to maintaining an informed, literate society in an age of increasingly sophisticated communication and technology.

In summary, this volume helps fill the void that exists between the views of the social critics who tend to dwell on the community college's shortcomings and between the defenders who feel that the community college can do no wrong. Certainly there is a middle ground where educational leaders can discuss issues and find solutions to those issues. This book, I feel, is a step in the right direction.

I wish to extend my thanks to those who helped bring this volume together. Arthur M. Cohen helped shape the idea for the book. As a friend and professional colleague, he listened, cajoled, and commented when needed and encouraged me to stretch my own thinking regarding the role of the community college. I appreciate the support of my colleagues at Piedmont Virginia Community College, especially P. J. Jenkins, Robert Ross, and Robert Templin. Donald E. Puyear, my friend and colleague, made a number of helpful suggestions as to how the volume could best serve leaders. I am deeply indebted to the authors who contributed to the volume. Finally, to my sons, Brandt and Andrew, for their patience and understanding and to my wife, Peggy, for her support and help, I am indeed grateful.

Charlottesville, Virginia   George B. Vaughan
August 1983

Contents

The Authors

George B. Vaughan is president of Piedmont Virginia Community College. He received his B.A. degree (1959) from Emory and Henry College in economics, his M.S. degree (1965) from Radford University in history, and his Ph.D. degree (1970) from Florida State University in higher education. In addition, he completed two years of postgraduate work in history at the University of Tennessee and participated in Harvard University's Institute for Educational Management. He received the Alumnus Award for Distinguished Achievement from Emory and Henry College. He is visiting professor of education at the Center for the Study of Higher Education, University of Virginia.

Vaughan's main professional role has been that of community college administrator. He served as dean of instruction at two community colleges and was founding president of Mountain Empire Community College, all in Virginia. Vaughan has published over thirty articles and reviews in numerous publications, including *Change, Community and Junior College Journal, National Forum, Community/Junior College Research Quarterly, Community College Frontiers,* and *Community Col-*

lege Review. He edited and contributed to the volume entitled *New Directions for Community Colleges: Questioning the Community College's Role* (1980). In addition, he has authored or coauthored several topical papers and monographs and has contributed chapters to several publications.

Vaughan formerly served on the board of directors of the American Association of Community and Junior Colleges (AACJC). He is currently a member of the executive committee of the President's Academy, an affiliate of the AACJC, and is a member of the editorial board of the *Community College Review.*

W. Clark Ames is assistant to the chancellor of the Maricopa Community College District, Phoenix, Arizona.

Alexander W. Astin is professor of higher education at the University of California at Los Angeles and president of the Higher Education Research Institute, Los Angeles.

Donald E. Barshis is executive director of the Center for the Improvement of Teaching and Learning, City Colleges of Chicago, Illinois.

Chester H. Case is director of the general education project at Los Medanos College, Walnut Creek, California, and visiting lecturer in higher education at the University of California at Berkeley.

Arthur M. Cohen is director of the ERIC Clearinghouse for Junior Colleges, president of the Center for the Study of Community Colleges, and professor of higher education at the University of California at Los Angeles.

Billie Wright Dziech is associate professor of English at University College, the University of Cincinnati, Ohio.

Paul A. Elsner is chancellor of the Maricopa Community College District, Phoenix, Arizona.

J. Wade Gilley is professor of higher education and senior vice-president of George Mason University, Reston, Virginia.

Thomas R. Guskey is associate professor of education at the University of Kentucky, Lexington.

Harold L. Hodgkinson is senior fellow of the Institute for Educational Leadership, Washington, D.C.

Dorothy M. Knoell is postsecondary education administrator of the Postsecondary Education Commission, Sacramento, California.

Robert H. McCabe is president of Miami-Dade Community College, Miami, Florida.

William R. Rhodes is a doctoral candidate in the department of higher and adult education at Arizona State University, Tempe.

Richard C. Richardson, Jr., is professor of higher and adult education at Arizona State University, Tempe.

Suzanne B. Skidmore is administrative assistant to the president at Miami-Dade Community College, Miami, Florida.

Robert G. Templin, Jr., is dean of instruction at Piedmont Virginia Community College, Charlottesville.

Issues for
Community College Leaders
in a New Era

Introduction: Community Colleges in Perspective

George B. Vaughan

During the 1960s and early 1970s community college leaders and speakers at national meetings almost always referred to the "community college movement" when discussing the community college. The implications were that some force greater than any single college or any single person was moving the community college toward its manifest destiny. As community colleges grew in number and as their successes multiplied with every passing day, or so it seemed, its leaders sought a basis for the movement.

When one thinks of movements, one tends to think of the heat of the battle; yet rarely has the community college led broad movements in society or even in individual communities. Rather, it has mirrored them. The community college's stance has often been one of synthesizer and it has played this role well: It has encompassed a number of social, political, economic, and educational movements within its comprehensive philosophy and shaped them into a profound statement about American democracy. The results probably qualify the development of the nation's community colleges to be viewed as a "movement." Thus its supporters, while often failing to interpret events and motives, would seem to be justified in using this term.

1

Past

Broad-based movements—whether religious, political, social, or educational—while looking to the future to fulfill their
destinies, seek their roots in the past. Roots give legitimacy to
present activities and provide the basis for future ones. The
search for roots often consists of identifying a leader or leaders, ascertaining significant events, developing a body of literature, and establishing some sort of framework or organization
with which the movement can be identified. A cynic might say
that if the roots of a movement cannot be documented, they
are invented. The search for roots by community college leaders
has seemed to stem not so much from a desire for historical
understanding as from an attempt to establish legitimate ties
with the past. Historical analysis had little place in the rhetoric
surrounding the community college during the 1960s. Contrary
to the popular mythology of that time, the community college
did not burst full-blown into being. Where does one turn, then,
in tracing the roots of a movement as diverse and as integrated
with American democracy as is the community college in the
United States? Should one turn to Thomas Jefferson who
wanted to place a college within a day's ride of all Virginians
and whose plan for public education in the state would have
opened the doors of public education to the masses on a scale
unprecedented in world history? Certainly Jefferson's belief
that talent and intelligence knew no social or economic barriers
fits well with the modern community college's philosophy as
did his desire to see "a school of technical philosophy to
which craftsmen in various fields of endeavor might come in the
evenings to receive instruction in the sciences applicable to their
occupations" (Wagoner, 1976, p. 34). Even community college
community services administrators can find much support in
the ideas of Jefferson. He advocated that "lectures should be
given in the evening, so as not to interrupt the labors of the
day" and that these lectures "be maintained wholly at the public expense." He even suggested courses for the pleasure gardener
(Koch and Peden, 1944, p. 647).

While much of what the community college does today is

compatible with Jefferson's views on education, it would be a mistake to try to tie the community college closely to Jefferson, for nearly two hundred years separate Jefferson's eloquent proclamation that all men are created equal from the time when equal access to higher education approached reality. American democracy, however, has been the shaping force in the development of the community college, and Jefferson is important as a symbol of that democracy.

Moving from the thinking of Jefferson to that of Justin Morrill, one finds a redefinition of what constitutes higher education in the Morrill Acts of 1862 and 1890 and in the land-grant colleges that resulted. The agricultural and mechanical colleges resulting from the Morrill Acts fought hard to legitimatize courses and programs previously excluded from higher education. Later, community colleges fought—and are still fighting—similar battles. The land-grant colleges would "reduce higher education to the lowest terms and give it the widest extension. In these literal people's colleges instruction should be adjusted to the average district school's standards" (Ross, 1942, p. 89). The land-grant colleges "reached a stratum of students for whom higher or even intermediate training would not otherwise have been available" (Ross, 1942, p. 133). In addition to its philosophical kinship with the early land-grant colleges, the community college borrowed the term *people's college* from them; the term became something of a rallying cry during the boom years of community college growth and is still popular today.

Both the thinking of Jefferson and the broadening of the base of higher education by the land-grant colleges were too far removed to provide the community college with the spiritual underpinnings required for successful launching. Instead, the movement originated with William Rainey Harper, an unlikely source: Harper was the first president of the Rockefeller-endowed University of Chicago. By 1896, drawing on the ideas of William Watts Folwell, president of the University of Minnesota, and Henry D. Tappan, president of the University of Michigan, Harper had established a junior college at the University of Chicago (Griffith, 1976, p. 14). As a result of his work at

Chicago and his influence on Joliet Township High School, Harper is viewed by many as the father of the public junior college in America. As much as anyone, he probably deserves this title.

Had not the break from the four-year university come at Chicago, however, it would surely have come elsewhere. For example, Alexis Lange, "the philosopher of the public junior college" (Griffith, 1976, p. 14), or David Starr Jordan, or the California legislation of 1907 (which authorized public school districts to offer the first two years of college work) shortly would have forced the break and thus the establishment of the junior college.

One of Harper's most important actions was making the distinction between upper- and lower-division work. Perhaps just as important to the community college was his leadership in making the university extension service an integral part of the University of Chicago, for the concept of serving the total community through extension services is central to the community college mission. Influenced by the Chautauqua movement of the late nineteenth and early twentieth centuries (Gould, 1961, p. 21), Harper brought to Chicago the idea that public service should be a part of the university's offerings and should be used for the improvement of mankind. Significantly, Harper influenced the development of the University of Wisconsin. The "Wisconsin Idea" defined the university's campus as the boundaries of the state. The community college applies this idea on a much smaller scale: Its campus is its service region. More important, the extension service instituted many courses and activities that are taken for granted by community colleges today.

If Harper was the father of the early junior college and Lange its philosopher, then Leonard V. Koos was its scholar. Koos published three volumes on the junior college in 1924 and 1925; he continued to write through the late 1960s. Perhaps just as important, Koos, while teaching at the University of Minnesota and the University of Chicago, taught such modern community college leaders as B. Lamar Johnson and S. V. Martorana. Koos's writings, along with those of Walter Crosby Eells, Alexis Lange, and, later, Jessee P. Bogue, provide the community college with a body of literature—a requirement of most broad social movements.

With its founding fathers, its historical documents, and a mission greater than its parts, the junior college needed an organizational framework. The organization began in 1921 with the founding of the American Association of Junior Colleges (AAJC) (Brick, 1964). The association was to serve as national spokesman for the growing junior college movement. Indeed, the junior college was primed to take advantage of the unprecedented opportunities that were to come its way at the end of World War II.

Once the war had ended, the nation faced the problem of translating the ideals for which it had fought into practical plans. Providing all Americans with the opportunity to obtain some form of higher education seemed a step in the right direction. But this was a radical idea during the years following the war. In America in 1947, only slightly over 18 percent of white males and less than 23 percent of white females had completed high school, and only 6 percent of the white population had completed four or more years of college. For the black population, the figures were even more dismal: Fewer than 9 percent of blacks had completed high school, and less than 3 percent had completed four or more years of college (U.S. Bureau of the Census, 1975, p. 380). Before the end of World War II, going to college in America was largely viewed as a privilege and not a right. With the passage of the G.I. Bill, returning veterans had the financial support available to attend college, and their education was seen as an entitlement. The pent-up demand for education, fueled by the G.I. Bill, created a demand for higher education unprecedented in the nation's history.

Higher education was only one of many areas that underwent change after the war. Demographics was another. The baby boom, with which educators are so familiar, saw the age group of fifteen- to twenty-four-year-olds increase by 68 percent between 1955 and 1970. This age group grew from slightly over twenty-one and a half million in 1955 to almost thirty-six and a half million in 1970 (U.S. Bureau of the Census, 1975, p. 10). These children, many of whose fathers served in World

War II or the Korean War, probably did not even consider whether going to college was a right or a privilege; they assumed, particularly after passage of the National Defense Education Act (NDEA) in 1958 and the Higher Education Acts (1965, 1968, and later amendments), that they could go to college if they so desired. Along with this came a demand for consumer products that seemed almost insatiable during the postwar decades: The real (adjusted for inflation) Gross National Product (GNP), which represents the best single measure of a society's wealth (or its ability to pay for services such as higher education) grew at an average rate of 3.95 percent during the decade of the 1950s, at a 4 percent rate during the 1960s, and at a 3.19 percent rate during the 1970s (U.S. Department of Labor, 1981, pp. 234–235). Further stimuli for higher education were the increasing need for skilled workers, which developed with wartime technology and continued; the increased rate of productivity; the decreased number of unskilled jobs; and several other factors. The stage was set for dramatic changes in American higher education during the period following World War II.

The two-year college was in an excellent position to take advantage of these propitious circumstances. One missing element was a national statement regarding the role community colleges might play in meeting the educational needs of postwar America. The sentiments for universal higher education were forcefully and eloquently expressed by the President's Commission on Higher Education for American Democracy. Reporting in 1947, the Truman Commission, as it is popularly known, advocated a network of locally controlled colleges which would place higher education within commuting distance of a larger number of Americans. The commission felt that as much as 49 percent of the population could profit from two years of education beyond high school. The commission used the term community college to describe these locally controlled institutions.

With the publication of the Truman Commission's report, the community college had its manifesto. The report was a clarion call for the nation to utilize the human talents of all segments of society. Symbolically, it was the final link in the chain of events that was to make the community college an integral part of higher education. The two-year college of the future was to be, for the most part, the public community college.

The demands for higher education in the 1960s worked to the advantage of the community college, for many four-year colleges and universities were literally bursting at the seams. If America was to fulfill the dream of universal higher education, some means were needed for serving the masses—particularly the academically undeveloped members of society. The community college served as the four-year institution's safety valve by enrolling students, who, for various reasons, were not prepared to enroll in four-year institutions. By relieving the pressure on the four-year colleges and universities, the community college permitted the nation to continue a policy of selective admissions based on merit. America had apparently reconciled its achievement-oriented society with its belief in equal opportunity for all.

Community colleges found state legislators in virtually all states willing to support the seemingly inexpensive community colleges with their politically appealing open door and their commitment to promoting the nation's free enterprise system. Legislative support at the state level resulted in the building of statewide (in fact, if not always in name) systems of community colleges. At the national level, the various student aid grants resulted in students being able to attend the state-supported community colleges with little or no cost to the individual. By keeping the cost low through state and federal aid and by providing a service that was valued by society, the community college again found itself in a highly favorable market situation. The nation's dream of open access to higher education had become a reality. (It is possible, however, that the demand for higher education, especially at the low-cost community college, was kept high through underpricing the service to the individual.)

A further advantage to the community college was that while having roots in the past, it was not bound by tradition to the extent that most four-year colleges and universities were. Consequently, it was able to try new things without the disruption that often accompanies breaking with tradition. Furthermore, the community college gradually shook its image of being grades thirteen and fourteen of the local high school and was accepted as a part of higher education. In many respects, the community college had the best of both worlds in that it was free to innovate while being accepted into the higher education family.

Developing as it did in the middle ground of society, where economic demands, political aspirations, and educational needs converged, the community college seemed to have virtually everything going for it—success seemed inevitable. Indeed, the merging of the various forces that shaped the community college was not the clash of town and gown for which American higher education is famous; to the contrary, it was more like love at first sight.

Present

Society's enthusiasm over the community college—so warm during the 1960s—has chilled a bit: Legislators are cutting funds; regulatory commissions and governing boards are cutting programs; the federal government is cutting student aid; administrators are cutting faculty. All is not well in the people's college.

While a problem-free golden era of community college development was never a reality, it seems, nevertheless, that today's community college leaders are faced with an inordinate number of obstacles and frustrations. In addition to the loss of funds, tuition increases and the limiting of enrollments threaten to change the constitution of the student population. The community college, in spite of its claim to uniqueness, still emulates the four-year college and university in many of its practices. Governance, once viewed as a means of raising faculty participation and professionalism, has settled down to a somewhat bureaucratic model; in some cases, it has substituted collective bargaining for faculty involvement. The mission is still unclear; as late as 1980, Edmund J. Gleazer, Jr., former president of the American Association of Community and Junior Colleges (AACJC) and long-time spokesman for the movement, saw as a major need the clarification of the community college mission.

Social critics claim that rather than promoting social mobility, the community college has served as a means of preserving the status quo. The issue of quality is again forcing community college leaders (and society in general) to raise John Gardner's question "Can we be equal and excellent too?" Indeed, community college leaders are now asking what role the community college has in raising the level of literacy in our society—and the Governor of Virginia claims that remedial higher education is a contradiction in terms. Some states are now labeling many community services activities in the community college as frivolous and therefore unnecessary.

Perhaps the community college has promised too much. During the 1960s, it tried to solve large social problems by pledging relevance, open admissions, special courses for all segments of society, low-cost instruction, and class meetings at times that were convenient for homemakers and full-time employees as well as for full-time students. Indeed, the community college seemed to be the Ellis Island of higher education, holding its door open to the poorly educated, the employed and the unemployed, the capable and the not so capable. But the open door of the community college, mirroring society at large, has not been able to eliminate poverty, unemployment, illiteracy, or social inequality. Rather than dwelling on unattained goals, however, this volume seeks ways to profit from past mistakes by putting them into perspective with issues facing community college leaders today.

Mission

How can today's leaders utilize the experiences of the past to build a better future for the community college and thus the nation? They can start by clarifying the mission of the community college. This mission is difficult to articulate for a number of reasons, among which are the following: it is constantly evolving and is thus in a constant state of flux; each college has its own mission, which, while it tends to mesh with many of the facets of the national mission as articulated by national spokesmen, nevertheless takes on a local flavor. Further, the change in

leadership at the national level in 1981, with Gleazer's retire-
ment and his replacement by Dale Parnell as president of the
AACJC, takes the movement in a new direction. For example,
Gleazer viewed the role of the community college as a catalyst
for community renewal; Parnell views the community college in
a more traditional way as a provider of services, working in partnership with business and industry to "put America back to
work." Finally, the mission has been unclear because community college leaders, instead of articulating the mission, have,
either out of fear of being misunderstood or ignorance of the
mission, tended to hide behind clichés, meaningless expressions,
or an all-conquering stance. These issues and others that distort
or obfuscate the mission are subtle and difficult to deal with.

Yet some recent events, while not necessarily clarifying
the mission, have brought it into focus as a topic of discussion
at national conventions and in the literature. One such event has
been the revision of the mission statement of the AACJC. In
1981, the board of directors, working with Parnell, clarified
and simplified the mission of the community college's national
organization and thus provided the basis for clarifying and sim-
plifying the mission statement of the local community college.
A second important event was the publication in 1981 of *Financing Community Colleges: An Economic Perspective* by
David W. Breneman and Susan C. Nelson. Published by the
prestigious Brookings Institution, this volume resulted in a national debate about the community college's mission. Breneman
and Nelson's critical analysis provided a much needed look at
the role of the community college by persons outside the movement and helped focus the attention of community college
leaders on the mission of their institutions. A third significant
event, and one that has not received the attention that it deserves, was the publication in 1980 of the AACJC/ERIC monograph, *The Impossible Dream? Financing Community College's
Evolving Mission*. Written by Richard C. Richardson, Jr., and
Larry L. Leslie, the volume gets to the heart of the current dilemma regarding mission. The authors avow that "to date, the
emerging conflict between institution aspirations for continuing
mission development and the restraints imposed by financing

arrangements designed to promote stability or even phased decline has not been confronted squarely" (p. 44).

While the above volumes and statements are useful and can serve as a basis for mission clarification, they will not be read by the general public and will only rarely be read by legislators. The role of interpreting the community college mission in a way that can be understood by the public and in a way that can be supported by legislators remains primarily the responsibility of the college president. This is as it should be; however, to date, much of what the mission is and what it can be is lost in the rhetoric served up by this leadership.

Robert H. McCabe and Suzanne Skidmore point to what appears to be a major reason for the fuzziness surrounding the community college mission. They surmise that "when viewed in the light of present day American society, all levels of the educational system have failed significantly to adjust as societal needs changed—the evolutionary process in education seems to have become 'stuck' in the 1960s" (1982, p. 3). There is some evidence to suggest that attempts to interpret the community college's mission are very much "stuck in the 1960s." For example, recently the vice-chancellor of a statewide system of community colleges told a group of deans that "working in the community college is more challenging and more interesting than working in any other part of higher education." The vice-chancellor's statement is typical of the view that tends to reinforce stereotypes rather than challenge the leadership. To illustrate further, literally hundreds of times each year community college presidents tell local service clubs and various other audiences that the community college "is unique," "is uniquely American," "cares about students," "serves the total community," and that its faculty members are "employed to teach and not research." These, and any number of similar statements, shed little light on the mission of the community college. Indeed, today even the local Kiwanis Club needs to hear more than glib, meaningless phrases if the community college is to be understood and supported. Legislators certainly deserve (and are demanding) more than warmed-over phrases when they are asked to appropriate the millions of dollars requested by community colleges.

What can be done to interpret the community college mission? Perhaps the most important thing is for those persons responsible for interpreting and selling the mission to realize that the community college may be as much in a watershed period now as it was in the 1960s. Or, as K. Patricia Cross hypothesizes, "the late 1970s and early 1980s represent a plateau between two periods of high energy and a sense of mission in the community colleges. The old ideals that sparked enthusiasm and the sense of common purpose in community colleges have receded, and new ideals have not yet emerged to take their place" (1981b, p. 113). Cross sees the potential for revitalization of the mission in such things as lifelong learning or in remedial education (p. 123). Once community college leaders realize that a vacuum exists between rhetoric and mission, they can begin to interpret the current role of the community college without relying on the clichés of the 1960s.

Is the community college's mission changing or is it simply shifting emphasis? Arthur Cohen would subscribe to the latter view: "The community college of the 1980s will not be qualitatively different from the community college of the 1960s or, for that matter, the 1940s. Although institutional leaders tend to emphasize one or another function at different times, the institutions themselves have not changed their precepts" (1981, p. 11).

Assuming that Cohen and others are correct in asserting that the community college role is relatively stable, what should be the rallying point for revitalizing the mission? To rally around one aspect of the mission, such as lifelong learning or developmental education as Cross suggests, is to focus too narrowly on the problem. A broader perspective around which community college leaders can rally, regardless of the emphasis on a local campus, is that of maintaining institutional integrity. Institutional integrity is threatened by several trends, each of which is explained in the following paragraphs.

The Quality Revolution. Will higher admission standards result in the exclusion of ill-prepared members of the lower socioeconomic groups, older adults, and others who see the community college as their only chance for a higher education?

To use quality as a means to exclude these segments would be a perversion of what the community college has stood for in the past two decades—open access. McCabe, the community college leader in the quality revolution, does not equate quality with higher admission standards. "Those who advocate increased standards for higher education by limiting admission make a serious mistake. . . . Retaining the open-door concept for the community college is more essential than ever. The nation cannot afford to give up on those who have academic skill deficiencies. America needs more, rather than fewer, well-educated individuals" (McCabe and Skidmore, 1982, p. 5). If institutional integrity is to be maintained, quality must not be interpreted simply to mean higher admission standards and higher academic test scores. Rather, it must be defined in terms that are compatible with the college's mission.

Partnerships with Business and Industry. As community college leaders move to form partnerships with business and industry, they must not let leaders from business and industry (or hospitals or any outside agency) dictate educational policy. Control of curriculum must remain in the hands of the educational leader.

Loss of Comprehensiveness. The community college's open door cannot exist without a comprehensive curriculum. As funds become tight and as community colleges experience new successes with business and industry, there will be a temptation to offer only those programs and courses that can show a profit. Community college leaders must resist this temptation. To let students enter the college without giving them a choice of programs is misleading and intellectually dishonest.

Loss of Funding for Community Services. Today, legislators are hesitant to fund recreational and personal-interest courses. Without funding, community college leaders are often unwilling to meet the community services commitment inherent in most mission statements. Leaders need to determine if community services are to remain a part of the mission, and if so, they need to seek alternate ways of funding them.

Increasing Costs to Students. As tuitions increase and as federal student aid becomes more scarce, members of the lower socioeconomic groups will find it increasingly difficult to attend the community college. Leaders must be sensitive to the needs of these groups and seek means to ensure that financial assistance is available for them. To exclude the members of lower socioeconomic groups is to abort a part of the mission that community colleges have performed so well in the past.

Abrogation of Decision-Making Powers. Fewer and fewer important decisions are being made by the campus administrator. Part of the problem is that community college leaders have not successfully distinguished between decisions educators should be making and those that rightfully should be made by legislators and external agencies. A challenge to community college leadership is to articulate its role in such a manner as to delineate lines of authority clearly. As encroachment on the campus decision-making process occurs, leaders must be prepared to fight. To abrogate willingly the right to make educational decisions is to trust institutional integrity to forces outside the community college campus.

If community college leaders interpret their mission in light of maintaining institutional integrity, it can be brought into focus and explained in terms that relate to the local campus as well as to the national scene and can be understood by the public as well as by local and national legislators—especially if objective criteria are used to demonstrate what the community college has accomplished and can accomplish in the future. To continue to promote the community college mission without bringing that mission into sharper focus is to gamble on a faith in the community college that the current situation does not support.

Perhaps more than any other factor, funding influences the shape of the mission. "Form follows function," a once-popular tenet of architecture, might be rephrased for the community college, "mission follows funding," especially in regard to aspects of the mission that any given college emphasizes. Breneman and Nelson (1981) give a good analysis of the role of funding in relationship to the mission, as do Richardson and Leslie (1980). Breneman and Nelson state the challenge to community college leaders aptly: "Community college leaders must draw upon the unique strengths of their own institutions as they seek to resolve the inevitable dilemma posed by changing missions and restrictive financing" (p. 215).

Community college leaders have always been very much aware of just how important funding is to the mission since almost all public community colleges' funding is based on enrollments. During the 1960s and much of the 1970s, preoccupation with enrollments became something of a mania among administrators, especially in statewide systems where one college was constantly compared with other colleges in the system. The comparison always related in one way or another to enrollments.

A number of examples demonstrate how funding influences the mission. The most common, and perhaps the most blatant, is the offering of practically every type of course for credit in order to receive state funding (Lombardi, 1978, p. 25). As the definition of a credit course was stretched to its limits, the mission of the community college became broader. Conversely, as states now redefine what constitutes a credit course, the mission will become more restrictive. Other examples are more subtle. For instance, in several states older citizens can now take courses for free. When senior citizens were counted in the funding formula and therefore generated state revenues for the colleges, they were aggressively recruited; when the law no longer permitted them to be counted in the funding formula, they were not only not recruited but were seen as a nuisance on some campuses.

Probably the best example of how funding influences mission is in the area of community services. If the state or locality funds community services or if the college is able to earn additional revenue through community services, the college emphasizes this aspect of the mission; if no funding is forthcoming, little emphasis is given to community services. Even in California, a state noted for its outstanding community services programs, community colleges have found their missions altered with the passage of Proposition 13, an act that has drastically cut the funding for community services. According to Ireland (1982, p. 11), the number of participants in community services activities has not declined markedly; however, "emphasis is placed on those programs that have the greatest potential to generate income and be self-supporting." In discussing the decline in certain types of activities, Ireland notes that "the most significant decline occurred in cultural events and community development activities, those programs that generally do not have a high capacity for generating income."

Does pointing out that mission follows funding merely state the obvious and thus preclude discussion? Yes and no. The implications of offering recreational and avocational courses for credit in order to boost numbers of full-time equivalent students (FTEs) are rather obvious to most community college administrators and even to some legislators. What is not so obvious is the shaping of the mission that can occur when funding is withheld. Although the community services mission has survived in California in spite of Proposition 13, in other states community services courses have declined in both number and variety. This decline has taken place not with a bang—or even a whimper—but in silence as many community college leaders have stood idly by. There is some evidence to suggest that developmental education may come under fire in some states. Will community college leaders passively accept cuts in funding that will mean that developmental education will no longer be a part of the mission? If so, what is next—the transfer function? If the campus leadership is to play a major role in charting the direction of the community college of the future, leaders must be sensitive to the role funding plays in shaping the mission and must seek funds for that part of the mission which they feel is worth fighting for.

Any realistic perspective for viewing the community college must deal with the question of who makes the decisions. Local control was (and in some instances still is) one of the distinguishing features of the community college. The Truman Commission of 1947 advocated local control, as have numerous state and local laws. Yet for many community colleges local control never existed, and if it did, it is less pronounced on most campuses today than in the past.

Community college leaders are well aware of the shift

from local to state funding and of the subsequent shift from local to state control. While funding is the major source of state control, it is not the only one. S. V. Martorana, a long-time and astute observer of state legislation affecting community colleges, notes that legislation does not have to be related to funding to affect community colleges. He points out that recent legislative trends have increased state control "while eroding institutional autonomy through measures that less visibly but effectively bound institutions through numerous procedural regulations" (Martorana and Smutz, 1981, p. 33). Martorana further notes that community colleges "are increasingly being caught in a web of legislation intended to apply broadly to other governmental entities as well as to community colleges" (p. 34). Finally, "what appears to be happening is that institutional activities increasingly have been constructed by a myriad of minor laws and procedural regulations rather than by broader policy direction" (p. 34). Loss of local control, then, is often subtle but nevertheless insidious. A well-known example of a policy that erodes local control but is not directly related to funding is that of state legislators granting collective bargaining rights to state employees. The result has been a restructuring of the approach to governance on many campuses and a loss of control over decisions that have traditionally been made independent of an outside agency.

In addition to the control over the campus exercised by the state legislature, both the executive and judicial branches make numerous decisions that affect the community college. These decisions range from statewide affirmative action plans to such seemingly innocuous policies as dictating the number of miles state employees (and thus those community college presidents who are state employees) may drive the state automobile.

One can point to numerous other instances where community colleges have been caught in the web of legislative, executive, and judicial decisions. The list is seemingly endless; it includes sunshine laws, tax laws, legislative reliance on staff reports (and thus the increasing importance of staff in the decision-making process), granting of more authority to higher education coordinating bodies, establishment of legislative watchdog committees, hiring freezes, budget cuts, and requiring colleges to generate more nonstate revenue (thus forcing tuition increases). The community college of the future will need to strike a balance between those decisions of external forces that influence campus activities and those decisions that are still in the hands of the local college and its governing board.

It is a truism that no organization is any better than its leaders. A theme of this volume is the role leaders can play in revitalizing the community college mission. The perspective this chapter brings to the role of leadership is therefore brief.

Many present community college leaders achieved their current positions as builders: builders of colleges, of departments of higher education, of bodies of literature, and of a community college philosophy. Several of these builders are still active, but instead of slaying the dragons associated with breaking bold new trails, they have to settle for swatting gnats and stepping on pismires that often inundate them in the form of laws, rules, regulations, and other less-than-exciting challenges. Neverthe-less, without inspired leadership there is little hope of rekin-dling that enthusiasm for community colleges that existed dur-ing the golden era of the 1960s and 1970s.

Community colleges have been fortunate in obtaining good leadership. In addition to the guidance provided by the "founding fathers" such as Koos, Eells, and others, the com-munity college has had a group of transitional leaders who bridged the gap from junior college to community college. Names such as C. C. Colvert, Joseph P. Cosand, Edmund J. Gleazer, Jr., Norman B. Harris, B. Lamar Johnson, John Lom-bardi, Leland Medsker, Raymond Schultz, and James Watten-barger come to mind. These men not only had roots in the past but were leaders during many of the community college's growth years. In addition to serving as spokespersons for the community college, they served as mentors for many of to-day's community college leaders (Vaughan, 1982a). The transi-tional leaders, as was true of the rest of the community col-lege movement, found circumstances favorable to their roles.

The W. K. Kellogg Foundation contributed significantly to developing the current body of leadership. From 1960 to

1974, the foundation gave $4,389,413 to the Junior College Leadership program; over 485 persons were fellows in the program and received financial support from Kellogg. Many of the transitional leaders were associated with the Kellogg programs in one way or another. The majority of the ten universities chosen to house the leadership programs are still turning out community college leaders. Graduates of the Kellogg programs found a ready demand for their services, for when community colleges were opening at the rate of almost one a week, administrators were in short supply.

The Kellogg program and other similar ones did much to train leaders not only through courses dealing with the community college's history and philosophy but also through courses in management, financing, use of computers, statistics, and legal issues, among others. Indeed, many of the leaders who emerged during the 1960s have been so successful that they are still active. While this speaks well of Kellogg's and other leadership programs, of the transitional leaders, and of current leaders, it still presents some problems.

The leaders who emerged during the 1960s are facing different problems now than they faced when both they and the movement were younger. One such problem is how to avoid "burning out." Factors that provided leadership opportunities earlier are now contributing to staleness, boredom, and exhaustion—especially among presidents. Many of the current community college presidents are still in their late forties or early fifties and appear to be "stuck at the top," with no place to go at a time when they are ready for new challenges (Vaughan, 1982b, p. 12). Moreover, the community college movement has matured and is not as exciting in some respects as it was during the boom years. Finally, it is not as easy to move from one position to another one as it was in the past (Vaughan, 1980, p. 12). If presidents are stuck at the top, many well-qualified deans will never get to the top because presidential vacancies are not readily available. While statistics tell us that a number of community college vacancies will be available in the future, the statistics do not tell of high interest rates, young families, and any number of other factors that militate against movement within the profession. If the community college leaders are to set a tone and pace that will kindle new enthusiasm, they must guard against burnout and work to revitalize themselves on their own campuses; to do less is to fail to revitalize the movement as a whole.

Conclusion

This chapter has briefly examined some of the forces in American society that have influenced the development of the community college. It has also shown how the community college has been shaped by events—often mirroring rather than initiating trends. American democracy has provided fertile soil in which the community college has thrived; in turn, the community college speaks profoundly for American democracy through its commitment to open access. Through this commitment, it has seized upon a basic American belief and parlayed that belief into practical reality, opening the door of educational opportunity to millions of people who were previously denied it.

The community college of the past has served society well, but there is no guarantee that the future will be as bright. Leaders must work as diligently in the future as they have in the past if the community college is to contribute its best.

Serving Today's
Diverse Students

Dorothy M. Knoell

The community college's reputation for excellence in teaching is due in large measure to its commitment to meeting the needs of students with highly diverse educational backgrounds and wider ranges of skills, abilities, interests, and motivations than are usually found among students in collegiate institutions. These colleges enroll students irrespective of their mastery of the basic skills needed for college-level work and help them progress as far as their motivation and ability will sustain them. In doing so, community colleges do not abandon academic standards or faculty expectations about student achievement. Instead, they practice flexibility in working with students who do not—and may not ever—fit the traditional model of a college or university student.

In many states, junior colleges developed as extensions of secondary schools, becoming grades 13 and 14 in public school districts. These junior colleges opened opportunities for higher education for large numbers of young people who were academically unprepared for baccalaureate-level work and for others whose immaturity, uncertain interests, or financial conditions made them poor risks for traditional, four-year colleges. So great was the success of the junior colleges in offering remedial and developmental programs and services for those not quite prepared for college that they were asked by their communities to take on ever more difficult tasks of instruction for

21

undereducated adults. Often the only floor for admission was age eighteen or high school graduation—with special provisions for some high school dropouts below age eighteen. California law requires its community colleges to admit all who meet the age requirement and who can profit from the instruction offered. The colleges' interpretation of the law has been that anyone who applies can benefit in some way from what is offered, regardless of mental capacity or previous educational attainment.

During the last few decades, junior colleges have become community colleges, at least in the public sector, and the concept of the community college has been expanded to include the notion of comprehensiveness. By the 1980s, community colleges had expanded their mission and function to such an extent that the only limitation on their offerings was that the curricula not exceed the first two years of college-level work. Students who enroll for two consecutive years are a minority in many institutions. Those who graduate from two-year programs often take longer than two years for many reasons, among them the need for remediation before starting a degree program, part-time enrollment, and uncertainty about choice of major or career. However, community college growth since the 1960s has occurred primarily among students who enroll for one year or less and who have other than associate degree or transfer objectives.

Definitions and Concepts

An examination of community college functions requires a clear understanding of frequently used terms.

Postsecondary Education. With the advent of the 1972 Amendments to the federal Higher Education Act of 1965, the concept of postsecondary education came into vogue in both statute and in the literature of education. But no clear distinction was made between postsecondary and higher education. Postsecondary education is assumed to include traditional higher education, adult education, continuing education, lifelong learning, and community education. It may be defined as any kind of organized instruction offered to high school graduates and others at least eighteen years old with no reference to its level of offerings or student qualifications. It may be offered both for credit and on a noncredit basis, as a curriculum leading to an associate or bachelor's degree or as a short-term program defined by student abilities and interests. In all ways, postsecondary education is viewed as more comprehensive and inclusive than higher education with respect to the nature of its purposes, students, programs, and institutions. Community colleges which are truly comprehensive are model postsecondary institutions under these concepts and definitions.

College-Level Work. Definitions of college-level work range from anything taken by a student enrolled in a college or university to only those courses that satisfy baccalaureate degree requirements. Community college courses not certified as baccalaureate-level instruction (that is, not for transfer) are sometimes regarded as less than collegiate. From this viewpoint, vocational, remedial or developmental, personal developmental, and community education courses would not be considered college-level work. Junior colleges, at least in California, were formerly authorized in statute to offer courses at the thirteenth and fourteenth grade levels. This reference to grade level was changed to lower-division level when they became community colleges in statute.

The decline in the preparation of high school graduates for college during the last decade or so, together with the increased enrollment of disadvantaged students, may have led to a decline in standards in college-level courses in institutions with open door admissions policies. Lower standards may mean that less content is covered, that fewer or less demanding assignments are given, that textbooks and other materials are changed to accommodate lower reading levels, and, of course, that grades are inflated or "withdrawals" are substituted for failing or unsatisfactory grades. The designation of courses as college level has more to do with their use in meeting degree requirements than with the level at which they are taught, particularly in community colleges with open door admissions.

Remediation. Remediation has been defined as courses

and support services needed to increase students' skills in reading, writing, and mathematics to a level at which students will have a reasonable chance of succeeding in regular college courses, including vocational, technical, and professional courses (California Postsecondary Education Commission, 1981b). This type of remediation has been a traditional function of community colleges serving young people whose high school preparation was not adequate for baccalaureate-level work. Students availing themselves of such programs were usually ready for regular college work after one semester, during which they often also enrolled for courses outside the areas of English composition and mathematics.

As community colleges have expanded access to postsecondary education, they have had to offer both more and different kinds of remediation for students with serious deficiencies in the basic skills needed for successful college work. Some colleges prefer to call these new programs developmental or preparatory as a means of distinguishing them from the remedial programs offered by four-year institutions. Students now served in community college programs range in ability from the functionally illiterate, many of whom are recent high school graduates, to students planning to transfer to a university who do not qualify for enrollment in a university-level course in English composition. Also under the umbrella of community college remediation are programs for undereducated adults who may be seeking high school equivalency diplomas and students of all ages for whom English is a foreign language. Thus remedial programs offered by community colleges may not all have the objective of preparing students for successful work in regular college courses. Some have the limited objective of functional literacy while others help students achieve the minimum basic skills needed for short-term vocational training. If postsecondary education is defined as any kind of organized instruction in which adults and other high school graduates participate, then all types and levels of remedial programs are postsecondary but not necessarily higher education.

English as a Second Language. Colleges and universities offering English as a foreign or second language (ESL) have traditionally taught it to students who are literate in their native language and able to succeed in college-level work in their own countries without remediation. In such situations ESL is taught as a college-level course, often for credit. Community colleges, however, have much more diverse groups of students who are in need of ESL, some of whom are literate in no language and need basic skills in English only to obtain employment or related training. Their students may include refugees of all ages, primarily from southeast Asia; young adults from migrant farm worker families, most of them Spanish speaking; nonresident aliens working toward two- and four-year degrees from American institutions; and immigrants from many different countries. Thus, community colleges may teach ESL as basic literacy, as remedial-level instruction, and as college-level foreign language instruction.

Vocational Education. Vocational education may be defined as employment preparation offered by both secondary and postsecondary institutions in programs leading to diplomas, certificates, and associate and baccalaureate degrees. Overlap exists between secondary school and community college preparation for many occupations and between community colleges and four-year institutions for others. In addition, area or regional occupational centers offer vocational training to both high school students and adults in many states. Nondegree-granting postsecondary institutions provide training for still other adults who are usually high school graduates. Community colleges offer the widest range of vocational preparation programs of all institutions, taking into account the number and types of jobs for which their students may prepare, the levels of training offered, and the length of time required to obtain entry-level job preparation.

When community colleges were still junior colleges, their vocational programs were terminal in the sense that graduates could not easily transfer from them to a baccalaureate institution. Moreover, federal funding for such programs was contingent on their being declared terminal. The concept of terminal is no longer applicable to community college programs although a large majority of vocational students, at least in California, are seeking short-term training for beginning or upgrading in jobs rather than longer-term vocational training leading to degrees or certificates (Hunter and Sheldon, n.d., pp. 3–5). With the exception of the various technologies, much of the vocational preparation offered by community colleges (such as secretarial studies or automobile mechanics) often is offered by secondary schools and area vocational schools. Community college students who enroll for only the vocational skills courses and have no additional preparation in basic skills or general education may have little advantage over high school graduates competing for the same jobs. Studies of job placement for community college students conducted by Pincus (1980) and Wilms (1975, 1980) have been highly critical of the poor results for vocational students. Few community college practitioners accept the findings and conclusions of either author. Nevertheless, there remains a need for information regarding the placement of community college students, especially of vocational students in short-term programs.

Community Education. Community or continuing education programs and courses, usually noncredit, are not accorded the same status as the transfer and occupational functions of the community colleges by either funding agencies or the general public. Community education has been defined as "courses of study in the liberal arts and sciences determined to be of public (versus private) benefit and designed to assist students and/or students' families to be more self-sufficient and more productive as citizens of the community" (California Community College, 1980, p. 14). Included under this function are personal development and survival (physical and mental health, citizenship, English for foreigners, and courses for older adults and substantially handicapped persons, as well as personal and career development), parenting and family support, community and civic development, and general and cultural courses. Although designated as noncredit courses, they may be offered for credit at the discretion of local governing boards if they meet state standards for credit. Standards that differentiate between credit and noncredit courses require that the former have instructional goals that are common to all students, enroll only students who meet prerequisites, provide for measurement of student performance and the assignment of a grade in the student's permanent record, and, of course, grant credit based on performance.

Community education courses may also be offered without credit, on an open admissions basis, by adult schools administered by unified or high school districts, extension divisions of four-year colleges and universities, and community agencies such as the Young Men's or Young Women's Christian Associations. Community colleges have become involved in this function as part of their larger effort to meet the educational needs of all adults in their communities, particularly those beyond traditional college age who do not want occupational or transfer courses. Taught in the noncredit mode, community education courses can be adapted to the educational levels, needs, and interests of the students at a particular time. Thus, community colleges, in their performance of the community education function, are postsecondary institutions serving adults with a wide range of abilities and interests rather than collegiate institutions offering courses at the lower-division level.

Choices and Limits

A paper prepared by staff of the California Postsecondary Education Commission in May 1981, *Missions and Functions of the California Community Colleges,* set forth a series of issues relating to these institutions which might be summarized in the question: What kind of institution should the community college strive to be in the 1980s? (California Postsecondary Education Commission, 1981a). The paper was written on the assumption that community colleges in California and elsewhere will be required to make choices and set limits in the 1980s because of new fiscal constraints. Differences among states in the nature of their two-year colleges are acknowledged, with the caveat that differences within many states are at least as important as differences between states. The need exists for postsecondary institutions to serve adults of all ages in courses and programs which should respond to their changing needs and for collegiate institutions to provide maximum possible access to both high-level technical education and the liberal arts and sciences which are required for baccalaureate degrees. The conditions for operating as a single institution—the community college—are at issue.

Myth of the Two-Year College. Junior colleges were established as two-year institutions with the expectation that they would offer the first two years of a four-year degree program and that an associate degree would be awarded to students completing these two years. The two-year college image appears to be less and less appropriate as students take more (or less) time to achieve their objectives and as curriculum planners find it difficult to limit associate degree requirements to about sixty units. Some of the reasons for lengthened time to earn the associate degree are: (1) the curricular designs in certain technological fields make it impossible to complete a program in two years; (2) it is unrealistic to expect students requiring remediation to complete a program in two years; and (3) a growing number of students are indecisive about their majors or uncertain of their educational motivation. Furthermore, large numbers of students are pursuing degree or transfer programs as part-time students: In California, over three quarters of all community college students are enrolled part time.

Community college students who enroll for only one semester or one year are becoming more numerous than those who enroll for two or more years. Increased enrollments of older students and those from disadvantaged, low-income family backgrounds have led to decreased interest in associate degree and transfer programs and a concomitant increase in interest in short-term programs leading to employment or skills in self-development, enrichment, or survival.

A longitudinal study completed recently in California showed that about 36 percent of community college students could be assigned to one of seven transfer prototypes, 36 percent to one of five vocational prototypes, and 27 percent to one of six special-interest prototypes (Hunter and Sheldon, n.d., pp. 3–14). Almost 70 percent of the transfer prototypes were regarded as serious transfers, including 22 percent who had majors

in vocational or technical fields. Among the vocational prototypes, more than three quarters had short-term employment
goals; only 14 percent were expected to complete degree or certificate programs in vocational or technical fields. Most of the
remaining students in this prototype were preparing for a second job or career; a few were taking courses to maintain their
licenses. More than 40 percent of the special-interest prototypes
were taking courses related to their hobbies or avocations, some
of which were in vocational fields. One quarter of the special-interest prototype students were called "education seekers" or
"perpetual learners" and were usually taking liberal arts courses.
The authors concluded that a very small percentage of students
in most prototypes enroll in or identify with programs prescribed by the college and that a large proportion are probably
not concerned with either grades or course credit, although all
were enrolled for credit. Students not interested in grades or
credit often withdraw before the end of the semester, whenever
they achieve their own objective or lose interest in the course.

Community colleges are organized and administered as
institutions of higher education insofar as (1) their calendar is
organized on the semester, quarter, or trimester system, (2)
they prescribe one- and two-year curricula leading to certificates, degrees, and transfer, (3) they award units of credit and
grades for courses completed satisfactorily, and (4) they adopt
policies and regulations which are more appropriate for young,
full-time students pursuing traditional objectives than for part-
time students with limited college objectives and outside activities which may detract from their participation in college. As
regionally accredited higher education institutions, community
colleges may have limited flexibility in responding to the educational needs of the adults in their communities, particularly if
most of their offerings are for credit.

Open Door Admissions. Carried to the extreme, an open
door admissions policy gives the right to attend a community
college and to enroll in most freshman-level courses to all high
school graduates and others at least eighteen years old. This
practice may be accompanied by voluntary assessment, counseling and placement, and liberal provisions for withdrawing from

courses. More moderate practices, which still fit into an open admissions policy, admit all high school graduates on the condition that they be counseled about their chances for success in the courses and programs of their choice and restrict the admission of high school dropouts to those who can demonstrate their ability to benefit from the instruction offered. Open admissions policies with no conditions are more characteristic of postsecondary adult schools, which adapt instruction to the level of the students enrolled, than they are of institutions of higher education, which are likely to set certain conditions for admission, including remediation in basic skills.

Three developments during the 1970s tended to foster unconditional open admission in community colleges. First, opposition to standardized testing for admission and placement increased. Such tests were viewed as ethnically biased and less than useful in predicting college success for students in general. Second, disadvantaged students began to question whether the remedial programs which worked well for students who were not quite ready for college work were equally effective for them. Short-term remedial programs were doubled in length and then expanded into a full curriculum for some disadvantaged students, at which point remediation became developmental education. Third, the adoption of policies of nonpunitive grading reduced the risk of failure for inadequately prepared students by allowing them to withdraw without penalty from courses which were too difficult and to enroll the following semester in different or less difficult courses. Some community colleges find it less costly to offer students open admission than to assess, counsel, and place them in courses and programs where they have a reasonable probability of succeeding.

Articulation With High Schools. Community colleges are both sending and receiving institutions: They send their transfer students to four-year institutions and receive a majority of their new students from local high schools. While there are occasional disputes between community colleges and four-year institutions, these institutions usually work together to ensure the smooth transition of community college transfer students into upper-division courses and programs. Four-year colleges and universities also work closely with secondary schools to improve student transition from high school to college, but community colleges seem somewhat ambivalent about articulating with high schools. There are several explanations for this ambivalence. First, there is a considerable amount of duplication in both level of instruction and content between high school and community college course offerings. Except in times of severe fiscal constraint, this condition is of relatively little concern since an important function of the community colleges has been to offer a second chance for higher education to students who are not prepared when they graduate from high school. Second, adults with a break in their education after high school graduation need refresher courses and support services from community colleges to help with their transition into higher education. Meeting the needs of such adults does not require articulation with high schools. Third, open admissions practices mean that community colleges usually do not prescribe a pattern of subjects to be completed in high school as a condition for admission; thus, they may not develop and make known to high school students their expectations about competency to be achieved before enrolling in college. Instead, community colleges tend to project an image of not caring about the kind or quality of preparation possessed by their new students; deficiencies can be made up when they enroll in remedial and other types of courses.

Remedial Education. Once the major responsibility of community colleges, remediation is now being carried out at most institutions of higher education. Evidence from many sources suggests that high school graduates are less well prepared in the basic skills for college now than they were a decade ago: Lower scores on high school competency tests, college admissions tests, and freshman placement tests are confirmed by faculty opinion about the lack of readiness of today's students. While the percentage of new students who need remedial programs has been increasing in four-year institutions, both the percentage and the intensity of that need have been increasing in community colleges. Recent high school graduates reading below the junior high school level enroll with the expectation of pursuing college-level courses and may be difficult to place in adult education programs. An unresolved issue for community colleges is whether a floor should be established below which remediation or developmental education would not be offered except as adult basic education and, if so, where that floor should be.

Community colleges are now beginning to move toward mandatory assessment of basic skills and placement in remedial programs. (Miami-Dade Community College is one example; McCabe, 1981). As they do so, they are confronted with a host of issues relating to the scope of such activities. Who should be required to undergo assessment and remediation? What levels and kinds of skills and competences should be expected? What about part-time students who have neither degree nor transfer objectives and who are enrolled in courses in which such skills are not needed? The issue for a community college is the need and desirability of having a minimum basic skills requirement that applies to all students, irrespective of their enrollment status, ultimate objective, and the nature of the courses they are taking. If no such need is found, a college may then ask whether it should specify different levels of competency for different kinds of courses and students, some of whom would be exempted from any such requirement. Institutions awarding the baccalaureate degree usually have common standards of competence which all new students must meet, especially at the freshman level. Since community colleges are both postsecondary and higher education institutions, the need to bring all students up to some minimum level is debatable.

Occupational Education. Occupational education in the community colleges overlaps and often duplicates programs offered under the auspices of other institutions. In many types of employment, there is little evidence of need for either high schools or community colleges to offer preparation which could not be done as well in on-the-job training programs. Various conditions have led community colleges to expand the scope of their occupational education offerings. Among them are high rates of unemployment among youth who would not usually attend colleges, increased interest among all youth in preparing for early employment, and poor preparation for education in the technologies and other high-skill areas among high school graduates. Enrolling part time, students focus on short-term vocational training leading to immediate employment and avoid instruction in basic skills and general education. Community colleges fulfill an important local need in expanding such opportunities for the underemployed and, in doing so, move further into the sphere of adult postsecondary education.

At the other end of the spectrum, community college transfer students may enroll in a sequence of occupational courses which carry transfer credit (Hunter and Sheldon, n.d., pp. 3-4). In California, occupational students have been able to transfer with considerable ease to California State University, which grants credit for all courses which the community colleges have certified as taught at the baccalaureate level. Four-year institutions are also trying to respond to increased student interest in preparation for employment, rather than for graduate school, upon receipt of the bachelor's degree. At the same time, students have been transferring in increasing numbers from baccalaureate-level institutions to community colleges to obtain the kind of job training not usually available at four-year colleges and universities. The appropriate division of responsibility between two- and four-year institutions for preparing students for the increasing opportunities for employment in the high-level technologies is not yet clear—in part because of a lack of information about the job placement of community college students compared with those who have had other types of preparation for the same jobs.

The Transfer Function. The number of California community college students transferring to the University of California and the California State University declined in fall 1981 to a level below that of a decade ago. The enrollment of recent high school graduates as first-time freshmen has remained fairly stable in each of the three branches of California's system, while the number of high school graduates has declined (California Postsecondary Education Commission, 1982). Many reasons have been offered for the decline in transfers; among them are changing student interests and demographics, increased

part-time enrollment, higher costs of attending a four-year institution, impacted programs and campuses in the university system, and poor articulation with senior institutions. The proportion of recent high school graduates enrolling in a community
college with the intention to transfer continues to be significant, probably as high as 40 percent (Hunter and Sheldon, n.d.,
p. 4), but little documentation exists concerning student goal
changes while in the community colleges or reasons for not
transferring after completing a transfer program. In any case,
diminution of the transfer function may serve to enlarge the
postsecondary functions of community colleges—nondegree vocational, developmental, and adult and continuing (or community) education.

The nature of community college enrollments in the future is unclear because funding levels for public higher education, including student financial aid, are uncertain. The decline
in numbers of high school graduates in the 1980s is expected to
produce spirited competition on the part of the four-year institutions to fill their freshman class spaces by recruiting students
who would have gone to a community college in the 1960s and
1970s. Failure to achieve their student affirmative action goals
thus far may also serve as a stimulus to four-year institutions to
recruit from ethnic minority groups. At the same time, students
who might attend four-year institutions face higher tuition and
fees, stricter eligibility requirements for student aid, higher admissions standards, and tough competition for admission to programs, such as engineering, that lead to job placement. Poor
economic conditions and a devalued public image of higher education also contribute to uncertainties about the size and distribution of enrollments among various types of colleges and universities.

Financial conditions in the first half of the 1980s may
well divert students from four-year institutions to community
colleges. Since community colleges are likely to be underfinanced
in relation to possible enrollment increases, they may be unable
to fund additional transfer courses or programs or unwilling to
give higher priority to transfer offerings than to community
education courses (which tend to be cheaper to offer). Since

many vocational programs are also expensive, particularly sophomore-level courses with low enrollments, students who are di-
verted from four-year institutions may find limited choices
available in the community colleges. Decisions and choices that
community college leaders make in the 1980s can have profound implications for the higher education of the nation's
youth.

Community Education. Community or continuing education is a relatively new, fast-growing function which threatens
to overtake the degree and transfer functions as community colleges respond to growing demands for short-term adult postsecondary education. A college which performs this function well
may find that its community has an insatiable appetite for continuing education programs, which, if not wholly funded from
user fees, will drain resources from important programs less in
demand. Community education has the advantage of being able
to respond rapidly to changing needs, some of which are non-
recurring.

Some students enroll first in community education programs, then move into programs leading to degrees, and ultimately transfer to four-year institutions. Such students tend to
be older, with a break in their education after high school,
undereducated in terms of their potential, and fearful of competition in classes with younger students. Community education
classes help them to gain confidence in their ability to compete
in college-level courses, to improve their study skills, and to explore their educational interests prior to choosing a program of
study. However, most students in community education are unlikely to move into regular college programs because they have
already achieved their formal educational goals, sometimes at
the baccalaureate or higher levels.

Conclusions

Community colleges function as both postsecondary and
higher education institutions. Both functions are appropriate to
comprehensive community colleges, and both are being done
well in many such institutions. The potential for conflict arises

when (1) the two kinds of functions are comingled or (2) the demand for community or continuing education increases to a point where it dominates other programs. The dangers in blurring the two functions include declining academic standards in the collegiate tradition and limited flexibility in responding to the needs of adults in the continuing education tradition. These dangers are most apparent when both purposes are pursued simultaneously through credit offerings. If the conflict between adult and collegiate education is difficult to manage, then community college leaders may need to differentiate sharply between credit and noncredit courses or to choose between the collegiate and the adult education functions of their colleges. (The chapter by Cohen offers additional observations on how noncredit courses might be approached.)

In times of fiscal constraint, the community college must set priorities and limit its activities to those priorities in order to maintain its reputation for excellence. This assumes that if community colleges choose to confine their functions to certain activities, public funding will be provided and students will seek to enroll. Unfortunately, public funding and student demand do not always coincide. Transfer programs for full-time lower-division students may be adequately funded through tax support but declining student attendance would soon reduce enrollments substantially. Demands from adult learners for personal development and vocational training may be increasing dramatically, but government rules will restrict the use of public monies for their support. Community college leaders must either accept the likelihood of sharply reduced enrollments or seek to alter the basis for public support of adult education. Neither of these tasks will be easy.

Community colleges are now two-year institutions only insofar as their prescribed curricula do not exceed two years of college-level work. Whether the institution is called a two-year college or not is less important than what the college communicates to its students about the length of time required to complete a particular program. Leaders should ensure that college personnel and publications accurately describe the normal completion periods for all students, including those requiring remediation. Community college leaders should also insist that programs not be unnecessarily increased in length for the sake of prolonging student attendance.

In most states, community colleges are committed to an open admissions policy, but current opposition to standardized testing for placement may mean unconditional admission. Remediation has always been an important function of community colleges; however, as the level of student preparation for college has declined, remediation has come to include adult basic education for the functionally illiterate. Vocational education is needed more than ever before, but more students are seeking short-term employment training, and fewer are willing to follow prescribed curricula leading to associate degrees and certificates. In some schools, community education is competing with degree-oriented programs for support. As a result of these many changing conditions, the transfer function may be in jeopardy.

Community colleges generally have not worked closely with local high schools to smooth student transition between institutions. If one accepts the belief that the educational success of any student is the business of all levels of public education, then several courses of action are apparent: first, the formal recognition of a common purpose and the organization among secondary and postsecondary institutions within a given region to deal with issues of student transition from school to college; second, the establishment of ongoing administrator-to-administrator and faculty-to-faculty discussions. The knowledge and skill required of students graduating from high school must be compared with that needed for success as a beginning community college student. Feedback to the high schools regarding the performance of their graduates at the college should be provided.

Society needs community colleges to provide opportunity both to young people in traditional programs and to adults with an awakening need for continuing education. If community colleges did not now exist, states would probably invent them—in a time of fewer financial constraints. If community colleges did not exist, however, states might well find it neces-

sary to invent not one but several new postsecondary institutions: one offering lower-division university programs for transfer students, another preparing students for highly skilled technology work, and a third committed to meeting the changing
needs of local residents for self-enrichment, personal development, and job training.

2

Keeping the Door Open for Disadvantaged Students

Robert G. Templin, Jr.

The winds of change are blowing on the community college in unexpected ways, and the effects promise both realization of potential and threat of great harm to its mission and function. The community college is rapidly becoming a predominantly middle-class college, accepted among white, educated, middle-income Americans as a higher education institution for themselves and their children. The positive aspect of such change is the promise of the community college's acceptance at last as a legitimate and valuable part of higher education recognized by and serving all segments of society. The danger is that many people for whom community colleges have been the last chance —the only chance—will no longer see these institutions as opportunities.

Faced with a depressed economy which makes attendance at any college increasingly difficult, many poor, disadvantaged, and minority students may be discouraged even from attending the relatively inexpensive community college. If, in addition, these students are confronted with reduced services and fewer program options because of the influx of middle-class students, then the poor are likely to believe that true access and educational opportunity have become mere slogans. As the middle class enters the community college in increasing numbers, the disadvantaged may find themselves squeezed out from the institution that once served them.

Enter the Middle Class

The major social forces acting upon community colleges and their students are the same forces affecting higher education generally: deteriorating economic conditions and the declining importance of higher education as a social priority in the eyes of state and federal legislators. High interest rates, unemployment, and continuing inflation have caused the cost of higher education to skyrocket at the very time when students and their families can least afford the expense.

State and federal governments confronted with recessionary conditions are projecting lower than anticipated revenues and many feel they have no choice but to reduce funds for educational programs. In the face of competing demands for declining resources, higher education is not perceived by most legislators as a critical area for increased governmental support. Federal programs to aid higher education have been either eliminated completely or cut drastically. Federal student financial aid programs in particular have been severely affected, and their future is uncertain. State governments, faced with their own federal cutbacks and declining revenues, are not contributing additional funds (after inflation) for expansion in education: They are finding it difficult to meet current commitments. In some states enrollment limits have been imposed and cuts in higher education budget levels already have been made.

Private colleges and universities are highly vulnerable during these times. Unlike their public counterparts, which can absorb part of the increased costs with public funds, private institutions have little choice but to pass on the larger part of their growing costs to students through greatly increased tuition charges. Between 1965 and 1980, private institutions averaged increases in tuition of 24 percent after inflation; public institutions averaged increases of 19 percent for the same period. Private colleges tend to have tuitions and fees nearly five times higher than those of public colleges (American Council on Education, 1982b).

As costs rise and the ability to pay decreases, enrollments in higher education will decline, students will shift in their enrollment patterns, or both. It seems reasonable to expect that students from upper-middle-income families may reconsider attending a private institution and choose a major state university instead. If this trend occurs it is likely that applications at major public universities will increase while they decrease at private institutions.

This pattern of shifting student enrollments has already begun to appear. Private institutions report a decline in freshman applications for 1982 while public research universities show an increase ("Applications for Fall Admission . . . ," 1982). The reasons given for the shifting enrollment are "recession, uncertainty of student aid, and big tuition hikes" in the private institutions (Magarrell, 1982, p. 1).

The shifting enrollment pattern is not likely to be expressed simply as a swing from private to public higher education. Flagship public universities faced with problems of declining state support and state policies which limit enrollments will likely raise their admission standards rather than increase enrollments. Consequently, the shifting enrollment pattern is likely to be downward throughout the entire structure of public higher education. There may be smaller enrollments at some of the public four-year colleges and comprehensive universities because of deteriorating economic conditions, increased student costs, and changing demographics, but there should be a downward shift of upper-middle-socioeconomic status students into these institutions as well.

For the community college, these economic forces and shifts in the enrollments of higher education have one important consequence: Middle-class students faced with increased costs and higher admissions criteria in some four-year colleges and universities are likely to consider the community college an acceptable alternative. They will begin to attend two-year colleges in increasing numbers.

In addition to the economic forces which are affecting all of higher education, there are at least five factors which are pushing community colleges toward becoming predominantly middle-class institutions.

1. Growth in Continuing Education Programs. Between 1970 and 1980, enrollments of part-time credit students in community colleges exploded by 157 percent to total nearly three million students. Since 1974 noncredit enrollments have grown by 206 percent, bringing the total noncredit student population to an estimated four million students. (American Association of Community and Junior Colleges, 1982). This phenomenal growth in part-time credit and noncredit students came primarily from middle-class learners. In North Carolina, for example, two-year institutions reported in 1979 that, except for those in basic education courses, continuing education students were typically from the middle-socioeconomic structure, representing a significant increase from the previous decade. Nearly 40 percent had family incomes in excess of $15,000 and had already had one or more years of postsecondary education (Shearon and others, 1980).

Throughout the 1970s, two-year colleges quickly became accepted places for learning among middle-class adults who attended mostly in the evening. These part-time middle-class learners did not originally attend two-year institutions as part of a traditional program of undergraduate education. Most were not interested in earning degrees; they wanted education in order to learn a job-related skill, gain personal satisfaction, or respond to life problems. As they attended, however, they exerted an influence over the character and curriculum of the institution. The values and needs of these students affected course offerings, times and locations of classes, and ultimately the academic requirements for degrees and certificates. As community colleges responded to their new middle-class clients, the demand for workshops, weekend classes, and new and varied course topics grew. During the 1970s, many adults who would not have considered sending their children to the local community college themselves became involved in its continuing education offerings. Today, these adult learners are looking for educational alternatives for their college-age children in a time of severe economic recession. As economic pressures continue and as parents become more familiar with the community college, it may prove an increasingly attractive alternative to four-year institutions for traditional middle-class youth.

2. Influx of Postgraduate Reverse Transfer Students. One of the fastest-growing segments of community college enrollment is among persons holding a college credential. Nearly 12 percent of all community college students in North Carolina have earned at least a baccalaureate degree (Shearon and others, 1980). In 1982, about 25 percent of the student body at one Virginia community college had already received a degree or certificate from an institution of higher education. Most of these postgraduate reverse transfer students were enrolled for career-related reasons and often represented one third to one half of the enrollments in high technology and allied health-related programs (Ross, 1982). It is reasonable to assume that most of these students are from middle-class backgrounds.

3. Growth of High-Technology Programs. These programs have attracted postgraduate transfers and other middle-class students with high career-related expectations. Rapid technological change during the past decade has produced an unprecedented demand for highly trained technicians in the fields of electronics, data processing, drafting and design, and instrumentation and other engineering technologies. Stemming from the significant development of microelectronics and the microprocessor, these technologies offer lucrative employment opportunities but also require a sophistication in knowledge and skill which has not previously been associated with community college curricula. Other fields, such as accounting, nursing, and many of the health technologies, require specialized knowledge and present employment opportunities similar to those in the high technologies. Evidence of a trend toward an increased emphasis on allied health and high-technology programs exists in community college graduation patterns. Between 1971 and 1978, associate degrees awarded in all curricula rose 63 percent, those in sciences or engineering-related programs increased by 116 percent, and those in the health technologies increased by 192 percent. (U.S. National Center for Education Statistics, 1980a, p. 30). Manpower projections for community college graduates in these fields continue to reflect a strong demand, with the health technologies increasing at a somewhat slower pace than before while high-technology occupations continue to increase at an accelerating rate (National Commission on Allied

Health Education, 1980; Harris and Grede, 1977). The outlook for employment in these fields remains high at a time when national unemployment figures approach those of the Great Depression.

4. *Growth of College Transfer Programs.* During the past two decades the previously dominant transfer function gave way to occupational programs and to continuing education courses as the traditional junior college broadened into the more comprehensive community college. Between 1970 and 1980, not only did transfer programs fail to keep pace with total college enrollments, but in some states the numbers of transfer students actually declined (Cohen and Brawer, 1982; Shearon and others, 1980).

At least part of the explanation for the decline of transfer education lies in the increase in access to baccalaureate programs at four-year colleges and universities in many regions at the same time as community colleges diversified the curriculum with occupational and adult education programs. Middle-class students seeking professional and managerial careers could afford the costs associated with attendance at public four-year colleges and state universities and chose that option. Less able and less affluent students had access to the baccalaureate degree through the community college; however, as the two-year college curriculum broadened, many chose or were tracked into technical, vocational, and remedial programs. The net effect of increased access to senior colleges and the broadening of the two-year college curriculum was a decline in the community college transfer function.

We may now expect to see, however, a renewed growth of the college transfer function. As economic conditions put tuitions at private institutions out of reach for many middle-class students, and as applications at major public universities exceed the spaces available, increasing numbers of middle-class students may be seeking the bachelor's degree through the community colleges' transfer programs.

Community colleges will probably respond favorably to the influx of middle-class transfer students because of the generally lower cost of offering transfer programs compared with occupational curricula. Increased educational activity in the liberal arts and general education will be welcomed as well, serving for some as an indicator of a much needed return of the community college to a more traditional collegiate mission (Cohen and Brawer, 1982).

5. *Quest for Legitimacy Among Community Colleges.* In the past, two-year colleges have been viewed by those in the university community, if not by themselves, as being second best colleges owing to their open door admissions policies and acceptance of less able students (London, 1978). The arrival of middle-class students with better-than-average college board scores and high school grade-point averages will be welcomed by community college faculty and administrators alike. The enrollment shift will signal to community colleges that their reputation for low-cost, high-quality education will have at last been acknowledged by those who may have previously rejected the community college.

The Educational Squeeze Out:
Exit the Disadvantaged

The influx of middle-class learners to the community college is not in itself a negative development. The problem is not that community colleges are becoming middle class but that they may be doing so at the expense of those who have traditionally looked to the community college for educational opportunity and social mobility.

In 1972, Jerome Karabel advanced the thesis that our stratified society was mirrored by a stratified system of higher education in which the community college played a unique role in serving the lower classes (Karabel, 1972). On the lowest rung of the hierarchy, it was the community college that gave access to higher education for the masses, especially the poor, minorities, and those of lesser ability. The expansion of community colleges allowed policy makers to respond at relatively low cost to demands for access to higher education while helping to preserve the selectivity and prestige of universities serving the more affluent.

As a result, the kind of institution students attend is closely related to their socioeconomic profile and their ability. Astin reports that "two-year colleges, four-year colleges, and universities follow a perfect hierarchical ordering with respect to the six background student characteristics we examined" (1982, p. 138). Astin's research shows that students attending public universities are twice as likely to come from families with incomes of $30,000 or more than are community college students, who in turn are twice as likely to have parental incomes under $15,000. He reports the same patterns for parents' educational levels and students' academic preparation.

Some critics charge that because of the stratified system of higher education, community colleges tend to perpetuate class inequalities in American society. However, most observers, including the critics, agree that community colleges have done a great deal to provide access to higher education where there was none before. Astin (1982, p. 152) points out that "it is probably true that, were it not for community colleges, many minority students would not attend college at all." In fact, he reports, *"Students from all minority groups . . , tend to be concentrated in two-year public colleges"* (p. 132, italics are Astin's). Millions of these students have taken advantage of the opportunity presented by community colleges and, in spite of the failures which can be cited, many have benefited from that opportunity.

Today, however, the community college is faced with a changing societal scene which is forcing the institution to reexamine its traditional relationships with minorities and the poor and indeed to reexamine its basic mission. Middle-class students are part of a downward shift in the enrollment patterns of higher education that could have a negative effect on the disadvantaged. Those traditionally served by the institution at the bottom of the educational hierarchy may be pushed out of higher education altogether. Karabel's explanation portrays the community college as an institution of limited opportunity for the poor, but the future may see a system of higher education with no opportunity for them at all. The disadvantaged will not be able to compete effectively against middle-class students on admissions criteria, will not feel welcome at the community college, and will not continue to find educational opportunities and services which meet their needs. Worsening economic conditions, declining student financial aid, and higher tuition charges will make it extremely difficult for poorer students to attend any institution at all, even the community college.

Though tuition and fees at community colleges tend to be less expensive than those at public four-year institutions, the gap is closing quickly. During the past fifteen years, tuition and fees at community colleges have increased by 106 percent after inflation compared to the 19 percent increase at public four-year colleges (American Council on Education, 1982b). Thus while the community college appears to be a bargain for middle-class students, its spiraling tuition and loss of financial aid resources may push the costs of attending out of reach for the poor.

Financial hardships will make it difficult enough to consider attendance at a community college. But faced with the influx of middle-class students, those from the lower class may find that there are fewer services directed toward their needs and less opportunity for entry into the programs they want. The cultural complexion of the community college itself may begin to change. Institutional values and attitudes are likely to take on an increasingly conservative, middle-class flavor which often projects an attitude of tolerance for, rather than receptivity to, lower-socioeconomic groups.

Initial signs of a downward shift in enrollments and the potential of an educational squeeze out along class lines are beginning to appear. Already the American Association of Community and Junior Colleges predicts enrollment demands upon community colleges far in excess of their financial ability to respond (Magarrell, 1982).

Typically, community colleges have attracted the poor and minorities to their campuses. In 1978, 42 percent of all Black students and more than one half of all Hispanic and American Indian students in higher education were enrolled in two-year colleges (U.S. National Center for Education Statistics, 1982a). In California, more than 80 percent of all Blacks and Hispanics who went on to public higher education immediately after graduating from high school in 1979 did so at a community junior college (California Postsecondary Education Commission, 1981a). Yet between 1978 and 1980, minority enrollments in community colleges began for the first time to fall in proportion to total enrollments (U.S. National Center for Education Statistics, 1982c). In the North Carolina system of fifty-seven community colleges and technical institutes, the socio-economic characteristics of credit students between 1968 and 1979 shifted noticeably toward the middle class (Shearon and others, 1980).

Will there be enough room for all the people who wish to attend the community college? If not, on what basis will programs be offered and students admitted? Should the transition of the community college to a middle-class college occur, will it be at the expense of the lower-income and disadvantaged student?

The increasing numbers of postgraduate reverse transfer students and the growth of high-technology programs provide good examples of how these questions manifest themselves as potential problems or issues for the community college. Because employment demand in the high technologies is great, demand for admission to these programs is also great. If admissions criteria are constructed along traditional lines, the postgraduate reverse transfer student emerges as a highly desirable candidate, often exceeding admissions criteria and having many other desirable attributes as well. Disadvantaged students have to compete not only with increasing numbers of recent middle-class high school graduates but also with persons already holding higher education credentials.

Another problem posed by the postgraduate reverse transfer student lies in the level of instruction. Instructors, faced with more articulate, able, and seasoned students than before, will be tempted to teach at a level challenging to the postgraduates but beyond the comprehension of disadvantaged students. Such students, once considered adequately prepared for a level of instruction associated with community college programs, might now face frustration and failure. Even if the lower-socioeconomic student can gain admission to a program, the presence of the postgraduate reverse transfer could diminish his or her chances for success.

A problem associated with access to high-technology programs is the length of time poorly prepared students might take to complete them. Student demand for these programs is typically high, yet employer expectations of what the finished graduate should be able to do makes it extremely difficult to take recent high school graduates with no previous experience and a minimum knowledge of mathematics, science, and communicative skills and hope they will finish a demanding program within two years. When the students considering such programs do not have the necessary background, they have little hope of success unless special remedial and support efforts are made on their behalf. Also, because of the rigorous demands upon students in these programs, associated but lower-vocational programs are often set on a separate curriculum track which is difficult to integrate with the associate-degree program. Thus, persons hoping to enter a high-technology program who are not as well prepared as middle-class students are shifted down to a vocational track which does not build toward a career in high technology but only toward an entry-level operator position with little career mobility. The examples are abundant: data entry operator rather than computer programmer, electronics-servicing repairman rather than electronics technician, nurses' aid rather than registered nurse.

A final danger with high-technology programs is that they are extremely expensive. Colleges with severely restricted budgets may choose to concentrate their program offerings in a cluster of technologically related curricula, dropping programs unrelated to these specialties. The results are likely to be a lessening of comprehensiveness and a loss of those vocational programs that have typically served disadvantaged students.

Problems associated with the growth of college transfer programs are also likely. As student demand for high-technology programs grows, and if community colleges institute traditional admissions criteria to select students for entry into these programs, disadvantaged students wishing to gain a postsecond-

ary education may be forced to choose general education transfer programs as a second choice. The prospect of success for
such students in these programs is not great (Astin, King, and
Richardson, 1980). Chances are high that they will not graduate, and if they do graduate the opportunities for successful
transfer are likely to be restricted. This is because larger numbers of community college students are likely to be seeking
transfer to senior institutions, which can be expected to have
fewer upper-division spaces available because of less attrition
among their own lower-division students.

Further issues and problems are raised when examining
community college continuing education programs. The bulk of
students served through continuing education courses is not the
undereducated or the disadvantaged. The typical community
college continuing education student is solidly middle class.

Participation of the upper and middle classes in continuing education is not a phenomenon exclusive to the community
college. Continuing education students at all institutions tend to
be twenty-five to thirty-four years of age and white, have one or
more years of formal college training, and have a family income
in excess of $15,000 (U.S. National Center for Education Statis-
tics, 1980b). Though Blacks and Hispanics together represent
nearly 12 percent of the total adult population, they constitute
less than 1 percent of all adult education participants. Not only
are these minorities underrepresented in contrast with the total
adult population, but the trend is toward even more serious dis-
parities between socioeconomic groups (Watkins, 1982). Cross
(1981a, p. 46), found that "the gap between the well educated
and the poorly educated is growing rather than narrowing." She
concludes that "with the new active and aggressive interest of
colleges and the professions in the continuing education of
adults, opportunities for lifelong learning are even more likely
to tilt in the direction of relatively well-educated young professionals."

Of all of the institutional factors contributing to the rise
of the middle-class community college, the community college's
quest for legitimacy is potentially the most damaging to minority and disadvantaged students. The tragedy in the making is

not merely that opportunities will be denied to the poor but that this may well be facilitated by the community college in its quest for legitimacy. As increasing numbers of able middle-class students apply to the community college for fewer and fewer vacancies, it will be tempting to establish admissions criteria which serve, not intentionally perhaps, to screen out minorities and the poor. Under the banner of higher admissions standards, institutional policies will stress earlier application deadlines and traditional measures of ability, both of which tend to work against the poorer and higher-risk students whose past academic records are weak and whose ability to finance higher education is uncertain at the time when admission decisions are made. Taking the more able student can seem to be the most prudent course of action under current circumstances. Middle-class students will tend to do better in their studies, be less likely to "stop out" or drop out, require less remediation, be more likely to graduate, and graduate sooner than the academically less able. However, graduating more and brighter students does not necessarily signify a higher-quality institution or an improved instructional process. It simply reflects the principle that advantaged students tend to be better prepared academically and to perform better than disadvantaged students. The danger is confusing improving quality with the abandonment of institutional mission. Apparent improvement in quality is not accomplished by real improvement in institutional teaching but is achieved through disassociation with groups traditionally affiliated with the community college.

Remedies

The examination of institutional factors contributing to the rise of the middle-class community college and the recognition that this may occur at the expense of lower-socioeconomic groups raises a number of critical questions for the community college.

The demand for high-technology programs raises these questions: How will community colleges respond to the demands of a changing technological society and yet maintain their comprehensive curricula? How can admissions policies for programs in great demand be set so as not to deny access to the poor and opportunity to the disadvantaged? How can institutions assure that poor and high-risk students are not being tracked into lower-technology and vocational programs?

The increase of postgraduate reverse transfer students raises these questions: Will postgraduate reverse transfer students have their traditional education at the expense of lower-class students? How many times will some people be served by the educational system before others have the opportunity to be served for the first time? How can community colleges guard against the level of instruction being oriented toward the postgraduate rather than the lower-division student?

The historical pattern of continuing education in America ıaises these questions: Will community colleges continue the trend toward serving the middle class disproportionally in continuing education classes? Will programs be increasingly responsive to the demands of middle-class adults or will new efforts be made by the community college to include the continuing education needs of less affluent adults as well?

The potential growth of college transfer programs raises more questions: Will the growth of college transfer enrollments divert funds from programs where a substantial proportion of students are from lower-class backgrounds? How can community colleges strengthen those transfer programs which enroll minorities and the disadvantaged so as to increase the rate at which these students actually transfer and earn the baccalaureate?

The community college's quest for legitimacy raises these questions: Will two-year colleges provide continuing support for developmental studies and counseling for disadvantaged students, or will these services be reduced in the name of raising academic standards? Will the disadvantaged and racial minorities find the community college a receptive and supportive environment, or will it be increasingly characterized as a white, middle-class institution where the cultural attitudes and values of lower-socioeconomic groups are less and less accommodated?

Analyzing the current higher education scene, forecasting the emergence of the middle-class community college, and raising a number of questions for institutions to confront are only preliminaries. Community college leaders can take positive steps now to avert the squeeze out of the poor, minorities, and other disadvantaged groups from the nation's two-year colleges.

The first step is to make every effort to understand who the students are that are presently being served by community colleges. A profile of students should be constructed using data on student characteristics such as race, age, sex, socioeconomic status, and academic ability. This student profile should be checked against the demographic census profile of the college's service area to determine which groups are and are not being served. The student profile should be contrasted with the profiles of earlier years to determine in what ways and how quickly the mix of students is changing. If appropriate student data are collected and analyzed on a program, institutional, and statewide basis, it should be possible for leaders to know whether or not the propositions set forth in this chapter hold true for their college or state system. It is important that community college leaders act on the basis of accurate information about who their students are and how their client population is changing.

The second step is to define what types of students should be served in greater numbers than are presently being served. Cohen and Brawer (1982, p. 64) state the issue succinctly: "Which groups have first claim on the institution? If enrollment limitations mean some students must be turned away, who shall they be? Those of lesser ability? Those with indistinct goals? Lists placing the categories of potential students in order from highest to lowest priority may have to be developed." The institution's board of trustees, faculty, and staff ought to become sensitive to the changing complexion of student enrollments in higher education and the community college. The issue of determining priorities in student enrollments should be openly discussed and debated. If the community college has a commitment to minorities, the poor, and other disadvantaged groups, then recruitment efforts and admissions policies will need to reflect this. Early applications and traditional standards regarding academic ability may not be relevant considerations.

The third step is to strengthen or develop programs and services for those groups defined as priority students. In particular, new financial aid programs will need to be developed within the state or the community itself. Banking institutions, business and industry, civic groups, and foundation support will need to be developed for grants-in-aid, educational loans, and work-study opportunities. Developmental studies will need to be evaluated for their effectiveness in assisting disadvantaged students and, if necessary, strengthened to produce the desired results. Degree programs and continuing-education courses will need to be evaluated in terms of their appropriateness to the meeting of needs of priority groups.

The fourth step is the formation of advisory groups made up of representatives from target groups. Community leaders, parents, present and former students, and potential students should be included. The task of such groups would be to advise colleges on the economic, educational, and attitudinal barriers that make enrollment and success in the community college difficult. An advisory committee made up of representatives from various disadvantaged groups could identify student needs and recommend appropriate institutional responses.

To be sure, the preceding four steps mark only a beginning of what will be necessary if community college leaders are to prevent their institutions from becoming middle-class colleges at the expense of the poor. Without special efforts such as those, the effects of current economic conditions will prevail, educational opportunity will be denied to disadvantaged groups, and the community college may no longer be the people's college.

3

Changing Status of Women

Billie Wright Dziech

In academic rhetoric, the story of women in community colleges often becomes a catalogue of disembodied statistics that bear little relevance to the lives of the individuals they describe. In reality, the story of women in "the people's college" is an account of success and failure, of hope and despair. The institution has broken and kept its promises, honored and overlooked its commitments to female staff and students. What it can or should offer them in the future must be determined by its performance in the past and present.

The most memorable glimpses of community college women often occur in the least expected places. One is a novel in which the central character, a Harvard graduate, finds herself teaching in the local two-year college. As the book ends, Mira, the heroine of *The Women's Room,* voices the confusion, resignation, and distress common to her colleagues (French, 1977, p. 686):

> August is nearly over. School will open in two weeks and I have done nothing, I have not read Chomsky . . . or found a better composition text. It doesn't matter.
> I am a good scholar, and in a different market, I could have done decent work, but in this one, it seems hopeless. Maybe I'll do it anyway, just for myself. What else do I have to do?

I guess I keep expecting that there should be
something out there that would make it easier to
be in here. Like the snails, you know? They don't
have to do anything except exist. This is not the
world I would have wished.

No, this is not, in many respects, the world many women
would wish. And Mira—mother, divorcee, teacher—exemplifies
the ambiguity of females caught in an unsympathetic world
they feel powerless to change. It is important to observe, however, that Mira's story ends during the 1970s. The tale of wom-
en in two-year institutions continues. It is worth following because the history of the community college, more than that of
any other educational institution in the United States, parallels
the struggles and the triumphs of women. It is a record of their
attempts to be recognized, to find "something out there," and
perhaps eventually to discover a place in the world as they wish
it to be.

Although the community college movement began early
in the century, its decade of greatest visibility was the 1960s. It
was a time of phenomenal growth and aspiration. Doors opened,
and minorities, the economically disadvantaged, and those in
need of remedial and vocational training walked through. Instead of isolating themselves, two-year colleges reached out into
their communities in efforts to learn as well as to teach.

Women were part of that experience. Some entered the
open doors and emerged bearing diplomas. But there were not
many of them, and most were on their way to low-paying, low-
status occupations. There were others who used the institution
sporadically in pursuit of what would eventually be termed
"lifelong learning," but that terminology would not be incorporated into the vernacular of higher education until the 1970s
when documents like the United Nations Educational, Scientific,
and Cultural Organization's Faure report raised academe's con-
sciousness about its need to assume new roles and responsibilities. In the meantime, the community college of the 1960s occupied itself nights and weekends with what some observers
perceived as merely preventing housewife boredom. There was
little awareness that women were a separate and unique constit-

uency, a constituency as much in need of direction into the mainstream of American life as minorities and the financially deprived.

During this era, women faculty and administrators were hired in greater numbers and awarded rank and tenure more rapidly in two-year institutions than were their peers in four-year colleges. This ostensible interest in women occurred as much from necessity as from choice. A shortage of qualified teaching personnel and the availability of money to all higher education institutions combined to limit the professional pool and afford baccalaureate and graduate schools the luxury of picking and choosing staff. They usually chose men. Community colleges, drawing heavily from the faculties of secondary schools, employed large numbers of women. There was little concern for sexual balance or equity.

Then came the 1970s and with them modifications in male and female roles so sweeping that society has not yet fully comprehended and assimilated them. On the American campus, affirmative action became a reality. To comply with federal and state regulations, institutions were compelled to correct inequities in recruitment, salaries, and advancement of women employees. Where they had previously constituted barely visible minorities, females became aggressive and demanding factors. They sought and often achieved improvements in support services and special programs and courses for women students. Though academe and the world were still not all that they might prefer, women were discovering the "something out there" for which Mira searched. They began to understand and to covet, though not fully to possess, power within the institution. But power was not so far off as it had been a decade earlier; by the end of the 1970s, the enrollment balance had shifted, and women had become the new majority in higher education.

Nowhere was this development more striking than in the community college, where the proportion of females enrolled full time increased from approximately 20 percent in 1973 to 52 percent in 1980 (Eliason, 1981). In the 1970s, women's voices were raised in protest; in the 1980s, those voices acquired a ring of power—the kind that institutions and bureaucracies understand best—the power of numbers. What the community college will become over the remaining years of the century will be inextricably linked to what women have been, are, and wish to be.

Female Faculty and Administrators

In some respects, community colleges appear curiously unaware that the past has disappeared and that things will never again be quite the same. Injustices are most apparent in the institution's treatment of female faculty and administrators. Examined carefully, the data on female personnel in higher education are extremely disturbing. In 1981, there were 64,759 male and 37,532 female full-time faculty members in community colleges, and there were 77,999 male and 54,970 female part-time instructors. When all ranks were combined, the average full-time male faculty member's salary in 1980–81 was $20,765—$2,093 more than that of the average female, who was paid $18,672 (Wohlers, 1982). The most frequently cited data on gender differences in higher education is that accumulated by the U.S. National Center for Education Statistics (NCES) for 1979–80 (Table 3.1). It provides further proof that the community college is not meeting its responsibilities to female faculty.

To defend current inequities against women, the community college usually relies on two approaches. One of these, employed throughout higher education, is to compare current statistics on the status of women educators with those of a decade or two ago. This is the academic version of "You've come a long way, baby." The other, peculiar to the community college, involves comparing data on female educators in two-year colleges with those in four-year institutions in order to prove the former's better treatment of females. The intention in both cases is to demonstrate that the community college woman is really not so bad off as she might be if she were someone else in some other place in some other time. In theory, one should derive encouragement from such improvements—but theory is far removed from reality, and the woman working in a dead-end

Table 3.1. Average Salaries of Full-Time Two-Year Faculty Members, 1979–80.

	Professors		Associate Professors		Assistant Professors		Instructors		Lecturers		All Ranks	
	Men	Women	Men	Women	Men	Women	Men	Women	Men	Women	Men	Women
Public and private, 9-month contracts	24,031	22,961	20,862	20,334	17,665	17,009	15,570	14,224	15,940	13,423	20,765	18,672
Public and private, 12-month contracts	26,594	24,427	23,229	21,968	19,541	18,205	16,166	14,516	17,471	16,608	19,904	17,475
increase in salaries (two-year), 1979–79 compared with 1978–79												
Private institutions	9.7%	8.4%	7.5%	5.6%	5.7%	6.6%	5.5%	7.1%	—	—	7.2%	5.5%
Public institutions	5.4%	4.3%	5.1%	6.1%	6.0%	5.2%	6.8%	5.1%	—	—	8.2%	7.6%
Change in number of full-time two-year faculty members, 1979–80 compared with 1978–79												
9-month contracts	+11.7%	+9.1%	+3.2%	+7.8%	-3.5%	0.0%	-7.1%	-5.9%	-7.4%	+2.3%	+0.1%	+1.2%
12-month contracts	+8.9%	+13.0%	-3.6%	+5.9%	+2.3%	+8.5%	+26.8%	+19.0%	0.0%	-14.3%	+4.9%	+6.3%
Women as percentage of total full-time two-year faculty members												
Private institutions	29.6%	23.3%	42.7%	32.5%	52.9%	38.8%	57.4%	53.8%	—	—	48.6%	41.3%
Public institutions	23.5%	17.8%	29.4%	30.6%	38.6%	41.6%	47.7%	47.3%	46.1%	47.4%	34.7%	36.1%
Public and private (combined)	23.8%	18.4%	29.9%	30.8%	39.3%	41.4%	48.4%	48.9%	47.4%	47.4%	35.2%	36.6%
Percentage of full-time two-year faculty members with tenure, 1979–80												
Private institutions	93.9%	89.7%	86.3%	70.0%	42.1%	32.1%	7.5%	9.7%	0.0%	0.0%	52.2%	37.9%
Public institutions	95.9%	96.6%	89.5%	88.8%	59.1%	56.2%	26.0%	21.6%	10.3%	2.9%	77.9%	67.1%
Public and private (combined)	95.8%	96.2%	89.4%	88.0%	58.6%	55.3%	24.8%	20.8%	10.3%	2.4%	77.2%	65.8%

Source: "Fact-File . . . ," 1981. Reprinted with permission of *The Chronicle of Higher Education,* copyright 1981.

position for lower pay than her male counterpart may not be particularly uplifted by hearing about how bad conditions used to be.

Whether women in community colleges today are better off than their predecessors or their peers in baccalaureate institutions is not a cardinal point when one examines the figures. What is significant is that female as compared to male faculty members are consistently outnumbered, outranked, and underpaid. There is no rank at which the average female's wages are commensurate with those of the average male. The discrepancy is understandable if males have been employed longer at institutions, but the system perpetuates existing inequities by paying male instructors more than females of the same rank. In the NCES analysis (Table 3.1), on the average, a woman faculty member with a nine-month contract receives $2,093 less than a man with the same kind of contract; a woman with a twelve-month contract receives $2,429 less than a man with a twelve-month contract. This condition is exacerbated by pay increase schedules. Men's average increases for 1979–80, compared with the preceding year, were 1.7 percent, for those with nine-month contracts, and 0.6 percent, for those with twelve-month contracts, higher than increases for women with the same kinds of contracts. These are not small differences. Higher percentages applied to higher bases widen a gap that is already frustrating and defeating for women.

The number of full-time female faculty did increase more than that of males in 1979–80. If it were somehow possible to hold all variables constant, the gains of 1.1 percent for women with nine-month contracts and 1.4 percent for women with twelve-month contracts would result in women's equal representation with men before another half-century passes. Most women would probably settle for equity of status in the present. The *Chronicle of Higher Education* ("Fact-File . . . ," 1981) reports that in private community colleges there are 6.3 percent more male full professors than female full professors. Neither are women equally represented in public institutions, where men with the rank of professor outnumber women by 5.7 percent. In the data on tenure, women's averages remain below those of men. Only at the instructor level in private institutions and the full professor level in public schools are there more tenured women than men.

Although the plight of women faculty is disturbing, that of female administrators is worse. In 1981, there were approximately 11,849 males and 5,887 females holding administrative positions in two-year colleges. The inequalities are much worse than this 2 to 1 ratio would indicate. The positions occupied by females are primarily low- and middle-level posts that seldom lead to advancement, and the men who hold them are typically paid only 80 percent as much as women with similar titles (Wohlers, 1982). Two-year colleges apparently have better records than other postsecondary institutions in selecting female presidents. In 1975, eleven women headed public two-year institutions; in 1982, twenty-one women headed such institutions. The 200-percent gain does seem enormous, but there are more than 1,000 public community colleges (Wohlers, 1982).

"Scratch a woman, find a rage," declares Marilyn French's Mira (1977, p. 462). The statistics remind women staff that although on the surface the community college has been a good place for them, it has not been good enough. Not good enough to recruit them, pay them, promote them, or tenure them equitably. Not good enough to lead instead of follow society's approach to women. Not good enough to challenge academic traditions and build an environment in which men and women can work as equals.

The community college's shortcomings with respect to its female employees are obvious. There are various proposals for correcting them, and it is important to distinguish those capable of producing genuine change from those which are overly theoretical and unlikely to effect immediate and widespread improvement in the condition of women faculty and administrators. One of the best publicized and most questionable of these theories is one popularized by organizational development and management "experts." Their basic thesis is that differential socialization of males and females accounts for the poor record of women in higher education. Academe is viewed as a male environment in which women can find success by avoiding certain female characteristics and by cultivating strategies outlined by the management theorists.

In recent years, descriptions of the differences in socialization and psychological development of males and females have become commonplace in academic and popular literature. No one is shocked any more to learn that women are taught to be less aggressive, assertive, competitive, team-oriented, and analytical than men. From Douvan and Adelson (1966) to Maccoby and Jacklin (1974), differences in the sexes have been documented and analyzed until such information has become an impediment rather than an aid to women. It is no service to female educators to assert unequivocally that they are different from their male peers, to imply that "feminine" characteristics are the source of their ills and that their success is contingent either on their mastering "male" behaviors or transforming the institution into some nebulous "female" image. One does not eliminate a stereotype by exaggerating its pervasiveness. There are no impressive data to prove that women who choose academic careers fit traditional female stereotypes. In fact, common sense suggests that women deliberately electing a male-dominated profession are probably anything but docile, passive, and dependent. Nor is there great credibility in the assertion that academe is a male environment. It is male dominated because there are more men than women in the profession. But there is no definitive proof that these men are representative of the traditional stereotype. On the contrary, there are studies (Aberle and Naegele, 1952) to indicate that the academic profession is not regarded by men as particularly masculine and does not tend to attract those inclined to stereotypic male behaviors.

The socialization theme can become a convenient excuse for academe's inequalities. Community colleges or women educators can invest time and money in programs to improve women's management styles, but they will have limited impact. Men have had greater success in two-year colleges not because they are that different psychologically but because they have numbers, history, and stereotypic myths on their side. Because there are more of them from whom to choose, they have greater opportunities for advancement. Because they have traditionally controlled the colleges, the institutional schedules and career models that have evolved are suited to male rather than female developmental cycles. Because too many have accepted the stereotypic myth that females are predisposed to humanistic and intuitive forms of knowing, women are at a disadvantage in an institution that values scientific and rational modes of inquiry.

Women are not the problem. The institution is. After more than a decade, condescension and inequities between the sexes continue in community colleges—primarily because a system and a network are in place and too many of us instinctively rely on them. Both the formal and the informal systems of academe militate against the progress of women. Neither is sacrosanct or impervious to change. Improvement in the status of female educators can be accomplished with commitment, sensitivity, and willingness to break with tradition. Informal networks that operate within and between community colleges bind individuals together and pave the way for shifts or advancements in professional activities. Because they outnumber women, men's networks have traditionally operated more effectively. Women in community colleges have been less isolated from one another than those in four-year institutions, but they still suffer from inadequate contacts within the system. This is especially true of those in male-dominated disciplines. Female educators need to build communication and support bases similar to those that have worked so well for their male colleagues over the years.

It is not enough that women devise their own support systems; male support is needed. Male networking operates so subtly that some men are unaware of its existence. Exchanges of information and support between friends occur naturally and are probably not intended to harm or exclude females, so contemporary males have been shocked to learn that they possess this informal but highly effective advantage over women. If males, especially those in power, can be convinced to analyze their networking systems, they may be encouraged to employ them on behalf of women.

Recruiting qualified women for faculty and administrative posts should be a priority both for those with formal responsibility for the task and those with network contacts. Too many community colleges assume that affirmative action implies adding a few words about equal opportunity to job descriptions. Affirmative action means far more; it means that the college is committed to search actively for females and minorities to fill open positions. It means advertising in public, professional, local, and national publications; using network contacts; attending conventions and meetings; and—not infrequently—reopening searches until there is a fair proportion of candidates. Recruitment of women is especially critical in community colleges where so many disciplines and programs are traditionally male. In areas in which the number of qualified women is seriously limited, institutions must begin to encourage their own female graduates of traditionally male programs to prepare for academic careers.

The assumption that sexual equity ends with better recruitment is erroneous. Equalizing the pay and status of women already in the system is also essential. The complex regulations and restrictions governing promotion and tenure in academe are procedures established by trial and error over time. That they coincide with stages in the life cycles of men should come as no surprise. Men, and a small number of "career women," wrote the rules. They did so at a time when few recognized that women might desire and need both careers and homes; and their inability to grasp that reality has effectively excluded thousands of women from advancement in academia. Most women are between twenty-five and thirty-five years old when they bear children—crucial years for establishing a career in academe. Men and childless women often have difficulty identifying with the woman who finds time running out for her both professionally and biologically. Two-year colleges operating on baccalaureate models have time restrictions for acquiring rank, tenure, and promotion. In such cases, "up-or-out" clauses in contracts can force women into incredibly painful choices between careers and motherhood. They also cost institutions the services of desirable professionals who cannot meet time schedules patterned on male life cycles. If a women can demonstrate that child rearing has temporarily inhibited her professional activity, she should be granted additional time to prove her worth to the institution. This does not constitute inequity to men. It does not require them to do any more than women. It simply acknowledges an unalterable dissimilarity in personnel, a dissimilarity that can be ignored only at the cost of injustice to females and loss to the institution.

There are other ways in which the dilemma of career mothers can be relieved. Daycare facilities, leaves, flex-time, and job sharing have been successful in business and industry. For all its claims of humanitarianism, equality of opportunity, and leadership, higher education has allowed rhetoric and tradition to prevent similar progress. Two-year institutions, because of their close ties to the community, are specially obligated to serve as examples. More research, discussion, and experimentation are needed to devise methods for better accommodating faculty and administrators (male and female) with primary child-rearing responsibilities.

Careers are established early in academe, and the individual forced to curtail her activities for any length of time finds it difficult, perhaps impossible, to re-enter the system and move in new directions. Promising women who seek administrative positions for the first time must face competitors with more extensive experience and credentials. Community colleges could equalize this gap by devising programs or internships to provide such women with the experience necessary to compete with those whose career patterns are more stable. There are excellent existing programs of this sort. The Summer Institute for Women in Higher Education Administration conducted by Higher Education Resources Services is only one of a variety of possibilities for colleges willing to commit resources to women who have potential. Without such commitment, the community college's options are limited. Until colleges acknowledge that quantity of experience does not always equal quality of potential, academic women must continue to wait.

Women are accustomed to waiting, but over the years it has become more difficult. They are, after all, representatives of the people's college, and they have asked very little of it. What they desire is equality of rewards and opportunities and access to positions that will allow them to prove their individual abilities and the worth of their gender to the institution and to society. The community college of the future is obligated as never before to grant them those rights.

Female Students

The world of the two-year college is not all that women faculty and administrators might like it to be, but it has been better for female students. Even more than their professional counterparts, they reflect the enormous and sometimes shocking changes that have occurred in the lives of women during the last decade. Their reasons for turning to the community college are well known. Compared to baccalaureate schools, it is usually economically and geographically accessible, its entrance requirements and schedules more pliant, its programs less time consuming for those eager to enter the job market. It has been able to respond to women students because its tradition of flexibility has allowed it to absorb and internalize societal changes more rapidly than other institutions. It has been accustomed to meeting the needs of nontraditional students and has, at least in theory, stressed the desirability of innovation in educating its diverse constituencies.

Women may be the most heterogeneous of the institution's constituencies. There is not a typical female college student, but at least three groups can be identified: (1) full-time homemakers, (2) displaced homemakers and re-entry women, and (3) young women immediately out of secondary school. Each has special characteristics and needs that the institution must seek to accommodate. Full-time homemakers, for example, "drop in" to the college to broaden their intellectual, cultural, or personal horizons. Displaced homemakers and re-entry women come to the institution with a greater sense of urgency and more severe time and monetary restrictions; they seek vocational skills and credentials that will provide better access to the work place.

Although the largest current enrollment increases are occurring among 30- to 34-year-old females (U.S. National Center for Education Statistics, 1980a), recent high school graduates provide new challenges because they both defy and fit tradition-al female stereotypes. The group of women just out of second-ary school has been infrequently analyzed but is worth examin-ing. Reared during the peak of the women's movement, the young female student reveals much about how women view themselves and about what they will ask of the community col-lege in the last years of the twentieth century. They are, in many respects, a curious group—neither as like or unlike males as one might expect. Probably the most comprehensive and reli-able data available on American college freshmen comes from the Cooperative Institutional Research Program, a joint project of the American Council on Education and the University of California at Los Angeles directed by Alexander W. Astin (Astin and others, 1981). Astin's data for 1981 demonstrate that com-munity college male and female freshmen are quite similar. Their major objectives and their primary reasons for attending college differ little. Both are concerned about career satisfac-tion, financial success, and raising families. The interesting di-vergences appear in academic capabilities (Table 3.2), education

Table 3.2. Academic Rank in High School (Percent).

	Men	Women
Top 20	20.7	29.2
Second 20	24.1	23.4
Middle 20	42.8	39.0
Fourth 20	10.8	7.4
Lowest 20	1.6	1.1

Source: Astin and others, 1981, pp. 15 and 31.

goals (Table 3.3), and probable career choices (Table 3.4). Even though women just out of high school are as well or even better prepared academically upon entrance to college, their educa-tional aspirations are lower than those of males. With one ex-ception, their highest occupational preferences are for tradi-tional lower-paying, lower-status careers. Apparently, the con-sciousness raising of the last decade has not had sufficient impact

Table 3.3. Highest Degree Planned Anywhere (Percent).

	Men	Women
None	2.9	3.9
A.A. or equivalent	16.5	22.5
B.A. or B.S.	42.4	38.5
M.A. or M.S.	25.0	22.9
Ph.D. or Ed.D.	4.6	3.8
M.D., D.O., D.D.S., or D.V.M.	2.8	3.1
LL.B. or J.D. (law)	1.9	1.6
B.D. or M.Div. (divinity)	0.6	0.4
Other	3.2	3.4

Source: Astin and others, 1981, pp. 19 and 35.

to convince even very young women that they can move beyond stereotypic choices.

There is one revealing item that was introduced in Astin's 1979 survey (pp. 30 and 46) and omitted from his 1981 survey of community college freshmen. Asked about future career plans, 96.5 percent of the men but only 57.6 percent of the women responded that they would prefer to be pursuing full-time careers ten to fifteen years after college. Even more revealing, 42.4 percent of the women as compared to 3.4 percent of the men expected to have only part-time careers or none at all at the same period. Of all the statistics accumulated by Astin, these may be the most thought provoking, for they indicate an enormous discrepancy between individuals who are very similar in other respects. To conjecture why such a large proportion

Table 3.4. Probable Career Occupation (Percent).

	Men	Women
Business (clerical)	0.4	*7.6
Business executive	*9.3	*9.9
Business owner or proprietor	*5.0	2.0
Computer programmer or analyst	*7.2	*8.0
Engineer	*22.7	2.4
Nurse	0.3	*8.5
Teacher (elementary, secondary)	1.3	*6.7
Skilled trades	*6.3	0.9

Note: Forty-three original choices; * indicates top five choices.
Source: Astin and others, 1981, pp. 22 and 38.

of women anticipate only part-time careers ten to fifteen years after college is not hard. If a sizable portion of contemporary women still view work as only one priority in their lives, it seems fairly clear that another must be home and family. Females who grew up during the women's movement retain much in common with older members of their gender. Both have complex and often conflicting role aspirations unfamiliar to males, who tend to focus on their careers.

As women attempt to maneuver between various roles, their educational needs change. The community college is uniquely equipped practically and philosophically to facilitate their movements between careers and life-styles. This is not to suggest that the task is simple. There are inadequacies and biases that must be overcome within institutions, and there are limited financial resources with which to work. Yet none of the barriers are insurmountable.

Women with primary responsibilities for children and homes must be educated under severe time restrictions. Institutions that choose to do so can ease their dilemmas, and many two-year colleges have demonstrated such willingness. On most campuses, the belief that education can occur only between the hours of 8:00 A.M. and 5:00 P.M., Mondays through Fridays, died years ago. More impervious to change but equally deserving of obsolescence are the traditional concepts of quarters, semesters, and credit hours. Liberal scheduling and credit formulas do not decrease the quality of education; they increase its efficacy by opening the doors of academe wider.

Better access to the institution also occurs where childcare facilities are available at limited cost. There is little validity in the contention that such services are too expensive. The community college has an invaluable resource in its own students, many of whom are preparing for careers in childcare. Women can be granted credit for work in such facilities, and costs can be structured according to individuals' abilities to pay. Institutions that can finance elaborate physical plants and athletic programs ought to be able to afford housing and personnel for the kinds of services that students need in order to remain in school.

The financial problems of displaced homemakers and re-entry women are often unique, but economic barriers can be eliminated if the institution cares enough. A number of studies (Brandenburg, 1974; Buckley, Freeark, and O'Barr, 1976; Eliason, 1978) have addressed the subject. Displaced homemakers, single mothers, and older women frequently enroll as part-time students. Although federal aid can be awarded to those registered for a minimum of six credits, many institutions have not made such money available. Widows and divorced or separated women are frequently ineligible for assistance because they are required to report their spouses' incomes from the previous year. Repayment schedules for loans may be unrealistic for women with families. In some cases, there are age restrictions on financial assistance.

The nontraditional female student seeking access to the job market through education finds herself in a difficult bind: She cannot achieve financial independence or security until she acquires the necessary skills and credentials; she cannot acquire the necessary skills and credentials until she possesses the financial resources to obtain them. Some men suffer similar problems; but men without specific skills have traditionally had greater access to and success in the labor market and are less likely to have been absent from it for long periods of time.

Community college leaders must seek appropriate and feasible solutions to the economic dilemmas of women. It will be necessary to abandon the notions that education is the private province of the young or that the completion of requirements in two years somehow constitutes education more worthy of assistance than that obtained in five. When its own funds are limited, an institution's ties to community, business, and industry may provide access to alternative-funding sources for students. The community college has pioneered in educational projects across the country. Evolving more creative methods of financing education should be one of its highest priorities in the years to come.

Imposing as it seems, relieving economic distress may be the least of the institution's worries in aiding women. Financial stress is tangible and can be confronted directly. Psychological needs are not so easily recognized or combatted. Yet they affect the performances of women students of all ages. Those who are older are more likely to require help in adjusting to life-style changes and in overcoming the effects of sexual stereotyping. They may be disconcerted by the unfamiliar environment of academe and torn between marital, maternal, and educational responsibilities. Internal conflict is not peculiar to older women. Perhaps the most comprehensive analysis to date of the psychological differences between males and females is that of Maccoby and Jacklin (1974). One of their most startling conclusions is that women of "college age" (eighteen to twenty-two years) exhibit less sense of control over their own fates and less confidence in their probable performances on school-related tasks than do men of similar age. They pose several theories to explain the phenomenon. Among these is that the period between eighteen and twenty-two years is when women feel most profoundly the conflict between gender and educational demands. Whatever the explanation, young women appear to be as prone to conflict as those who are older.

These women, far more than faculty and administrators, require education and counseling about the consequences of female stereotyping. To accomplish this task, community college leaders must exhibit greater diligence than they have in the past. If they do not, the open door will continue to revolve and then shut on women who have not resolved gender conflicts and learned to cope in the aggressive world of the classroom.

The institution claims to have dealt with such issues by introducing courses and programs in women's studies. The value of these is obvious, but they may not be the most viable or pervasive means of solving the problem. Women's studies courses allow the institution to acknowledge that it recognizes women's past endeavors and encourages their future contributions to society. But they can exert little influence on the perceptions and behaviors of those who move in and out of academe without the time or the interest to elect such courses.

Informal instruction can be as effective as formal education. The community college, with stress on teaching and nurturing functions, should be especially sensitive to this. Every classroom—not just those specializing in women's studies—is a forum, and every teacher committed to establishing equality for women and minorities can use that forum. Some disciplines invite discussions of gender differences and problems more readily than others. This is the reason that the humanities and psychology are essential for all students. Yet even those disciplines which do not encourage consciousness raising about gender can contribute to the progress of female students, whose self-esteem rests partially on recognizing that women have made significant contributions in every field of endeavor. If teachers and textbooks neglect to convey that information, students will probably never learn it. And they will not believe it unless they are given the opportunity to observe successful women in the disciplines to which they are attracted.

Beyond concern for its faculty and administrators, the institution possesses responsibility for its students. It cannot fulfill its obligation to those who are female if it refuses to provide them with successful role models. As long as its own women employees remain a lower-status minority, it will send a message to both males and females that, rhetoric and special courses aside, women really are an inferior lot.

Gender conflict and stereotyping provoke not only psychological but also vocational dilemmas for women. The traditional position of the community college has been that women should be allowed access to any program, even those typically occupied by males. It has generally fulfilled its promise to permit women such opportunity, but the time has come to move from a passive to an active role. Eighteen-year-old female freshmen and middle-aged housewives do not choose academic programs independently. Their choices result from complex pressures exerted by sexual stereotypic myths along with the opinions of counselors, clergymen, teachers, parents, relatives, and peers who may subscribe to these myths. In selecting a career, a male is advised and a female is admonished.

Institutions have devised elaborate testing programs to determine prospective students' proficiencies in language and mathematics. They have taken great care to inform them about extracurricular opportunities. But few question students' vocational choices or attempt to educate them about the effects of stereotyping on career decisions. If the community college is serious about equity for female students, it must actively inform women about and recruit them for nontraditional vocations. It must educate them about the dangers of sexual stereotyping and encourage them to make independent career choices. It must guard against an environment in which neglect, stereotyping, or harassment dissuade women from exploring new careers and life-styles. Discouragement comes in a variety of forms—from biased texts and resource materials to parochial instructors and counselors. The task of the community college is to eliminate the impediments so that women will have genuine freedom to choose their own lives.

Institutional responsibility does not cease once women have been recruited and have graduated. A degree is one thing, a job another. Women have learned this through sometimes bitter trial and error. Much of the research (Briggs, 1978; Kirby, 1981) implies that educational recruitment without commitment to satisfactory job placement may be as bad as no opportunity at all. The community college has unique ties to business, industry, and government that can be used to increase training and employment opportunities for students and to guarantee them smooth entries into nontraditional as well as traditional occupations. One of its most exciting challenges in the years ahead will be to demonstrate that its creativity and innovativeness can be employed to solve even the pragmatic concerns of its students.

Conclusions

Serving students—female as well as male—is, after all, the primary function of the people's college. In the years to come, it must provide practical support for female students. It must maintain open admissions standards so that re-entry women will not be prevented access to education. It must assure that scheduling and credit procedures are flexible enough to meet the needs of diverse and often overextended constituencies. It must mobilize all of its resources to guarantee that counseling, child-care facilities and financial aid are available to nontraditional

students. It must attempt to combat the effects of gender stereotyping and to move women of all ages into the mainstream of
America's labor force.

In so doing, community college leaders must be prepared
to have their own female staff regarded as representative of
their attitudes toward women. It must move more rapidly to
establish equity in rank, tenure, and pay for male and female
academicians. It must actively recruit women faculty and administrators so that sexual imbalances in staffing will moderate.
It must be flexible enough to incorporate female as well as male
life-cycle patterns into career models. It must offer contractual
allowances for childrearing and opportunities for women with
interrupted careers to gain experience and expertise.

Perhaps the best way to summarize the task confronting
the community college at the close of the twentieth century is
to say that it must give women courage to risk themselves in a
world of prejudice and unforeseeable change. If things are not
as women "would have wished," then higher education must
provide them with the spirit and the skills to survive and to create a world more to their liking. It will be a place where both
sexes can finally feel at home. The classicist Dorothy Sayers
(1971) made this point in 1938 in an address to a women's society:

> "What," men have asked distractedly from
> the beginning of time, "what on earth do women
> want?" I do not know that women, as women,
> want anything in particular, but as human beings
> they want, my good men, exactly what you want
> yourselves: interesting occupation, reasonable free-
> dom for their pleasures, and a sufficient emotional
> outlet. What form the occupation, the pleasures
> and the emotion may take, depends entirely upon
> the individual. You know that this is so with your-
> selves—why will you not believe that it is so with
> us? The late D. H. Lawrence, who certainly cannot
> be accused of underrating the importance of sex
> and talked a good deal of nonsense upon the sub-
> ject, was yet occasionally visited with shattering
> glimpses of the obvious. He said in one of his *As-*

> *sorted Articles,* "Man is willing to accept woman as
> an angel, a devil, a baby-face, a machine, an instru-
> ment, a bosom, a womb, a pair of legs, a servant,
> an encyclopaedia, an ideal or an obscenity; the one
> thing he won't accept her as is a human being, a
> real human being of the feminine sex." "Accepted
> as a human being!"—yes; not as an inferior class
> and not, I beg and pray all feminists, as a superior
> class—not, in fact, as a class at all, except in a use-
> ful context. We are much too much inclined in
> these days to divide people into permanent cate-
> gories, forgetting that a category only exists for its
> special purpose and must be forgotten as soon as
> that purpose is served [p. 33].

It is probably necessary at this moment to categorize, to examine the needs and desires of the sexes as if they were different
and unique. For now, they may well be. But tomorrow when
the community college has accomplished the "special purpose"
of moving its women into the mainstream of the institution and
society, the categories can be forgotten, and men and women
will be able to get on with the challenge of being simply human.

Providing
Remedial Education

Donald E. Barshis
Thomas R. Guskey

The name, though not the concept, of developmental education is reasonably new in the academic marketplace. It is the encompassing term for the compensatory educational experience provided by colleges for increasing numbers of their students who are ill-prepared for traditional entry-level college curricula, as well as for the various vocational and technical programs characteristic of two-year colleges. The term gained prominence in the early 1970s (Roueche and Wheeler, 1973) and derives from Carl Rogers's "whole person" approach in psychotherapy (Rogers, 1961). Since then, developmental education has found proponents across the educational spectrum who believe that the "whole person" focus is necessary to provide a significant educational experience for the nation's increasing numbers of poorly prepared and poorly motivated students. Roueche (1980, p. 5) expresses the global implications of these ideas when he argues that "the goal of competence must be expanded beyond verbal literacy and computational skills. It must include more than word skills, figures, and economic rewards. We must raise awareness and promote creative growth to such an extent that holistic literacy becomes the common aim of the individual and society, congruence and harmony are the norms, and the quality of life is enhanced for all."

76

The pervasiveness of the developmental education movement has been documented by Cohen and Brawer (1982) who have verified Morrison and Ferrante's finding (1973) that most of the nation's community and junior colleges have some sort of developmental, preparatory, or remedial program. During the 1970s as these programs proliferated and became more comprehensive, critics, both inside and outside academe, have become more visible and vocal. Questions are continually raised about the reliability of data reported in different program studies. Counselors fret over the damage that academic tracking does to the self-concept of the already failure-prone student. Defenders of curricula and academic standards argue that both areas suffer because of the negligible long-term effect of compensatory efforts. College administrators, state legislatures, and the public complain about the costs of providing literacy training at the taxpayers' expense for students who have shown no indication that they can be educated. It is time to ask some hard questions about the assumptions, practices, and results of these programs; to define the still unresolved issues in clear, propaganda-free terms; and to answer those critics who would see developmental programs end, cut back, or relegated to sectors other than higher education.

There has always been a certain proportion of college freshmen who have been unprepared for the college-level curriculum. Rudolph (1977) notes that colonial colleges were beset by this problem in the early part of the eighteenth century. Special programs or courses designed specifically to help these students can also be traced to the nineteenth century (Cross, 1976). While higher education has seen fit to serve the underprepared student for some time, the number of such students has increased dramatically during the last decade, taxing the resources of the nation's colleges greatly. Hechinger's sobering study on national literacy (1977) presents us with the reality of a nation of high school graduates, over half of whom cannot read beyond the level required to graduate from grammar school. This population is mirrored in the declining levels of preparedness among college freshmen. While high school grades have remained constant or shown an increase, scores on national examinations taken by the college-bound, such as the Scholastic Aptitude Test and American College Test, have shown a gradual and consistent decline since the mid-1960s (Roueche, 1980; American College Testing Program, 1966–1981).

Traditionally, public and private four-year colleges and universities have restricted admissions on the basis of scholastic aptitude and secondary school records. This has left the community college with its open admission policy as the only institution of higher learning available for students from poorer academic backgrounds. Estimates of the proportion of entering community college students who need some sort of academic remediation vary from institution to institution. Some are as low as 25 percent (Cohen and others, 1973), others as high as 70 percent (Barshis, 1982; Gold, 1977). Lombardi (1979) predicts that the proportion of entering students needing remediation of some sort will reach 50 percent of the total enrollment in the next decade, a figure that may be too low according to Roueche's findings (1982) from a study on Texas community colleges.

Students ill-prepared for college-level work are often referred to as "high-risk" students though other euphemisms abound. Whatever they are called, these students have been perceived as less likely than their better prepared counterparts to succeed in any given college course and consequently less likely to continue through a standard sequence of courses from term to term (Romoser, 1978). Academically, these students lack a solid educational base for success. They have poor study habits and lack basic reading, writing, and computational skills (Kraetsch, 1980). Most have had less than favorable learning conditions during their elementary and secondary school years. Most are from the bottom third of their high school class (Campbell, 1981). Psychologically, these students have little confidence in their ability to learn and generally suffer from a low self-image. In class they are seldom active participants and are reluctant to admit they need help (Friedlander, 1981–1982). In the major urban areas, these are largely minority students whose educational and psychological handicaps are exacerbated by economic, social, and racial factors.

That there is a need for compensatory education programs, developmental or otherwise, to serve a vast number of American students who have been ill-served by their prior educational experiences seems obvious. The improvement of social and economic conditions within the nation is a likely outcome of improved national literacy. Whether community colleges are the logical place for these programs may provoke some disagreement, but as long as an open admissions policy remains part of the community college's mission, as long as the community's priorities can direct the institution's priorities, then these colleges, as Cohen and Brawer (1982) point out, have the responsibility to teach their students the skills required for them to succeed.

Key Assumptions

Three key assumptions underlie most community college developmental education programs, and these assumptions have remained relatively unquestioned as designers concentrated on the practical problems of setting up model programs. The first is that the increasing population of inadequately prepared students who come to the nation's community colleges is educable —that is, that under appropriate conditions, such students can be prepared to learn well in college or vocational and technical curricula. The second assumption is that these appropriate conditions can be provided in an efficient manner with the resources available to community colleges. The third assumption is that the community college is the most appropriate place to provide the developmental education experience. The unquestioned acceptance of these ideas has provided program critics with pertinent issues for their concern. They deserve a closer look.

Educability of Students. In her seminal study of the "new students" entering institutions of higher learning under an open admission policy, Cross (1976) defends the educability of this population. When these students are provided with instruction that is appropriate to their needs and when they are given help in overcoming learning difficulties, the large majority can have successful learning experiences. As a result of such conditions, they develop a positive view of their own learning capabilities and can be motivated to complete their original goals and plans for higher education (Guskey, Barshis, and Easton, 1982).

Studies in recent years have shown that the teaching and learning strategies associated with "mastery learning" (Bloom, 1968, 1976) are one way to provide students with favorable conditions for learning. Although there are a number of variations of mastery learning, most involve conventional group instruction followed by periodic feedback and corrective procedures to bring the majority of students to a high standard of learning for each section of a teacher's course. In addition to improving student achievement, these strategies also have been shown to result in increased motivation for further learning and marked reduction in course attrition rates among students in community colleges (Guskey and Monsaas, 1979).

Many institutions have also managed to improve conditions for learning by attacking the very structure of the traditional learning environment, which is characterized by group instruction carried out within rigid time constraints. "Open-entry, open-exit" instructional sequences, contract learning, credit-granting individualized learning centers, credentials for life experience, and self-paced instructional packages delivered in a variety of nontraditional ways (radio, television, newspapers, and computers) have all helped to bring instruction closer to the ideal of a one-to-one student-teacher ratio. Unfortunately, because it is sometimes difficult to provide these conditions in a cost effective way, program designers are driven back to traditional structures and more remote approximations of the ideal.

We can probably assume the educability of ill-prepared students under appropriate and supportive learning conditions such as those described, but educational leaders must work within compromising realities. They are subject to the pressures of results-oriented and cost-conscious boards, often unsympathetic or ill-informed state legislatures, state educational guidelines that fail to allow for creativity and flexibility in programs, and restrictive contractual arrangements with faculty and professional staff. Community college leaders must therefore work to effect change whenever possible within such restricting forces, never lose sight of the ideal of serving their community populations, and submit to compromise only when resources necessitate it. This compromise may mean limiting the number of students who can be served through comprehensive developmental programs, limiting the time they have to fulfill the objectives of the programs, establishing criteria for entry into a mainstreaming program, and creating other alternatives for other kinds of students.

Sufficient Resources. The majority of developmental programs today were launched with the idea that they could be accommodated and sustained by their parent institutions that adequate resources would exist within the traditional educational structure to meet program needs. These resources include personnel such as faculty and counselors, course and program design capability, an incentive structure for students (such as credit for courses), and sufficient academic support services beyond the classroom.

This assumption of local sufficiency has not prevented many institutions from seeking all the assistance possible—federal, state, local, and private—to aid in the initiation or development of model programs in compensatory education. The principle behind most funding programs, at least those of recent vintage, is that a receiving institution will aim toward the institutionalization of the funded program within a few years. All too often, however, the funded programs vanish and the project personnel return to the unemployment rolls when the funds run out. Local college personnel will have to become involved if funded programs are to enter the regular curricula and services of the college. And the colleges will have to provide the specialized assessment, counseling, curriculum design, staff development, tutoring, or academic advising that generally characterizes funded efforts.

This raises the question of whether the principal services staff—administrators, faculty, counselors, and academic support staff—are actually qualified to work with developmental students. Even if they are, there remains the issue of whether the top academic and fiscal administrators will provide the unified, coordinating leadership to initiate and maintain a comprehensive developmental education program that by its nature requires cooperative effort among the various academic and administrative departments. Because resources exist in an institution does not guarantee that they can be organized effectively to create the optimum conditions for learning essential for a successful program.

Appropriateness. Most community college mission statements contain the provision of remedial or compensatory education as one of their five or six principal functions (Breneman and Nelson, 1981). Gleazer (1980) argues that community colleges must evolve into community-based learning centers as their next logical phase of development. These centers will provide the specific literacy training required to prepare citizens for jobs and fulfilling lives. Roueche (1980, p. 3) speaks of the community college of the future "with its track record in developmental education" as "the college of diversity. It is the institution to which the poor, the disaffected, the hard-core 'losers' will turn for aid in exploring the options that will give them a better chance of survival in an increasingly hostile and complex world." There is no question that developmental education is currently part of the community college function, and some educators predict significant future growth in that function.

Breneman and Nelson, in their critical examination of community college financing (1981, p. 50), note that "the public benefits from remedial education seem substantial, but the costs are also likely to be high in view of the high-risk nature of the students. The question of how many times society must pay for basic education poses a reasonable challenge to postsecondary remedial programs. If the view prevails that remedial education is not the proper function of community colleges, then the efficient level of subsidy would be zero—either the courses should not be offered at all, or only on a self-supporting basis. It is more likely that remedial education would be deemed a proper function of community colleges and its public benefits would be considered worth their full cost."

The issue then is not whether the community college

should serve developmental students. Instead, the issue concerns degree: what share of a college's dwindling resources should be allocated for developmental students, and should those resource expenditures adversely affect the college's transfer or vocational and technical functions? Individual institutions must set their priorities, subject always to the priorities of funding agencies, to accommodate developmental students. But proponents of developmental education programs should beware. Institutional priorities can shift, assumptions can change in time if complacency over a program's place in the institutional hierarchy leads to inattention and failure to reaffirm its value through solid evidence of success.

Practices and Outcomes

Shifting our emphasis from the assumptions underlying developmental education programs, we will examine some of the principal practices within these programs and the results these practices are purported to yield.

First, some of the terminology most often used to discuss developmental education needs clarification. Confusion often results from the interchanging of terms such as developmental, remedial, compensatory, basic, and corrective. Lombardi (1979) has provided a useful paradigm that makes developmental education the umbrella term under which he places four categories of developmental curricula: pretransfer, handicapped, remedial, and adult basic education. This model recognizes the distinction first developed by Roueche and Wheeler (1973) and modified by Cross (1976) that separates remedial and developmental education on the basis of specific focus (correction of deficiencies versus development of skills *and* attitudes) and intended outcome (entry into programs one was previously ineligible for versus growth as a functioning, self-assured human being). The model also avoids unproductive comparisons between the two terms and avoids bias against the more limited remedial. By seeing remedial as a kind of curriculum and curriculum as but one part of a college's total developmental education effort, the Lombardi model provides a useful perspective from which to examine the ways in which developmental education is carried out in American community colleges.

We have noted that the majority of American colleges have some kind of developmental education effort. The most common approach is the remedial course in one of the basic skills areas of reading, writing, or mathematics. Students deemed deficient in one or more of these requisite skills are placed in appropriate remedial courses designed to bring their performance to college-level standards. Quite often, as Roueche points out (1981–82), the students are simultaneously programmed into regular college courses requiring the skill being remediated. This practice negates the effect of the remedy. Faculty in the regular college courses may either fail such students or lower standards and base their grades on judgments about the undemonstrated potential of the student. This subjectivity in grading is well known among American educators: It creates faculty unwillingness to grade on student performance, along with a variation of the primary and secondary school practice of "social promotion." It has contributed to the overall decline in student literacy, the wholesale inflation of grades, and the increase in unrealistic student expectations that plagues postsecondary educators today.

Remedial courses in themselves are not the problem. In fact, considerable evidence exists (Cohen, 1973; Cohen and Brawer, 1982) that the courses actually achieve what they set out to achieve: they remedy a specific problem. The issue is how the courses fit into a total student program, given the commonplace among educational researchers that "transfer of training" does not automatically occur across the curriculum (Cross, 1976). Remedial courses must be supplemented and not countered by the other courses in a student's program. In addition, remedial courses have been shown to increase in effectiveness (Cohen and Brawer, 1982; Barshis, 1982) when attended by tutoring and other academic support services. Remedial curricula show the greatest results when incorporated into a larger human development framework.

The other curricular approaches suggested in the Lombardi model—pretransfer, handicapped, and adult basic education—suffer from the same limitations, albeit of different degrees, as the remedial course approach. Pretransfer and adult basic education courses have the advantage of a direct test of effectiveness: entry into the transfer course or successful passing of the General Education Development (GED) examination. Curricula for handicapped people are almost always accompanied by supportive services and are still in early stages of development. Pretransfer students are likely to bring fewer problems and needs with them when compared with their remedial counterparts, necessitating fewer attendant services. Adult basic education courses, while rarely accompanied by support services, are generally kept to an appropriate level of difficulty to meet student needs and are almost always attended by part-time working students. Remedial courses still have the largest enrollments and are most frequently offered as the first mainstreaming efforts to bring poorly prepared students into college or vocational programs (Lombardi, 1979).

Another curricular approach, one not suggested by Lombardi's model, is the "regular courses plus services" approach advanced by Cohen and Brawer (1982): Students are allowed to enroll for regular courses, though the number of courses is restricted, and are required to avail themselves of academic support services. Bloom (1980) has argued that major gains can be realized in regular courses by providing maximum time for specific learning tasks through creative use of mastery learning strategies and support systems. Should students fail despite such help, Chausow (1979) and others have argued that they may still profit by repeating the course a second time, rather than taking it in a diluted remedial version. Roueche (1978) has countered that this approach is akin to diagnosing a severe heart ailment in a patient and then treating him or her as an outpatient and advising a jogging regimen as therapy. Yet the approach of Cohen and Brawer may prove to be the most attractive, and perhaps the only, alternative if external funding is restricted.

Other practices in developmental education short of a comprehensive program include special orientation sessions, summer skills institutes, walk-in learning resource centers, clinics, and alternative schools. Many of these practices have elaborate documentation of success, particularly since so many were funded with public or private grants. But the fact that none of them is an alternative of national significance to the comprehensive model suggests that a piecemeal approach to developmental education is not the answer.

The questions raised over the years about the adequacy of a pure curricular approach have led many colleges to adopt comprehensive programs in developmental education that provide students with a total, integrated package of services. La Guardia Community College's exemplary program, begun in the early 1970s, was soon followed by a number of equally ambitious efforts to address the human development needs of students. Often these programs were started under grants from the once bounteous coffers of federal Title III programs. Comprehensive programs in diverse community college districts such as Monterey, Colorado Springs, Fort Worth, and Charlotte, along with La Guardia in New York, have produced considerable literature on the number of services that could be crammed into a student's experience. The results showed apparent success—and the expected amount of questionable data. Out of various descriptions of these exemplary programs (Roueche and Snow, 1977; Beal and Noel, 1980), there emerges a reasonably consistent pattern. Most successful comprehensive developmental program models have five common elements: (1) thorough assessment leading to appropriate placement; (2) qualified and committed faculty teaching in the program; (3) appropriate curricula suited to the needs of the students and leading to appropriate subsequent steps in the college's program or network of referrals; (4) focused academic support services, such as tutoring and counseling; and (5) program evaluation and thorough documentation of results.

Our concern in examining these characteristics of successful programs is to distinguish actual practices with demonstrable results from idealized procedures that fail to contend with the realities of community college life. Our approach is necessarily indirect; very few colleges have documented their inadequacies. We have been guided primarily by our own experiences as developmental educators, program evaluators, and avid conference goers (where much of the truth in education is discussed candidly in and out of workshop sessions).

Thorough Assessment. Much of the good work being done in community college preregistration assessment is overshadowed by the nightmare of poor and often destructive practices that pass for assessment. Almost every community college instructor has a personal horror story about some poor soul who wound up in an advanced elective section while concurrently enrolled in a developmental reading course. Most poor assessment practices can be traced directly to low priority valuing and poor leadership at particular institutions, declining resources for testing and counseling, a "body count" approach to recruitment and registration, abdication of involvement in the testing function by academic departments, and faculty prerequisite structure in entry-level courses.

Many researchers have concluded (Roueche, 1981–1982; Herrscher, 1977) that entering students must be screened carefully to determine if they possess all the necessary skills—and, if possible, the attitudes—for collegiate study. Communication and quantitative skills are the core of a student's academic survival strategies, closely followed by self-esteem (Mink, 1976) and self-direction in learning (Knowles, 1975). Most model developmental programs purport to have embodied these findings into the assessment phase of their programs. Many colleges proudly point to required Nelson-Denny Reading Tests for all incoming students, to writing samples graded by local English department members, to comprehensive orientation programs where new students undergo quantitative skills examinations and self-concept tests. While these are all exemplary practices and create a very professional image of a developmental education program that cares about knowing who its students are, a closer look at these testing practices reveals some recurring problem areas.

Required reading tests are necessary aspects of preregistration assessment, but what kind of placement decisions are based on them and why? The Nelson-Denny is the most widely used placement test in community colleges (Roueche and Snow, 1977), but it fails to measure levels below the sixth grade, and the grade-level discriminations are themselves based on questionable criteria, according to the review of the test in *Eighth Mental Measurements Yearbook* (Buros, 1978). The test is rigorously timed; even a few extra minutes can produce a wide variance in grade equivalent scores. In the two years since it has been used as the primary placement instrument by the City Colleges of Chicago, five of the seven colleges either have requested use of another instrument or have found it necessary to give some sort of followup test to verify placement into the colleges' two-tier developmental education program. The Nelson-Denny may yield useful placement information if a college has only one level of developmental education programming, but even then it affords little diagnostic information about student reading problems. The moment assessment personnel begin exploring alternate testing instruments, however, they begin to face the problems of cost, testing logistics, and comprehensiveness of assessment for all entering students.

Mass registration in larger community colleges, particularly those whose funding levels are determined by head count, militates against comprehensive assessment programs. Part-time students, late registrants, and advisees of ill-informed faculty regularly fall into the cracks of any comprehensive assessment effort. Skills assessment requires consistency in administration of programs; few community colleges with large enrollments, in our experience, have managed to attain this consistency. The integrity of a college's developmental education program is bound to suffer, and students with the greatest need often are not served.

Another weak area in assessment is the use made of the information garnered. Ideally, student records should list pertinent information about student deficiencies, attitudes, learning styles, and the like. These records should then serve as a guide to the college developmental program staff charged with providing services to the student. In practice, student records are seen briefly during registration or advisement and possibly in individual counseling sessions that attend comprehensive developmental programs. But concerns about student privacy, uncoordinated student services, and the sheer weight of bureaucracy in large systems and programs quite often keep valuable information from those who might best use it to improve their services to the students. Only aggressive program leadership can ensure that information acquired becomes information used to help students.

A final area of concern in preregistration assessment and placement is the questionable link between the specific objectives of developmental courses and services and those levels of skills and attitudes being assessed. How often have students found themselves in total developmental programs on the basis of a single reading test score which may have been low only because of testing conditions or over-reliance upon rigorous timing? Because testing is both costly and time consuming, far too many institutions are trying to find that all-purpose testing instrument which will yield an accurate measure of students' verbal and quantitative skills in one stroke. Care instead should be given to creating flexible programs into which students are placed based upon specific assessment directed toward the objectives of the specific program. And the student should always have the option of being able to withdraw from the program if he or she has been wrongly placed.

Qualified and Committed Faculty. A national study (Beal and Noel, 1980) discovered that a caring attitude on the part of faculty and high-quality teaching were the two principal reasons that community college students stayed in school. Spann (1977, p. 31) has argued for the carefully trained developmental specialist, "a person who believes that students can learn and will learn if given the proper environment; he believes that a student brings his whole self to school (not just his mind) and that as his teacher he must respond to the student as a whole person. A teacher who responds to the whole person must not only possess the ability to provide student-centered instruction but must acquire appropriate helping skills to work with the student personally." As has been the case with education throughout its history, the teacher plays a pivotal role, perhaps more so for high-risk students who have not benefited from their previous educational experiences.

Workable comprehensive developmental education programs depend on their faculty. A number of developmental studies departments have gathered expert faculty together into single cross-disciplinary units. Other colleges have given faculty special assignments (often with incentives such as reduced work loads) to work with high-risk students. In fact, if we were to limit our reading to developmental education's advocacy literature, we would think that faculty availability for developmental programs was hardly an issue, that cadres of eager, qualified, caring mentors filled community college faculty ranks. Sadly, such is not the case.

One of the critical problems facing new as well as established developmental education programs is the acute shortage of faculty resources. Community colleges are not short of faculty, but the regular faculty are mainly tenured and entrenched in jobs they have been at for years. As Cohen and Brawer (1982, p. 237) have noted, "traditional faculty members remember their college in the 1950s and early 1960s, when they had well-prepared students. They may feel nostalgic, perhaps even betrayed because the conditions under which they entered the colleges have changed so. At the same time, they may be pleased that the segregated compensatory education programs remove the poorer students from their own classes. . . . Nonetheless, the teachers in the compensatory education programs run the risk of becoming pariahs, similar in that regard to occupational education instructors in the pre-1960s era." The pervasive wish among faculty for the days when college students came with the requisite skills, when elective classes flourished, when teaching was essentially a matter of dissemination of carefully prepared content, helps to explain why there is a shortage of appropriate faculty for the high-risk student. It helps to explain as well the outright hostility of some traditional faculty to the high-risk students and their problems. These instructors resent the recommendations of developmental education theorists such as Roueche, Cross, and Spann that teachers in developmental programs need to interact personally with their students. In fact, they strongly feel that faculty responsibilities do not necessarily include friendships and personal involvement with students.

The increasing number of underprepared students entering the open doors of today's community colleges make the high-risk student everyone's problem—and responsibility. While remedial courses are rapidly replacing both electives and college entry-level curricula, developmental education program coordinators are faced with faculty who lack either the interest or the skill to work with high-risk students. Simply assigning these people courses and expecting them to figure out how to succeed does both them and their students a great disservice. The proliferation of staff development efforts in community colleges across the country, efforts that emphasize new pedagogical strategies and mentoring practices, points to a necessary retooling of faculty resources.

Appropriate, Sequential Curricula. A thornier issue of developmental education programs concerns the most appropriate curriculum for high-risk students. Lombardi's categories fail to indicate specific course descriptions, emphasizing instead audience and overall outcome. What should constitute the preliminary educational experience in college for high-risk students who have every expectation, based on their high school experiences, of moving right into college curricula? Developmental education curricula cannot be simply a restatement of primary or secondary school courses with a college label affixed. The students have not learned needed word-attack skills, cannot understand main ideas, fail to produce literate and interesting sentences, cannot organize a series of thoughts into unified and focused paragraphs, and cannot calculate or solve word problems requiring some abstract reasoning skill. Primary and secondary school education has not worked for them, and the courses in a model developmental education program must address this fact of life.

Despite disagreement among educators as to the appropriate content for developmental studies programs, there is some consensus about the general characteristics of the courses. Herrscher (1977) argues that courses should have a sound rationale, a clear set of performance objectives, a direct relation to the college's assessment program, alternate learning activities tied to the course objectives, opportunities for revision, and postassessment consistent with objectives and learning activities. Block and Anderson (1975) focus on objectives, sequential learning units, diagnostic testing with many opportunities for correction, and summative or evaluative testing based on what was taught. Roueche (1980) opts for curricula with utility, relevance, multisensory capability, and a cross-disciplinary thrust. Over and over, these and other educators emphasize the need to specify what is to be learned, to give students every opportunity to learn it, to evaluate the students on what has been taught, and to envelop the entire process with valuing. How does this translate into specific courses?

Most developmental education curricular programs build around the nucleus of basic skills courses in communication (reading, writing, speaking) and quantification (usually, a calculations review course). Often block programming is used. Block programming means structuring curricula into groups of courses —for example, developmental reading, writing, and math—with twenty-five or so students concurrently enrolled in all the courses in a block. Many colleges fill out the program with a human development course that combines the overall emphasis upon improving self-concept with useful reviews of study skills, test taking, personal career planning, and the like. Others use pretransfer courses, either in vocational and technical areas or general education disciplines, to complete the student's program. In either case, the added courses should be conducted at reading and writing levels consistent with students' entry abilities, and they must reinforce the basic skills courses. This is usually accomplished by instructors team teaching blocks of courses under the leadership of a program coordinator. Block programming allows the teaching effort to be integrated with the academic support services available at the college.

Does the cognitive component of most comprehensive model programs really help to achieve overall program goals? Are its students integrated into college-level programs? Do they experience personal growth? Do they develop as whole persons? There are no easy answers to these questions. Roueche (1980) and others want developmental curriculum to include cultural history, esthetics, and other affective contexts recently brought to light by brain science research into right-hemisphere learning.

Block (1971) cites a number of mastery learning theorists who believe that we have only scratched the surface in teaching traditional subjects successfully because of our poor pedagogical practices. Cohen and Brawer (1982) urge the use of liberal arts courses, perhaps even at the expense of effective basic skills curriculum, with limited numbers of credit hours and massive support services.

Whatever the curricula, developmental studies must lead students somewhere; they must avoid repeating the failures of past education. There is no clear answer as yet as to what is the best curriculum. In the reality in which we must function, a certain level of cognitive skill is still expected of college-level students, but so is the ability to self-direct one's life and learning. Whatever a school is able to do well and whatever integrates with its institutional mission and other curricula might serve as a first step in determining its best developmental curriculum.

Focused Academic Support Services. One of the results of the grant origins of many comprehensive developmental programs is a network of services and learning supports that might not otherwise have emerged from within the resources of the colleges. Many of these support services have been embraced by the colleges and incorporated into their fiscal priorities. A number of large community college systems (California and Illinois, for instance) receive specific additional state money for academic support services such as tutoring and special counseling. Other systems keep these costly services by actively pursuing grants; still others enter into cooperative arrangements with local senior colleges and graduate schools through intern programs. Whatever the source of these services, most are deemed essential to the success of their programs.

Focused academic support services are specifically integrated into the assessment, placement, and curricular efforts of the comprehensive program. Counselor aides work with program coordinators during assessment periods to provide proper orientation and explanation of programs and curricula to prospective students. Often, these same paraprofessionals take major responsibility for placement testing and specialized counseling. Tutors in programs with focused resources actually sit in classes and work with instructors to develop and provide curriculum supplements, often supplying feedback to instructors using mastery learning strategies (Caponigri and others, 1982). The tutors build close personal relationships with students and take on the larger function of mentor or "learning manager." These tutors can have a marked positive effect on improving student retention (Lenning, Sauer, and Beal, 1980). Counselors and their assistants can directly provide ongoing focused support to the student during the comprehensive program in several ways: through personal counseling and academic advisement, self-guided careers exploration workshops, study skills seminars, academic monitoring and prescriptions for improvement, courses in personal development, and assistance in cutting through the bureaucracy attending financial aid and other administrative services. A focused resource program can bring valuable academic assets such as libraries, computer-supported instruction systems, such as Programmed Logic for Automated Teaching Operations (P.L.A.T.O.) or Miami-Dade's Response System with Variable Prescriptions (R.S.V.P.) system, and individualized instruction centers into full use by those students who need them most.

The alternative to a focused academic support service program is the traditional set of student services, such as counseling offices, libraries, and tutoring centers, available to students at most community colleges across the country. These resources often are quite excellent in design and staff, but they fail to make a significant difference in developmental student performance because they rely upon student initiative for their use. The high-risk student most in need of help lacks the motivation and information to make best use of these services. Vitalo (1974, p. 34) has observed that "(a) untrained students cannot effectively discriminate which individuals are best able to offer them help in their efforts to learn and grow, (b) untrained students do not function at high enough levels of communication skills to be of help to one another in times of crisis, (c) untrained students do not function at high enough levels of communication skills to facilitate each other's learning, (d) untrained students tend to be unsystematic in their approach to problems and issues, and (e) uncounseled students tend to lack

definitive career goals and directions which have been sufficiently scrutinized and confirmed by solid investigation." Thus, the
academic support services personnel must not passively wait for
students to come to them; they must seek out students and actively engage them in the available services. A likely byproduct
of such active service is the judgment by students that the institution's faculty and staff possess the caring attitude found by
educational researchers to be the principal reason why students
stay in school (Beal and Noel, 1980).

Of course, developmental programs with focused academic support services must have the appropriate personnel to
staff those programs. Finding such people becomes increasingly
difficult as funds get tighter and more programs turn toward
part-time staff members to fill their positions. Community colleges face particular difficulties because they do not have a pool
of upperclassmen from which to draw, and most of their students are already working. Staff development programs become
crucial to provide the in-service training needed, putting a further drain on scarce resources. Educational leaders must look to
the total costs of adequate support services and let that factor
help determine the scope of the program. Focusing the support
services to the needs of the highest-risk students will necessarily
decrease their availability to other students. Again, reality forces
leaders to become pragmatic and set hard management priorities
on the use of scarce resources. The results may be less than the
best possible program for a particular group of students, but
those students exist alongside other students with their own
needs for support services.

Program Evaluation and Documentation. Developmental
studies programs that have attracted most national attention
have also published glowing reports about the continuing successes of their students. The Educational Resources Information
Center (ERIC) indexes are filled with summary papers on program results. In a recent meta-analysis of developmental education programs (based on techniques expounded by G. V. Glass
in 1976), researchers studied 504 documents before arriving
at their final pool of 60 comprehensive evaluation documents
(Kulik, Kulik, and Shwalb, 1982). It is obvious that develop-

mental educators are aware that their continued existence depends upon their accountability for time and resources spent. But what are the standards for accountability against which developmental educators are to be judged? Is student retention in a program an adequate measure of that program's success? Is a gain of several grades in reading level during a semester satisfactory? What if the student started at a fifth-grade level and is still unable to begin college-level work? The very practice of using before and after testing with standardized reading tests is, as Cross notes (1976), highly suspect, especially if the examiner uses grade-level improvement to demonstrate a cause-effect relationship between the developmental effort and grade gain. Is grade-point average at the end of the program an adequate measure of success when grades themselves have been rendered meaningless as predictors of student success (Sharon, 1972)?

The situation may not be as bleak as Cohen and Brawer (1982) paint it—with advocates of absolute performance standards lining up to do battle with defenders of individualized standards and lifelong learning. It is true that the most outspoken proponents of the "whole person" approach in developmental studies see criteria for determining a program's success beyond the traditional ones of retention, grades, test scores, and next-term achievement. The enthusiasm these educators show for mastery learning pedagogy with its emphasis on clear standards of performance suggests a solution to the problem of which standards of accountability to apply to developmental programs. The national movement toward specific exit standards for developmental courses, which suggests ways of documenting such standards (competency testing using a variety of testing formats), is a healthy first step toward countering the relativity of evaluation in the last decade.

Issues Facing Developmental Educators

As educators—administrators, faculty, and support staff—move through the 1980s, they must face and resolve a number of currently unsolved problems. Most of the pressure on community colleges over developmental education will come from concern over funding. Tough economic times normally send more people to schools for possible retraining or upgrading of their skills. But those same tough times find available money for social programs being cut, and education always feels the pinch. Though community colleges will benefit from increasing numbers of nontraditional students, these students will demand more from developmental program resources. Will legislatures continue to provide the money to community colleges to maintain or increase the level of developmental services? If the economic pie does not get any bigger, will these funds be provided at the expense of those allocated for traditional college programs? The Illinois state legislature recently mandated that remedial and developmental education no longer be done in four-year colleges and universities and made it a primary responsibility of the community college system. This decision will be tested fully if and when its budgetary implications are realized in critical areas such as allocations for student support services and funding levels for remedial courses. Will the senior institutions be willing to give up some of their support service money? Will they be able to serve their traditional population as well without funded remedial and developmental resources? What will senior institution enrollments look like without the numbers of ill-prepared students they are currently aggressively recruiting?

The future of community college developmental education includes the need to create close ties with the secondary schools which provide its new students and the senior institutions which receive its transfer students. National competencies efforts, such as the College Board's Project EQuality (Redmon, 1982), can provide direction for educators at all three levels in creating a unified educational effort centered around a common understanding of what constitutes competency in college-bound students. A healthy exchange among the three levels of schools can lead to the necessary pooling of information and resources that will give high-risk students some chance at both consistency and quality in their educational experiences. Progressive community college leaders can initiate the exchange by convening counterparts from other institutions to begin creative planning on ways to match one institution's expectations of student ability with another's capability to produce such a student. Subsequent sessions should involve the principal service providers—faculty, counselors, support staff—and might include valuable resource-pooling efforts similar to those between vocational-technical community college programs and the industries they serve.

Efforts to link community college developmental programs and the private sector need to be improved if the national literacy problem is to be addressed. The more comprehensive assessment techniques become, the more they can be put to use by business and industry, which sorely need ways to improve the skills and overall competencies of their workers. The New York Economic Development Council's support of mastery learning training for academic personnel demonstrates the interest of business and industry in helping to generate quality workers for their employment rolls. The better developmental educators become in their accomplishments of creating skilled, complete human resources, the more likely they will be to receive both support and requests for further service from the communities they serve.

Almost all the issues that need to be worked on internally by community college educators stem from the tension between traditionalists and evolutionists. The traditionalists regard the transfer function as the primary mission of the community college and, grudgingly in recent years, have added vocational and technical education. Their ranks are filled with theorists, faculty, legislators, trustees, and members of the general public. The evolutionists, following Gleazer's lead (1980), see the next logical step in the development of the community college to be true community education, where the emphasis on lifelong learning will move the institution away from its rigid structures and expectations. The tension between these two camps is reflected in many specific issues that need to be resolved, such as faculty roles (specialist in content versus manager of learning), types of pedagogy (lecture and discussion versus high-engagement strategies), curricula (basic skills versus holistic focus), and program accountability (absolute performance standards and mainstreaming versus individualized learning and personal growth).

There are no easy answers to these problems. We have tried to present the broadest possible picture of the complexity that is community college developmental education; it is in that continuum that educational leaders must function. College administration may think that developmental education is one of the most important things a community college should be doing, but trustees, students, faculty, and the community may have other priorities (Cross, 1981b). This is the reality in which decisions—and compromises—have to be made. Developmental education programs are part of community college life and, no doubt, will be for some time. High-risk students continue to find reason to come to community colleges for another chance at learning, and many of them are apparently pleased at what they find. But many are not. We need to keep those failures before us. They will keep us honest and self-analytical and make us willing to change. As we move through the 1980s, others will keep telling us to do better. As serious educators, we have to listen and, in this serious business of developmental education, do better.

5

Reformulating General Education Programs

Chester H. Case

It is widely acknowledged that the community college is in a period of transition. Vital and challenging questions are being raised about its proper mission and goals, as this volume attests. Answers to these questions will shape the essential character of the community college for years to come. One such critical question has to do with the general education function of the community college. As has been the case with other segments of postsecondary education, the community college has embraced general education in principle and rhetoric but has delivered it poorly.

The improvement of general education should be a concern of highest priority for the community college because general education is an essential, even indispensable, function of the community college. Community college general education needs reformulation in order to overcome its present shortcomings and limitations, but it does not need reinvention. There is an extensive literature and a body of experience to draw upon. There are well-known and often-proclaimed principles of community college general education that scarcely can be improved upon. These principles urge that the community college educate for citizenship in a democratic, pluralistic society; that it promote in the learner knowledge of self and society; that it complement specialized and vocational education; that it promote in the learner knowledge, skills, and attitudes conducive to a lifetime of learning.

While there is no need to reinvent general education, there is, nevertheless, a need to restate its ideals and to find effective means of translating them into effective programs. To do so, the community college must take up the challenge of reformulating general education. Reformulation means to recast the best of past and present ideas into new forms that are workable, practical, and consistent with the comprehensive, open door policies of the community college.

Promulgating yet another set of goals or yet again rewriting a college's general education requirements will not accomplish reformulation. Reformulation will be a major undertaking. It will challenge faculty and administrative leadership of colleges and districts to develop for their colleges the best elements of philosophy, goals and objectives, organization, curriculum and pedagogy, resources and personnel, and program development and implementation that can be combined into workable and effective programs. If it is pursued over time with tenacious leadership and an adequate commitment of resources, the outcome of a reformulation project should be a clearly identifiable, coherent curriculum integrated into an effective program well suited to its college.

Contemporary General Education

General education, as commonly practiced, is not general. It is not tied to a commonly accepted body of knowledge that all the college's learners ought to know. It is not wrapped up in a consistent, widely accepted definition, and it is not implemented in widely accepted and recognized models. Typically, it is not anchored to a philosophical base that expresses the institution's convictions about the role of the college, the needs of society and the learner, and the part that general education should play in the overall educational plan of the institution. It is not, except in all too few instances, an operational program that offers a body of curriculum deployed into a clearly identifiable set of courses that cohere around shared concerns and beliefs and demonstrate in their integration the interrelationships of knowledge. General education is not a concept that lends itself easily to quantified evaluation, nor is it a concept that can be readily communicated and justified to an audience that wants to see a positive benefits/costs ratio. Cohen and Brawer (1982) observe that, while there is a plethora of definitions of general education, there is no consistency among them.

Though there are variations among colleges in their general education offerings, a pattern is discernible. The findings of a survey of community college deans help sketch in the outlines of this pattern (Hammons, Thomas, and Ward, 1980). Of the responding colleges, 87 percent offered "a general education program or components with general education goals" that fell within the definition given by B. Lamar Johnson (Johnson, 1952, quoted in Hammons, Thomas, and Ward, 1980, pp. 23–24): "that part of education which encompasses the common knowledge, skills and attitudes needed by each individual to be effective as a person, a member of a family, a worker and a citizen. General education is complementary to, but different in emphasis and approach from, special training for a job, for a profession, or for scholarship in a particular field of knowledge."

The survey found that courses taught under the label of general education were mostly of one type: the subject-centered course taught from the viewpoint of a single discipline. A much less common type was the student-centered course organized around themes or problems and taught from the viewpoint of several disciplines. Even less common were core courses required of all students and taught within an integrated program. Typically, courses were offered in the conventional curricular areas of social science; communication; natural science; arts and humanities; mathematics; and health, physical, and family education. The ordinary means by which students were compelled to choose courses among those listed as general education was through the rationale of the breadth requirement. Breadth requirements obliged students to sample courses from the various disciplines, thus achieving a kind of "breadth" in their exposure to learning. This approach is frequently referred to as the "cafeteria" approach. Breadth requirements are usually tied to the expectations, real or imputed, of colleges or universities to which community college students transfer. A community college may have general education requirements that go beyond the breadth requirements called for by transfer institutions, but the general education and transfer programs are sometimes virtually the same thing.

The subject-centered, single-discipline course is likely to be an introductory course to a field designed with that field's prospective major in mind. It might be a survey course, but it would probably not be a course framed specifically upon general education goals and principles. In content and methods of instruction, it would likely be oriented to a transfer institution and therefore tend to be imitative of the lower-division university course. It is unlikely that these courses would have interrelationships among them.

Community colleges speak of their "general education programs," most of which can be termed nonprograms when *program* is correctly defined. A program should have institutional recognition, some form of organization, a set of goals and objectives, and the means to accomplish them. Instead, general education is commonly a list of courses categorized by departments or divisions and regulated by a body of policy and requirements. At a larger college, literally hundreds of disparate courses might meet general education requirements. Other than simply giving a learner some breadth and variety of experience in different fields of study, the distribution approach seems to serve no other general education goal.

There are exceptions to this prevailing pattern: colleges and districts that have envisioned what general education might be and have made the commitment necessary to carry out their vision. They are relatively few in number, but important. In 1980, when Hammons made his survey, he found only two instances of colleges that were making "significant progress" toward achieving general education goals. These were Miami-Dade and Los Medanos colleges. Since Hammon's survey was made, there has been an upsurge of interest in community college education, as elsewhere in postsecondary education. Were an inquiry made today, more exceptions to the prevalent pattern probably would be found.

The prevailing pattern of community college education can be best accounted for by a convergence of many influences.

General education has fared badly in the university and four-year college as well as in the community college. In his history of the curriculum of higher education, Rudolph (1977) speaks of the many forces and adversities that have plagued general education over the years. He finds important sources of influence in the changing social order, changes in the nature of knowledge and truth, the university movement and department-alization, specialization and the free-elective system, the rise of faculty power, and shifts in student interests and choices. General education is a worthy ideal of long and venerable standing in higher education, he observes, but it is waging a losing struggle. "The challenge of the curriculum today is to create an environment that is friendly to the production of social critics and that is responsive to a concern with values and the human experience. General education courses have sought to keep alive such a concern in the specializing, vocationalizing university, but the general education movement is hopelessly engaged in the artificial respiration of a lifeless ideal" (p. 288).

The community college is, of course, a far different institution in respect to mission, organization, tradition, and other aspects than the "specializing, vocationalizing" university Rudolph speaks of. In the community college, general education is far from "a lifeless idea," but it is under serious threat. Specialization afflicts the community college in the form of subject matter compartmentalization; vocationalism, construed as single-minded concentration on training for entry level skills, is gathering momentum.

The community college is not alone in its concern for general education. The Carnegie Foundation for the Advancement of Teaching in its survey of American higher education (1977) called general education "a disaster area" badly in need of reform. Boyer and Levine (n.d., p. 1) caught the circumstances of general education in the metaphor of the "spare room" of academia's house, disarrayed and untended, serving many purposes and hence none well. A source book compiled by the General Education Models Project commented, "it is no longer news that general education is in disarray," and went on to say: "What is news is that debate has turned to action" (Association of American Colleges, 1980, p. 1).

In addition to being influenced by factors that have shaped general education in all postsecondary institutions, general education in the community college has been shaped by factors peculiar to itself. In speaking of the history of the community college curriculum in general, Cohen and Brawer (1982) offer an interpretation that can be applied to general education in particular. They point to certain changes in the community college and count them as losses. These include the integration of the curriculum, sequence of the curriculum, and continuity of student attendance. In a passage that tells of the arrival of the "smorgasborg" approach to the total curriculum, Cohen and Brawer (1982, p. 311) comment on the problems of general education as well: "Confronted on the one side by universities wanting better prepared students and on the other by secondary schools passing through the marginally literate, captives of their own rhetoric to provide programs to fit anyone's desires, the community colleges erected a curriculum resembling more a smorgasborg than a coherent educational plan. What else could they do? Their policies favored part-time students dropping in and out at will, whose choice of courses was often made more on the basis of convenience in time and place than on content. Their funding agents rewarded career, transfer, and continuing education differentially."

The prevailing pattern of general education took root during the period of rapid increase in the number of colleges. Why did not the numerous new colleges, presented with the once-in-a-lifetime opportunity for a new beginning, install imaginative and effective programs in general education? Perhaps one reason is that during the period of most rapid growth, interest in general education was on the wane throughout postsecondary education. Also, replication of existing curricular patterns and organizational arrangements was the order of the day. This meant the installation of departmental structure and breadth requirements by new institutions in imitation of existing institutions.

Other influences were at work. Transfer institutions directly or indirectly influenced what was to be taught, how it was to be taught, and according to what standards it was to be taught. Instructors, for their part, went ahead and taught what they knew and wanted to teach by methods that were familiar to them. The result was the typical subject-centered, single-discipline course oriented to the prospective major in the field.

Once installed and staffed, the curricular and organizational arrangements pertaining to general education resisted change. Departmental organization frustrated attempts at interdisciplinary innovations. When innovations were made, they were typically made in the form of experiments that did little to disturb deeply rooted patterns. More often than not, the innovations soon faded away, and their founders lost enthusiasm and reverted to their home disciplines and departments. Student protests demanding relevance and self-direction challenged the narrowly conceived versions of common learning enforced by required courses. The already weak concepts of general education was further diluted as more courses were added to distribution lists. Decisions as to what courses were considered to be general education were often made by political processes of accommodation and compromise rather than by application of criteria derived from a college's general education philosophy and goals.

Once a general education pattern has become institutionalized, it is difficult to change. The college deans surveyed by Hammons, Thomas, and Ward (1980) perceived barriers to change, which they ranked in the following order of importance: (1) resistance of the present faculty to change, (2) difficulty of organizing a new approach, (3) difficulty in obtaining credit for transfer, (4) inability to recruit specially trained faculty, (5) difficulty in locating appropriate instructional materials.

We should not be surprised that faculty would resist change, nor should resistance be seen as a necessarily negative response. It is axiomatic that the prospect of change is threatening to routines, habits, and, accustomed patterns. My experience prompts me to mention several more barriers to change. They are: inadequate exercise of will by key administrators and faculty leaders; lack of a comprehensible, attractive, and inspiring "big picture" of what the change is supposed to lead to; and inadequate or counterproductive staff and organization intended to carry out the change. If a proposal to change general education lacks leadership, vision, and suitable process, faculty resistance will be a reasonable response to unreasonable expectations.

The deans ranked difficulty of organizing a new approach as second in importance. A large part of this difficulty is attributable to the departmental form of organization, which frustrates attempts to develop interdisciplinary curriculum and to bring faculty together across disciplinary boundaries. An absence of departments facilitated the development of the general education program at Los Medanos College. At the outset, the college planners recognized that departments would be an impediment to the envisioned general education program. Thus, departments were not included in the college blueprints for organization and governance.

Considering the number and strength of the influences that have shaped general education and that make it resistant to change, reformulation has to be recognized as a difficult challenge. Yet, there is a basis for guarded optimism in the existence of the general education programs that are exceptions to the prevailing pattern. They demonstrate not only that this pattern is not an inescapable inevitability but that the combination of leadership, resources, and a worthwhile vision can bring change. The current interest in reforming general education appears to be gathering momentum, and this should lend encouragement and support to college leaders who are considering it. Strengthening general education programs will strengthen the community college itself.

General Education As It Might Be

There are problems of generalization inherent in any writing about the numerous and varied community colleges of the nation: Any generalizations should be read with the certainty of exceptions in mind. Moreover, suggestions made here are intended as points of departure for discussion and possible adaptation to a college's project for improving its general education program, not as prescriptions. To illustrate points and provide examples, I will draw upon Los Medanos College's general education program with which I have had long and direct involvement. Our successes and progress, our failures and false starts, may have instructive value for others embarking on similar projects. If any wisdom is to be derived from Los Medanos College's nine years of experience in working toward a coherent, integrated general education program, it is that no one college's model should be touted as a model for all colleges and that each college must ultimately work out its own unique arrangements in the unique context of its own history, personnel, resources, institutional character, clientele, and community.

A general education program needs to have at its base a set of goals. The following are examples of goals basic to any general education program:

1. To provide the opportunity for the learner to learn about self, society, and the physical and natural world.
2. To help the learner develop skills in communication and relating to others.
3. To lead the learner to explore values and ethical issues confronting the individual and society.
4. To teach effective means of participating in society and promoting its welfare.
5. To illustrate and explore the significance of interconnectedness of life and events on the planet.
6. To direct the thinking of the learner to the future as well as the past and present.
7. To promote skills, knowledge, and attitudes conducive to a lifetime of learning.
8. To explore the content and modes of inquiry of humankind's important fields of study.
9. To teach about knowledge.

A general education program should promote learner skills, but it should not attempt to provide service that is better provided by well-organized and -staffed developmental education programs. Skill development should be pursued at a more complex level and within the context of a given field of study. At its best, skill development and subject mastery should be intertwined tightly. Reading and writing skills at the basic literacy level are best addressed by specialists in developmental education programs outside the general education program. At Los Medanos College, general education courses provide an assessment of reading and writing skills and refer learners to tutors and developmental workshops. General education courses also incorporate the use of reading and writing as tools of effective learning. These courses enhance the learner's skill development by teaching methods of solving problems, thinking critically, and using creativity.

If a goal is so abstract or idealized as to defy translation into realistic learner outcomes, it should be amended or discarded. A statement of learner outcomes will specify what the learner should be able to show as gain in the domains of learning—cognitive, affective, or psychomotor—as the result of receiving instruction in the course. It is important for general education courses to be able to show a clear linkage between goals, learner outcomes, and course content and methods of instruction selected to elicit these outcomes. Besides effecting a salutary demystification of the purposes of general education courses, requiring the stipulation of learner outcomes in a course outline is conducive to clarity of curriculum design and provides a basis for course and program evaluation.

My experience leads me to believe that there is an elusive but distinctive general education approach to curriculum and instruction. This approach follows the axiom that while liberal arts bends the student to the subject, general education bends the subject to the student. The general education approach disposes an instructor to comment on the *how* as well as the *what* of learning and to seek connections and relationships among what is being learned. The general education approach regards the learner's education as a process, the essence of which is well captured by Cohen and Brawer (1982, p. 132): "General education is the process of developing a framework on which to place knowledge stemming from various sources, of learning to think critically, develop values, understand traditions, respect diverse cultures and opinions, and most important, put that knowledge to use. It is holistic, not specialized; integrative, not fractioned; suitable more for action than contemplation."

The process takes place within the learner. Hence, general education should be student centered. Course content and instructional procedures should be selected, organized, and pre-

sented in a curriculum that invites learners to expand their capabilities, knowledge, and awareness as thinking, feeling, and acting members of society.

The curriculum should include courses from social and
behavioral sciences, physical and biological sciences, communication, humanities, and mathematics. A general education course
must maintain its intellectual and disciplinary integrity by pur-
veying an understanding of its discipline. Yet, it should use this
knowledge more as a means to explicate concepts, to expand
upon themes, and to explore problems and issues that face the
individual and society than to lay down the beginning foundations for a potential major. However, a prospective major should
be able to get a good perspective on a given discipline from a
general education course.

By its goals, design, and instructional procedures and by
its common concerns with other general education courses, each
course in the general education curriculum should be readily
identifiable as a general education course. However, it can be
difficult to determine if a course is properly labelled general
education or not.

To help solve this problem, Los Medanos College derived
from the college philosophy and general education program
goals a set of eight criteria that a course must satisfy in order to
be labelled general education. These criteria, along with a procedure for applying them to proposed courses, were developed
through a project funded in part by the National Endowment
for the Humanities. This project, nearing completion at the time
of this writing, extended over three semesters and was organized
into three stages. In the first stage, the criteria were generated
by a study group of faculty and administrators. In the second
stage, courses were rewritten in light of the criteria, which then
were applied to determine which courses qualified. In the third
stage, courses were field tested, further refined, and the criteria
reapplied. The final step in the third stage will be the evaluation
of the criteria themselves for effectiveness and appropriateness.
The criteria are:

1. Intradisciplinary: Does the course address that which is
    common among courses in a disciplinary family (such as

sociology, anthropology, and sociology) and show intercon-
nections among these fields?

2. Modes of inquiry: Does the course teach the characteristic
    means by which knowledge is generated and tested in the
    discipline?
3. Esthetics of knowledge: Does the course invite the learner
    to experience the joy of learning and the beautiful aspects
    of that knowledge?
4. Implications of knowledge: Does the course include consid-
    eration of the societal, ethical, and change-inducing impli-
    cations of knowledge in its field?
5. Reading and writing: Does the course utilize reading and
    writing as tools for learning?
6. Effective thinking: Does the course teach attitudes and
    strategies for effective, critical thinking—such as detecting
    fallacies, problem solving, evaluating evidence, or using in-
    tuition and taking risks?
7. Creativity: Does the course introduce creativity in terms of
    product as well as process and encourage individuals to ex-
    plore their own creative potentials?
8. Pluralism: Does the course help learners understand the
    character and consequences of pluralism in a democratic
    society, include contributions to the discipline and society
    of minority persons and groups, and encourage respect for
    diverse views?

These criteria cause all general education courses to address a
common set of concerns in ways that are reasonable and appropriate to a given discipline. A criterion may be satisfied by the
content of a course, by instructional methods and materials, or
by both.

The general education program should be the centerpiece
of a community college's master educational plan because it is
the central function of that plan. General education is what all
persons granted a degree should have in common. The general
education program, for all of its centrality, however, ought not
to claim precedence over other college components but instead
mesh with them in mutual support. It should integrate with the
counseling and guidance, developmental education, career devel-

opment, occupational, and majors programs. By focusing sharply its scope and activities, it can resist proliferation of function.

The curriculum of the general education program should be organized in a compact, integrated pattern of relatively few, well-designed courses that meet criteria derived from general education philosophy and goals. Mechanisms and policy should defend against the proliferation of courses and assure that the criteria are satisfied both by newly proposed courses and by courses already being offered. Courses should be numerous enough, however, to allow for some degree of choice by learners. In addition to courses from various disciplines, a general education program needs required core courses to ensure that learners have the opportunity to share common learning experiences.

The Los Medanos College program provides one possible model for a general education program structure. This model is ambitious. It is organized into three main parts called *Tier One, Tier Two,* and *Tier Three.* The learner takes twenty-six units per semester of course work within the three tiers.

Tier One is comprised of twenty-five courses representing the six areas, or disciplinary families, into which the college's academic curriculum is organized—namely, behavioral science, social science, language arts, humanistic studies, physical science, and biological science. To be included in Tier One, a course must satisfy the criteria listed earlier. A learner takes six disciplinary courses, one from each area, plus a two-unit core course in social science called "Social Order and Institutions" for a total of twenty units.

Tier Two is a three-unit interdisciplinary core course titled, "An Ethical Inquiry into Societal Issues." Multiple sections of this course are offered by instructors representing a variety of disciplines. It is team planned but not team taught. Major societal issues are explored, each receiving two to four weeks attention within an eighteen-week semester. The issues to be studied are selected by a college-wide committee that includes students and administrators as well as instructors. Currently, the issues under study are: energy and the environment, economic and population growth, nuclear weaponry, equality and justice by race and sex, and the search for societal and individual values. Instructors facilitate examination of each issue by following a strategy of inquiry developed for the course. The strategy, called "ethical inquiry," follows these steps expressed as questions addressed to an issue under study: (1) Is there a problem? (2) What is the magnitude and what are the characteristics of the problem? (3) What are alternative solutions to the problem? (4) What are ethical implications of the alternative solutions? (5) Where do you (the learner) stand on the issue? Learners plan, carry out, and report in writing a self-directed study of some aspect of an issue, following the ethical inquiry strategy. This course is concerned with the development of skills of locating, organizing, and reporting information as well as critical thinking and study.

The Tier-Three courses are intradisciplinary. They are designed to focus tightly on an aspect of a Tier-One societal issue. Tier-Three courses are designed by instructors who have gone through the staff development seminars preparatory to teaching and who have taught Tier One. The topics of Tier-Three courses are meant to be changed from time to time as important issues arise and instructors create new courses. Each Tier-Three course is designed along a common format and must be approved by a committee. As in Tier Two, learners write a paper using the method of ethical inquiry. So far, course topics have included science and values, nuclear and alternative energy, minorities, crime and violence in modern society, ecology, social change and the future, and biomedical ethics.

A general education program should be staffed by instructors from every discipline who understand thoroughly the program goals and principles. They should be willing to develop the knowledge and skills that contribute to effective general education instruction, meeting and working together regularly in professional staff development activities to enhance their teaching skills—especially the facilitation of discussion—and to work on curriculum, share information and ideas, review, evaluate, and where necessary, institute corrective planning and revisions in the program.

A general education program should not be a "breakaway

unit" operating independently of the rest of the college. General education should be the business of the whole college. How a specific college works out its organizational arrangements will depend on its circumstances. But any arrangement should be able to provide for program coordination and for planning and evaluation activities. The program should be able to promote the loyalty of instructors, gather resources, establish relationships with other functions of the college, and maintain administrative and faculty support.

Reformulation Processes

Reformulation is essentially an orchestration of strategies for guided change. To be effective, it will demand leaders who are willing and able to make the necessary commitments of energy, time, stamina, and resources. The way in which reformulation is pursued will have a powerful influence on its outcome. A reformulation project should take into account the college's readiness and capability to change.

The leaders of a college need to make an assessment of the readiness and capability of the college to undertake reformulation. An inventory of preconditions favorable to prospective changes as well as factors unfavorable to change needs to be made. This kind of assessment can be expressed as a series of questions: Do the personnel of the college perceive a necessity for change? Is there dissatisfaction with the present arrangement? Is the college facing serious problems, perhaps even survival issues, because of enrollment declines, changes in student characteristics, or shifting expectations at transfer institutions? Are resources available? Are the college leaders willing to go far beyond the pro forma in their support of reformulation? Can leaders in both faculty and administration be counted on to do their homework and seriously study general education? Will the top administrators be willing to take the risks inherent in initiating a major change? How willing are leaders to empower the group that undertakes the hard work of planning for reformulation and to accept the possibility that its plan may very well "rock the boat"? Is there a reasonable, open-minded attitude about the essentially experimental nature of reformulation? Is there a realistic understanding of what will be required by way of time and resources?

Clearly, reformulation cannot be taken lightly. Planned well and pursued energetically, reformulation will send waves of change ramifying throughout the college. The project will reach to the foundations of the college's philosophy and challenge the status quo in both the formal and informal aspects of the college's organization. If preconditions favorable to change are not present or are insufficient, then the first step toward reformulation will be to cultivate them. Reformulation can begin on a small scale and enlarge as momentum gathers. At a college with propitious preconditions, reformulation can begin on a larger scale.

A philosophical base is an indispensable element for reformulation. From it are derived program goals; from the goals are derived principles essential to the design and operation of the program. These principles provide guidance in making decisions and in solving the innumerable problems that arise. Learner outcomes, for instance, can be derived systematically from the philosophical base. Decisions on what courses should or should not be considered general education can be made more effectively and consistently using criteria rooted in the philosophy.

The Los Medanos College experience provides a useful illustration of the value of a philosophic base. Well before the college opened, an advance planning group concluded that the general education program should be central to the college's educational plan. Philosophic postulates concerning the nature of learning, society, and schooling were hammered out and a philosophy of general education was derived. General education, it was concluded, should be education for survival of the individual and the society. The program envisioned was to be integrated and interdisciplinary. It would encourage self-directed learning, lead learners to explore ethical aspects of societal issues, and advance the belief that knowledge should lead to action. The philosophy, principles, and goals were written out in detail (Collins and Drexel, 1976). This philosophical base has continued to provide a bench mark to guide the program in its implementation and subsequent revisions.

A reformulation project starts with assessment, but it begins formally with the establishment and activation of a work unit, called a "task force," "study group," or "committee." This unit needs to have the full endorsement of the college chief executive officer. It should be broad based and staffed with a cross section of faculty and administrators who can bring to it skills in group process, research, and writing. From the unit's inception, important processes, such as building ownership in the project and laying a base of shared understandings and experiences, will be at work. This unit runs the risk of self-insulation and separation from the rest of the college. Rather than functioning as a separate entity within the college, it can work more constructively as a subsystem interfacing and interacting with other college subsystems.

The unit should research demographic information and characteristics of the college's learners, such as learning styles, skills, and curricular choices. It should also research the history, norms, social structures, and informal organization of the college itself. To add to the knowledge base of the project, information about general education projects at other colleges should be sought out. Visits to such projects can be useful.

At the start, possible problems can be anticipated. Jerry Gaff (1980) has compiled a helpful list of forty-three "potholes" that might be encountered by a project on the road to general education reform. He categorizes them under the following headings: misconceptions about the task, erroneous task force procedures, mistaken concepts of general education, misunderstood notions about program planning, faulty methods for securing approval of proposals, illusions about program implementation. Awareness of these "potholes" along with an information base about the college and its clientele will be important in planning project activities and program design.

A reformulation project will pass through stages as it moves towards its goals. The first stage will involve defining the task, clarifying expectations, setting a time frame, gathering information, and conceptualizing program outlines. The second stage will attend to the translation of broad concepts into operational plans. At this stage, the roster of participants in the project might well change, as visionaries detach themselves from, and planners attach themselves to, the project. The third stage will involve implementation, in-progress evaluation, and corrective planning. At this stage, the roster may change again as some planners leave the project while "doers" arrive to design and teach the reformulated courses and to make refinements and revisions in the program. The fourth stage will be concerned with maintaining the program in a dynamic steady state, which includes evaluation, corrective planning, and adaptation to changing circumstances and new needs.

Movement through these stages cannot be hurried, and if experience is an indication, it will likely take longer than anticipated. Any reformulation project should have a generous time frame. Los Medanos College, in its eighth year, had only reached the outskirts of the maintaining stage. (This is perhaps longer than another college might experience, inasmuch as major revisions were made in the program to correct flaws in concept and design and to introduce new program features.) A reformulation project should be open ended and evolving—a perpetual experiment even at the maintaining stage. Backing out of dead-end approaches, identifying and correcting errors, acknowledging failure, and moving on to further development should be accepted as positive, legitimate, and appropriate program business.

Los Medanos College added strength to its program when, in response to an intensive evaluation of one aspect of the program by faculty and students, it abandoned a one-unit, semester-long intradisciplinary course known as the *generic* course. This course attempted, in too brief a time period and in too disjointed a fashion, to present the major concepts and generalizations of each of the six families of disciplines and simultaneously to explore societal issues and concerns. From the evaluation process and decision to abandon the course came a curriculum development project in which a study group of students, faculty, and administrators invented the Tier-Two and Tier-Three courses of the present program. These courses have perpetuated the best parts of the defunct generic course and have enabled the program to carry on commitments established in the college philosophy and general education program goals.

This can be said categorically: No reformulation project and no general education program can succeed without staff development. A reformulation project is ethically unsound and lacking in wisdom if it expects college personnel to become effective in general education instruction and curriculum design without adequate college support in the form of staff development. Consider the instructor accustomed to a professional lifetime of teaching subject-centered, single-discipline lecture courses. No matter how willing or conscientious, this instructor will find it difficult to satisfy criteria that call for an interdisciplinary, student-centered course that teaches about knowledge as well as transmitting it, attends to skill development, and inquires into values and ethical implications of societal issues.

The staff development component of a general education program should be conceptualized and conducted as a continuing process. Once a large-scale program is under way, all functions need to be in operation simultaneously: While new instructors are being recruited and prepared, others are participating in supportive activities concurrent with their teaching, and others are exiting from the program to resume teaching in their home disciplines. In the recruitment and preparation phase, workshops and seminars could meet regularly to discuss and provide practice in instruction, curriculum design, and selection and preparation of materials, as well as to discuss the philosophical base of the program and its implications for teaching and learning. In the support phase, teaching faculty and administrators could participate in workshops and seminars in which information and experiences are shared, demonstration and practice sessions held, curriculum critiqued, and peer support and affirmation given. The teachers would be teaching one another an essentially interdisciplinary curriculum on general education. The exit phase provides for a positive, amicable disengagement of an instructor from a general education assignment and facilitates the transition to another teaching assignment.

Benefits Versus Costs

Whether initiated on a small or large scale, reformulation of community college general education will be a difficult and time-consuming task that puts heavy demands on the resources and personnel of a college. Why would a college want to embark upon such a long-term and arduous task? The prevailing pattern of general education can be seen as a pragmatic equilibrium between what is demanded by the college clientele and what the college is able and willing to offer—a de facto statement of what is possible. For all its shortcomings, it seems to work well enough to at least satisfy transfer functions. Also, vexing questions arise when reformulation is contemplated. Does society really want the community college to become serious about general education? Will sufficient numbers of students choose to take general education courses? Will reformulation disrupt agreements with transfer institutions? Would a reformulated general education program price itself out of the education consumer's market by its challenging standards, requirements, and expectations? Will unexpected, additional problems in finance, enrollments, and demands for accountability arise to frustrate a reformulation project and wash away any progress that might have been made?

Before undertaking reformulation of general education, a college's leaders need to be convinced that the benefits outweigh the costs. A general education program vitalized by reformulation benefits a college by providing a cohesive element within an otherwise disjointed curriculum. The process initiates a college-wide dialogue on its mission and goals, and, as the general education function is defined and clarified, other college functions also are defined and clarified. Perplexing issues of quality and standards can be addressed more systematically and productively when a general education program has clarified its goals and expectations and can stipulate learner outcomes. The "value-added" approach to evaluation can be more appropriately used when a program is well defined. A strengthened general education program can have a strengthening effect on liberal arts programs by introducing learners to fields in ways that capture their interest and encourage further study and continuing enrollments. Likewise, vitalized general education strengthens the transfer function by providing for the transfer student a breadth and depth of preparatory learning in subject matter as well as skills that far exceed the narrowly specialized courses in the prevailing pattern.

Benefits can be anticipated for faculty. Implicit in the reformulated general education concept are an expanded faculty role and an opportunity for participation in decision making and policy formation. As instructors acquire the skills, knowledge, and attitudes requisite for effective general education instruction and establish working relationships with other college units, they expand their professional competencies and scope of activities. The role of instructor takes on additional, enhancing attributes. As the competencies and knowledge base of general education instructors expand, their participation in decision making becomes more essential. They will be in a better position than current instructors to be proactive and anticipatory in their participation in college affairs.

Staff development workshops and seminars can create the opportunity for searching discussion among faculty and administrators. As teachers teach teachers in the staff development program, the heretofore elusive ideal of a "community of scholars" can begin to be realized—except that it would be more accurately described as a "community of learners" because the unifying element is not original scholarly research but the study of teaching, learning, and curriculum. Other parts of the college's curriculum will enjoy vitalization as general education instructors bring interesting and innovative curriculum design and methods of instruction to their nongeneral education courses.

There are costs to be incurred in the reformulation of general education, of which fiscal costs are only one variety and probably not the most telling. Reformulation is inescapably a process of change. Disturbances in the status quo and uncertainties about the outcome of the process will exact costs in morale and productivity. Other costs will include organizational and interpersonal stresses. Reformulation will certainly generate conflict, which, even if contained and put to the service of constructive ends, is costly in time, energy, and emotion. Also, reformulation would coerce students, faculty, and administrators into new patterns, and coercion is costly, regardless of the ends to which it is directed. Costs can be measured in the time, energy, and emotion consumed in the resolution of conflicts, abatement of anxieties, eliciting of cooperation and compliance, and in the establishing and explicating of a rationale that convincingly justifies the reformulation project.

A heavy cost will be borne by the chief administrative officers, especially the president of the college, who will need to dedicate considerable time, energy, and attention to the project in addition to developing a deep understanding of its philosophy, principles, and goals. Deans, division heads, and department chairpersons will incur additional stresses and work loads. They will be required to balance the demands of managerial tasks against the necessary work of leadership in the pursuit of reformulation. Stress for some will be intensified by the need to share authority with faculty as well as by the ambiguities, open endedness, and possibility of surprises in reformulation processes.

The costs and doubts about the prospects for effective reformulation may seem to outweigh the benefits. However, the balance will tip strongly in favor of reformulation, in my opinion, when several further prospective benefits are considered. A general education vitalized by reformulation could shore up the eroding collegiate function and bolster a college's claim to comprehensiveness. Vitalized general education programs across the nation could add positive support to the welfare, even survival, of society as more and more learners expand their awareness of the world they live in and become accustomed to exploring ethical aspects of societal issues with knowledge and skill. We cannot overlook, either, the ethical burden incumbent on the community college to contribute through effective general education to this democratic, pluralistic, and changing society. After all, there are close to 1,300 community, junior, and technical colleges in the country, available and accessible, proudly proclaiming the ideology of "democracy's college," "the people's college," "the college of opportunity." What other institution is in such a strategic position to serve society and the individual through general education?

6

Strengthening Transfer Programs

Alexander W. Astin

Any examination of the community college in terms of the part it plays in the U.S. higher education system will necessarily emphasize the transfer function. It is principally through the transfer process that community colleges are linked to other higher education institutions; moreover, most of the systematic evidence concerning the effectiveness of the community college in fulfilling its role in the larger society is derived from studies of the transfer process.

Since I am likely to be regarded as an outsider in traditional community college circles, it may be useful to say a few words about the personal perspective from which I approach this task. I see myself primarily as a social scientist and research administrator who has focused most of his professional energies during the past two decades on the study of American higher education. My main hopes for this research are to deepen our understanding of American higher education and to find ways to improve and strengthen it. This latter aim has in recent years led me to become actively involved in the dissemination of research findings to those audiences of policymakers and educators, including community college leaders, who are in a position to effect constructive change.

The Transfer Function

Some readers may object to focusing on the transfer process on the grounds that the transfer student today represents

only a small fraction of the total community college population. Indeed, in my graduate seminars, which are frequently attended by community college administrators from the Los Angeles area, I often hear that transfer students represent only a
"trivial" or "insignificant" subpopulation of the total student
body in local community colleges.

While it is true that transfer students account for a
smaller proportion of community college enrollments today
than in earlier years, the transfer student population is substantial when looked at from a national perspective. For example,
community colleges enrolled 617,000 students—about 36 percent of the total number of full-time, first-time freshmen entering colleges in the fall of 1981. This represents virtually no
change since 1971, when the figure was also 36 percent (583,000
students). Of equal significance is the fact that nearly all of
these freshmen entering community colleges (96.5 percent) in-
tend to obtain a degree, and most (76.5 percent) aspire to at
least a bachelor's degree. More than a third (35.7 percent) report
plans for graduate or advanced professional degrees (Astin, King,
and Richardson, 1980; Staff of the Office of Research, 1971).

These facts make it clear that the community college's
role in the education of students pursuing the bachelor's degree
is just as important as it used to be, if not more so. The common misperception that the community college's role in the
transfer process is declining no doubt stems from the tremendous increase in vocational, part-time, and nondegree-credit
enrollments during the past ten or fifteen years. In other words,
even though transfer students represent a declining proportion
of community college enrollments, the community college's
"piece of the action" in educating baccalaureate-oriented students has not diminished.

The findings of our program of studies of student development in American higher education, carried out over the last
seventeen years, may offer help to those community college
leaders interested in enhancing the transfer function. Contro-
versy over our empirical research has been generated by our
longitudinal studies of student persistence or retention. To put
these studies in proper perspective, it may be useful first to review the design and scope of our research.

The basic tool for the research has been our Cooperative Institutional Research Program (CIRP), which was initiated in 1966 at the American Council on Education (ACE) and has been carried on since 1973 jointly by the University of California at Los Angeles (UCLA) and ACE. The CIRP conducts both an annual national survey of freshmen entering higher education institutions of all types and periodic longitudinal followups. The survey sample includes some 300,000 first-time freshmen; followups usually involve smaller groups of students, with the number depending upon the particular problem being studied and the available funding. An important thing to keep in mind about CIRP studies of dropouts is that they are limited to students *who entered institutions with the intention of completing at least a baccalaureate degree.*

In a typical longitudinal study, a *dropout* is defined as a student who entered college as a freshman with aspirations for at least a bachelor's degree and who at the time of followup did not have a bachelor's degree and was not enrolled somewhere in pursuit of that degree. All others are classified as persisters. (Such a definition, it should be noted, tends to overestimate the actual number of persisters.) In these longitudinal studies we use multivariate statistical analyses to control a wide range of characteristics of the entering freshmen, including high school rank, ability test scores, parental income, parental education, educational aspirations, study habits, values, and attitudes and expectations about college. The massiveness of these studies—in terms of large samples and large numbers of variables—is necessitated by the fact that student development is a highly complex process involving many interacting variables. The multivariate analyses needed for unraveling the various causes and effects in this research process require both longitudinal data as well as large numbers of cases and variables. In addition, the extraordinary diversity of American higher educational institutions requires a relatively large sample of institutions in order to represent the full range. (For more details on the methodology used in these studies, see Astin, 1975; 1977.)

Our basic methodology involves computing for each student a dropout proneness score based upon all of that student's entering characteristics. In a typical study, we control from 75 to 100 different characteristics of entering freshmen. As you might guess, test scores, high school grades, and educational aspirations carry a major weight in determining dropout proneness. Dropout proneness scores are then aggregated separately for students exposed to different kinds of environments, say— commuters versus residents or two-year colleges versus four-year colleges—and compared with the actual dropout rates for the same students. Environments where the actual dropout rates exceed the expected dropout rates are considered to foster attrition, whereas environments where the actual rates are below the expected rates are said to foster persistence. For students who start out pursuing the bachelor's degree at a two-year public college, we find the actual dropout rate (57 percent) exceeding the expected dropout rate (45 percent) based on entering student characteristics. In four-year public colleges, the actual dropout rate (28 percent) is somewhat lower than the expected rate (32 percent) based on the entering student characteristics. These results suggest that, on the average, a baccalaureate-oriented freshman who enrolls initially at a community college has a 16 percent better chance of becoming a dropout than a comparable student who enrolls at a public four-year college.

We find a number of other environmental situations which affect the student's chances of dropping out. One of the most interesting ways to keep students in college now is through jobs. Students who have part-time jobs while enrolled in college have a better chance of finishing than comparable students who have no jobs. This effect is particularly strong if the student lives on campus. Here we have a case where the facts clearly contradict the folklore: Having to work while attending college does not hamper the student's academic progress but rather enhances it. We should add a note of caution here, however. The beneficial effects of work diminish as the number of hours worked exceeds twenty, and if the student has a full-time job the effect is actually reversed: Students who have to work full-time have a decreased chance of finishing college in contrast to students who have no jobs. In short, it would appear that jobs represent a highly effective way of combating attrition, *provided* that the number of hours worked is limited to twenty per week.

Another highly effective way of cutting down on attrition is for the student to get away from home and to live in a dormitory on campus. The positive effects of dormitory living on persistence occur in all types of institutions and among all types of students regardless of sex, race, ability, or family background. As a matter of fact, our data show that the absence of residential facilities is one of the reasons for the relatively high attrition rates among students who attend community colleges. Thus, if we take into account the student's place of residence and work status in computing our expected dropout rates, the discrepancy between expected and actual rates among community college entrants drops from 12 to 7 percent.

Students who join social fraternities or sororities are also less likely to drop out, as are students who participate in extracurricular activities. Involvement in sports—particularly intercollegiate sports—has an especially pronounced effect on persistence. Other activities that enhance persistence include participation in honors programs, participation in the Reserve Officers Training Corps (ROTC), and participation in professors' undergraduate research projects.

Students are also much more likely to persist if they are heavily involved in their academic work or if they interact frequently with faculty. These results suggest that, on the negative side, students who seldom or never make contact with faculty members or who show little involvement in their academic work are likely to drop out. Clearly, if ways could be found to get students more involved in academics and to interact more frequently with faculty, significant reductions in attrition rates might be possible.

More recent studies of college impact (Astin, 1977; 1982) have given us an opportunity to assess the consequences of dropping out, as far as it affects the student's personal development. In the past few years, it has become fashionable in some academic circles to rationalize the act of dropping out, to employ the term *stopping out,* and to argue for the supposedly therapeutic value of attending college and then dropping out. There is little question that, for some students, leaving college without completing a program of study may be highly beneficial to their personal development. But our research shows clearly that such students represent a very small minority and that students usually leave college for negative reasons: boredom, finances, poor grades, and so forth. Positive reasons, such as a good job offer, are given by less than 10 percent of the dropouts. My feeling is that the term *stopout* all too frequently represents a rationalization for educators: It is easier to believe that students are taking time off to "find themselves" than it is to confront the limitations of institutional programs and policies.

Our longitudinal data revealed a number of behavioral consequences of dropping out. Some of these are self-evident: Students are denied entry to many challenging and well-paying occupations that require baccalaureate or graduate training, such as medicine, law, teaching, engineering, social work, and many science fields. Even among those dropouts who eventually complete college, occupational entry and subsequent progress are delayed. From a national perspective, dropping out represents a loss of talent and a waste of limited educational resources. From the perspective of the student, our research highlights a number of other more subtle consequences of dropping out. Students who fail to finish college are much less likely to show the usual developmental changes associated with continued attendance: increased interpersonal and intellectual skills; and greater self-esteem, tolerance, and open mindedness.

The greater than expected dropout rates among baccalaureate-oriented freshmen entering community colleges is not an isolated finding from a single study. Similar results have been reported from independent samples of men, women, whites, Blacks, Chicanos, Puerto Ricans, and American Indians. Further, the results have covered various intervals of time ranging from two years (Astin and Cross, 1979), four years (Astin, 1975), and nine years after college entry (Astin, 1982).

Strengthening the Transfer Function

Reactions from community college officials to our empirical studies of the transfer student have been decidedly mixed. Many community college faculty and administrators feel that our results underscore the need for community colleges to revitalize their transfer function. I have engaged in numerous personal exchanges with such individuals with the aim of identifying possible ways to improve the chances that baccalaureate-oriented students can ultimately realize their degree aspirations. A very different kind of reaction has come from a few administrators and individuals from community college organizations. They have discounted our research as methodologically suspect or questioned our motives by suggesting that we are "out to get" the community colleges. These "defenders of the faith" apparently feel that it is essential to refute any suggestion that there might be areas where community colleges need to strengthen or improve their programs. For those community college leaders who believe that our findings signify the need for reexamining community college transfer programs, there are a number of steps that might be taken to strengthen these programs.

Although we are often not aware of it, those of us who must make educational decisions as part of our professional responsibilities are implicitly basing these decisions on some theoretical ideas about what alternatives are likely to work best in certain situations. This suggests that if a viable theory about student persistence and retention could be formulated, it could serve as a kind of mental guide for community college leaders as they develop short- and long-term strategies. That is, if the community college administrator has an operating concept of how students persist—of what it is about student behavior that facilitates or inhibits their ability to implement degree plans—then this theory could presumably enable that administrator to choose the best courses of action from the available alternatives.

If one examines the various environmental factors that research has shown to affect student retention, a clear-cut pattern emerges. This pattern has led to the formulation of a more general theory about persistence, which might be very useful in guiding the thinking of community college leaders when they attempt to design programs for reducing attrition. The key construct in this theory is the notion of student involvement. Briefly, the theory states that the more students are involved in the academic experience, the greater their persistence and learning; the less involvement, the less learning and the greater chance that students will be dissatisfied and drop out. Involvement is not an esoteric or mysterious construct. It is manifest in how much time and how much physical and psychological energy the student invests in the educational process. Clearly, the factors already mentioned that enhance persistence appear to reflect greater student involvement: having a job on campus, living on campus, studying hard, interacting with faculty, joining student organizations, participating in extracurricular activities, and so forth.

As a general operating concept, the administration of a community college should strive to formulate policies and programs that encourage students to get more involved—to invest more of their total time and effort in the educational process. There are many ways to facilitate involvement, and a good starting point would be a thorough examination of the institution's information system. What kind of information concerning student involvement (or lack of involvement) is currently available to key institutional personnel? Do classroom instructors and faculty advisors regularly have access to data on students' academic involvement and academic progress? Do personnel administrators periodically receive information on students' extracurricular participation and social life? Do appropriate data get disseminated in a timely and comprehensible form? Do administrators take the initiative in surveying faculty and staff needs for information on student progress and development? Is the administration responsive to requests for better information? Since there are probably few, if any, community college administrators who can respond affirmatively to all of these questions, evaluation and improvement of the institution's information system appears to offer a useful means to encourage greater student involvement.

How does one go about identifying those students who are most likely to drop out? Considering the limited resources available for counseling or other special help in most community colleges, being able to identify as early as possible those students who are most likely to drop out is a critical task. Our studies reveal a number of factors that influence students' chances of dropping out. For the entering student, the most important are high school grades, degree aspirations, and religious background. Freshmen with good grades, plans for postgraduate degrees, Jewish parents, and Jewish religious preferences have the best chance of finishing college, while those with poor grades, plans for only a bachelor's degree, Protestant parents, and no religious preference have the poorest chance. Next in importance are good study habits, high expectations about academic performance, highly educated parents, being married (for men), and being single (for women). Other characteristics that are significant but less influential are high scores on college admissions tests, being Oriental, being a nonsmoker (for Black students, being a cigarette smoker is strongly associated with dropping out), and growing up in a moderate-sized city or town.

In addition to identifying individual students who are most likely to drop out, obtaining estimates of dropout proneness can also be extremely useful in institutional self-evaluation. My first major study on college dropouts (Astin, 1975) included in its appendix a table which would allow individual institutions to estimate what their dropout rates ought to be, given the characteristics of their entering students. Judging from the correspondence I have received since the book appeared, a number of institutions of varying types have made use of these estimates in self-study. There is no reason why community colleges could not employ such an approach in trying to evaluate the effectiveness of their own efforts to reduce student attrition. Even though community colleges as a group appear to be less successful than four-year institutions in assisting baccalaureate-oriented students to realize their degree objectives, there are no doubt many community colleges that are quite successful in such efforts. Comparing their actual dropout rates with expected rates based on entering characteristics would be one way to identify such institutions. A careful examination of the programs of those institutions might provide important clues as to how other community colleges might reduce student attrition.

A related use of estimates of dropout proneness in community colleges is political. In my judgment, community colleges frequently get a "bum rap" when legislators or other public officials cite the high dropout rates. Simply comparing drop-

out rates of different kinds of institutions with
account the kinds of students they attract in th
clearly invalid and likely to penalize those institu
roll the least well-prepared students. In my own
example, the actual dropout rates of communit
dents are twice those of students at public four
(57 versus 28 percent). However, the estimated ᵣₐₜₑₛ
based on entering student characteristics are also considerably
higher for community colleges (45 versus 33 percent). And
when the entering student's place of residence and work status
are also taken into account, the differences in expected dropout
rates between community colleges and public four-year colleges
are even greater (50 versus 32 percent, respectively). By reject-
ing simplistic comparisons of dropout rates and insisting instead
upon the use of carefully derived expected dropout rates, community college leaders can force policymakers to make more
valid and fairer comparisons between different types of public
institutions. Indeed, it may even be possible by using such data
to demonstrate that certain community colleges are actually
more effective than their four-year counterparts in promoting
student retention.

My personal view is that some of the difficulties that
transfer students encounter in community colleges are created
by the fact that, particularly in recent years, community colleges have come to serve an increasingly diverse constituency
that includes adults, part-time students, and vocational students, as well as the transfer student coming directly from high
school. It may well be that the transfer programs have suffered
as a result of the community college's effort to serve an increasingly diverse clientele.

A particularly important feature of this diversity is the
tremendous increase in the enrollment of minority students in
community colleges during recent years. Thus, whereas community colleges enroll about 33 percent of white freshmen, they
enroll 39 percent of Black and 53 percent of Hispanic and
American Indian freshmen (Dearman and Plisko, 1980). In recognition of this fact, and in view of the high attrition rate
among minority transfer students, the Commission on the Higher

ducation of Minorities recently recommended the establishment of a "transfer college within a college." Such a college would make it possible to bring together all students aspiring to a baccalaureate so that they could be exposed to the same kind of intensive educational and extracurricular experiences commonly available to students at residential institutions. The commission also suggested that funding formulas may have to be revised to strengthen this "college within a college."

The need to differentiate different subpopulations within the community college also relates to the involvement theory. In all likelihood, involvement is a much more serious issue for the transfer student coming directly out of high school than it is for adults and part-time students. Under these circumstances, establishment of a transfer subcollege or of other special programs within the community college that are designed specifically for the transfer student may help to enhance the involvement and persistence of these students. These transfer-oriented programs might include special orientation, academic advisement, career counseling, and—perhaps most importantly—much more intensive monitoring than would be indicated for most of the other student subpopulations.

Given the fact that most community colleges serve a predominantly or exclusively commuter population, our research on the effects of student residency poses a serious challenge: Lacking residential facilities, how can institutions be administered so as to maximize student involvement and minimize student attrition? Is it possible to simulate the residential experience, at least for those eighteen-year-olds coming directly out of high school in pursuit of a bachelor's degree? While the appropriateness of any attempt to simulate the residential experience will vary depending upon the resources and needs of the particular community college in question, the options are, nevertheless, numerous: weekend or week-long residential "retreats," more cultural events on campus, improvements in parking facilities, required office hours for faculty, regular conferences between students and advisors, organized study groups, improvements in campus recreational facilities, expansion of on-campus employment opportunities, organized tours of potential transfer institutions, and expansion in number and size of student clubs and organizations. Community colleges can establish closer relationships with neighboring residential colleges and universities. Involvement with neighboring residential students will present community college students with many cultural and social opportunities that are not available on their own campuses. Student activities directors should work to obtain discount tickets to entertainment and athletic events held on neighboring campuses. Moreover, cooperation between the faculty and administration of the community college and the residential college will give community college students a feeling of being a part of the higher education community. An excellent analysis of possible alternatives was published in July of 1977 by the Educational Facilities Laboratory under the title, *The Neglected Majority: Facilities for Commuting Students.*

No matter how sophisticated the community college's approach to the transfer process, one would expect a certain loss of students simply from the physical move and the paper work involved. The incumbent undergraduate in the four-year institution has only to show up each year at the same place and approximately the same time to complete his or her undergraduate education. The Airlie House Conference several years ago produced a number of specific recommendations designed to smooth the transfer process (Association Transfer Group, 1973). While there is no point here in reviewing these recommendations in detail, suffice it to say that many of them are still not implemented in many states. A great deal more effort is needed, particularly in areas such as interchangeability of credits and grades.

Our longitudinal research suggests that much attrition occurs before the transfer process is undertaken. Indeed, there is some evidence suggesting that students who manage to make the transfer to the senior college actually have a better chance of completing the baccalaureate than do native students in the same college (Astin, 1975). This would suggest that a major effort needs to be focused on the preliminaries leading to transfer. Most critical, of course, is counseling and advisement. My colleague at UCLA, Fred Kintzer, has recently produced evidence suggesting that we might be able to facilitate the transfer process significantly by doing a much better job of advising students and, in some instances, by simply dispensing better information at critical times during the students' first and second years (Kintzer, n.d.).

Enhancing Quality

Even if community colleges are successful in reducing student attrition and facilitating the development of transfer students, they will continue to be unfairly penalized by an image problem that derives from the fact that they are part of hierarchically organized public education systems that are dominated by major research universities. California's three-tiered public system is the most obvious example, but some form of hierarchy exists in almost every state. This hierarchy is manifest not only in differential admissions policies but in funding patterns. Thus, in 1977-78 community colleges across the country spent an average of $2,909 per student for educational and general purposes, compared to the $3,251 spent by four-year public colleges and the $4,638 spent by public universities (Astin, 1982, p. 143). (These figures have been adjusted to take into account the greater cost of graduate and professional education.)

By traditional quality standards, community colleges are consigned to the bottom of the academic pecking order: Compared to four-year institutions, they have less well-prepared students, fewer Ph.D.'s on the faculty, smaller libraries, and lower expenditures per student. The obvious fallacy in the use of such criteria, of course, is that they reflect something about what an institution *has* but very little about what it *does*. Although I have personally campaigned against the use of such indexes and have even produced some empirical evidence suggesting that they have little if any validity (Astin, 1968b), most educators persist in assuming that the institutional hierarchy is a valid reflection of relative levels of educational quality.

The Commission on the Higher Education of Minorities made a major recommendation regarding testing and grading practices which, if implemented, could go a long way toward debunking these traditional notions of academic quality. Briefly, the commission recommended that all institutions, including universities, four-year colleges, and community colleges, revise their traditional testing and grading procedures to reflect and enhance the "value-added" mission of the institution. By *value-added mission,* the commission meant the primary obligation of all higher education institutions to enhance the cognitive skills and personal development of the student. In value-added terms, the quality of an institution is based not on the performance level of the students it admits, but on the changes or improvements in performance that the institution is able to effect in its students.

In actual practice, the value-added approach would work something like this. Newly admitted students would be tested to determine their entering levels of competence for purposes of counseling and course placement. These initial test scores would be useful not only in providing both students and faculty with information about the student's specific strengths and weaknesses but would also constitute a baseline against which to measure later student progress. Following the completion of appropriate courses or programs of study, the same or similar tests would be readministered to measure student growth. Differences between initial and later performance scores would provide students, faculty, and institutions with critical feedback on the nature and extent of student growth and development. Unlike traditional course grades, which do not necessarily reflect what students have learned but merely rank them in relation to each other at a single point in time, before-and-after testing indicates whether, and to what extent, students are actually benefitting from their educational experience. Results from many years of research on human learning suggest that such knowledge of results for both students and teachers would greatly enhance the effectiveness of the teaching-learning process.

The value-added approach does not depend on the use of any particular assessment method. Objective tests, essays, interviews, departmental examinations, work samples, performance examinations, and many other approaches might be appropriate, depending on the content and objectives of the course or program in question. Some readers of the commission's report have suggested that the commission was anti-test. Quite the contrary.. If anything, the commission was advocating more rather than less assessment, including, when appropriate, the use of nationally standardized examinations. The commission's objections to current testing and grading practices concerned the nearly exclusive reliance on such devices for screening and the infrequent use of them to measure improvement in the performance of individual students.

Another common misconception about the value-added approach is that it will somehow reduce academic standards. *The value-added approach is not a substitute for academic standards, nor does it require any change in such standards.* The notion of academic standards ordinarily refers to the absolute level of performance or competence that students are required to demonstrate in order to earn credits or degrees. If necessary, the same measures used to assess value-added education can also be used to define whatever academic standards the institution chooses for itself. In fact, defining academic standards via such measurements would provide a much more rigorous and far less ambiguous set of standards than current academic standards based solely on relativistic course grades. Moreover, initial test scores would provide both students and professors with concrete information on just how much each student needs to improve in order to reach certification or graduation standards.

There is some research evidence suggesting that course grades can be very misleading indicators of individual student progress. For example, some students who learn very little from a course can still get A's if their level of knowledge or preparation at the beginning of the course is sufficiently high. Many students who earn B's or C's, on the other hand, may actually have benefited much more from the same course. Without before-and-after assessments, there is simply no way to know whether, and how much, each student is actually learning.

The same problems occur with one-time standardized testing given at various educational exit points. Can high schools take the credit if their students do well on the Scholastic Aptitude Test (SAT) or American College Testing Program (ACT)?

How do we know that these students weren't already performing at a relatively high level when they first enrolled as ninth or tenth graders? And can undergraduate colleges legitimately take the credit if their seniors perform well on the Graduate Record Examination (GRE)? How do we know that they weren't already high performers when they first started college?

A special appeal of the value-added approach is that by capitalizing on a well-established fact of human learning (the feedback principle) it offers the possibility of significantly enhancing the educational effectiveness of institutions—without large investments of additional resources. Some educators may be inclined to question the feasibility of the idea on the grounds that faculty members would be unable to implement it. If individual professors are willing and able to assess student competence at the end of a course (through final examinations and the awarding of course grades), why cannot they also assess competence at the beginning of the course? Assuming that a course already has a final examination, the simple addition of an initial test is all that would be required to implement the value-added approach. While much of the value-added assessment could occur in individual courses, assessment of growth in general skills, such as writing and critical thinking, could be carried out at the institution-wide level. Among those institutions that require entrance or placement examinations, the value-added approach could be implemented simply by the addition of a followup test at the exit point.

These value-added recommendations have particular relevance for the concepts of quality and effectiveness as they apply to community colleges. If institutions were judged by how much they added to their students' cognitive functioning rather than by how well their students functioned at the time of admission, there would be no reason why community colleges could not achieve a level of quality comparable to that of any other kind of institution. The more selective research universities, on the other hand, could not continue to argue that their programs were of high quality simply because their entering students were better prepared. In this regard, it is not surprising that some of the most vigorous resistance to the commission's value-added recommendations has come from people associated with elite institutions.

Conclusions

Even though many contemporary community college spokespersons are inclined to downplay the transfer function, current data on enrollments show that the community college's responsibility for the education of persons aspiring to the bachelor's degree is just as important as it has ever been. Although many longitudinal studies suggest that attainment of the baccalaureate may be more difficult for students who begin their undergraduate studies in community colleges rather than four-year institutions, there are a number of remedies available to community colleges that offer promise of strengthening the transfer function. Since it appears that greater student involvement is the key to retention, there are a number of options available to community colleges that seek to encourage greater involvement and, hence, greater retention among their transfer population.

As long as educators persist in equating academic quality with traditional measures (entering student ability, expenditures, libraries, and so forth), community colleges will continue to fare poorly when judgments about academic quality are made. On the other hand, if traditional testing and grading procedures are abandoned in favor of a value-added approach to assessing student development, community colleges will compete on a more equitable basis with other kinds of institutions. As a matter of fact, it may well turn out that many community colleges may surpass four-year institutions when judged in value-added terms. In short, it appears that community colleges have little to lose and a great deal to gain by pioneering the adoption of a value-added approach in their testing and assessment procedures.

-»» **7**

Redirecting Student Services

Paul A. Elsner

W. Clark Ames

No genuine consensus exists about the nature of, need for, or direction of community college student service programs. A model for change seems to elude most leaders. Those who believe that student services have never been needed more than at the present are also urging that such services be vigorously overhauled and reshaped. Others question the value and relevance of student services. Many student services professionals themselves feel beleaguered, unappreciated, and misunderstood. They do not feel that there is a promising future for them in times of tight budgets.

Leaders of community colleges and student personnel staffs agree on one point: student services need to be redesigned. The student services function needs an infusion of new ideas, new approaches, and a new reason for being.

Student Services Past and Present

Some historians would argue that student services were never more pervasive than during the colonial college era (Fenske, 1980). The classical curriculum was defined and followed in relatively consistent patterns from college to college. Each college sought to produce a "man of God" who was schooled as much or more in culture and religious doctrine as in basic academic skills. The fervor with which these colleges approached moral education was not matched in their concern for other aspects of students' lives. Both Cowley (1964) and Brubacher and Rudy (1976) present evidence that students in the colonial era were often left to fend for themselves, forced to huddle in unheated residence halls, left to cope with deplorable food and other living conditions which no contemporary student would tolerate.

Many of today's student services were originally performed by the college president. As colleges became more complex, presidents delegated more responsibility to the faculty. Brubacher and Rudy (1976) point out that President Eliot appointed the first dean of men at Harvard in 1890 to relieve the president of "disciplinary duties." Eventually, such additional positions as dean of women, director of housing, and dean of admissions were formalized.

The history of student services in higher education centers around three developments. First, student services functions were lodged in the area of discipline. In its in loco parentis role, the college assumed responsibility for the conduct and moral well-being of its students. A second kind of student service function was often initiated by students themselves. Greek letter societies (housing and social functions), intercollegiate athletics, literary societies, and other activities contributed to the quality of student life. These activities became formal student service functions when colleges began to exercise control over them. A third set of student services grew out of the needs and demands of special interest groups. These are still evolving though at a slower pace than during the 1960s or early 1970s. The most recent entrants into this category are women returning to school and handicapped students. If there is a common thread in the history of student services, it is the importance of the special interest needs that motivate the establishment of new student services.

What kinds of student services do community colleges offer today? Based on a study of 123 junior colleges supported by the Carnegie Corporation, the American Association of Junior

Colleges (1965, p. 15) offered a definition of community college student services as "a series of related functions to support institutional program, respond to student needs and foster institutional development." This study demonstrated that student service functions were "woefully inadequate" and that the traditional functions of admissions, orientation, and counseling were neither uniformly integrated nor adequately supported. The findings of this study shaped thinking about student personnel services for several years.

The student services movement has been built around a loosely connected series of personal human development philosophies—philosophies which have had an unimpressive impact on community colleges. Attempts to operationalize these growth and development functions have been offered by Chickering (1969) and Astin (1968a). They offer the promising but rather impractical suggestion that managing the environment will effect certain student changes. Delworth, Hanson, and Associates even speak of "campus ecology management," which "calls for a shift in perspective and attitudes of student service personnel. The historical concern directed toward individual students must be awakened to include the total campus ecology. The new 'set' should include providing and designing opportunities, supports, and rewards to foster full student development" (Banning, p. 224, 1980). Can anyone question why the student personnel movement has an identity crisis?

At a recent faculty meeting the senior author was taken to task by a faculty member who said that it was disconcerting for him to see so many specialists with titles and job descriptions that made it impossible to tell what they did. He said, "I am a teacher of English. People know what I do and where I do it and, generally, how I do it." This is an important point. We can appreciate the need for a title that reflects what a profession is. Admittedly, the title for any profession or field does not begin to reflect the diversity of opportunities that are available to a person in it. Perhaps that is one of the generic difficulties with the student services movement: It has too many sources of entry and too many similar, yet distinctly different, types of preparations for practitioners.

This profession is relatively young, perhaps fifty years old, and no longer needed as the enforcer of in loco parentis on community college campuses. There is great diversity in how counselors are deployed. Some colleges put a heavy emphasis on individual counseling; others put emphasis on teaching such classes as career exploration. The service philosophies of the counselors themselves vary according to their personal inclinations. Student services are seldom integrated with the instructional program. Faculty tend to be suspicious of student services, seeing them as competitors for scarce dollars that support the instructional program as well as their own welfare. Administrators see student services as desirable so long as they do not compete with other services, can rely on grant money or receive federal support, and do not utilize the general college fund.

The student services professional may be viewed as an indispensable partner in the development of students and curriculum or as simply a serviceperson who can easily be eliminated if the budget gets tight. Perhaps student services personnel represent a luxury we can no longer afford. In states where collective bargaining is intense, the issue of the need for student services has been forced: Where do these professionals fit when contracts come into play?

The inability of student personnel professionals to articulate a well-argued, documented, and convincing case for themselves has hindered them greatly. They have been further betrayed by the educational theorists who have lulled them into a false sense of professional equilibrium.

There is no doubt that gifted student services practitioners exist and that tremendous services have been provided by student personnel programs in community colleges. The irony of the student personnel professional's dilemma in the community college is that he or she often represents the only genuinely responsive segment of the college toward new constituencies. Examples abound: the skilled counselor who works with handicapped students, specialized advisors who work with veterans, the women's center coordinator, the retired senior volunteer program director who works with senior adults in a sensitive and understanding manner, and the student activities coordinator who provides numerous and diverse services. Often, the student's only social contact with other students is the student clubs or the student activities promoted by such persons.

The dilemma arises when we try to document the impact of student services on our students. We at Maricopa Community College recently posed some questions to the student personnel professionals in our system: What is the currency of student services? What is the coin of your realm? Since there is no transcript which documents the impact of student services workers, how can you show that what you do is an important component of the college's operation and an important part of the community college's mission? The basic issue underlying these questions is whether or not student services in community colleges are partners with the instructional program or whether they are supplemental to that program. If they are partners, they are indispensable. Some of us, who seem to be critics of the student personnel movement, do not believe there is much middle ground: the partnership either exists or it does not.

The typical student services worker in a community college could probably be characterized as beleaguered, unappreciated, under the budgetary knife, scorned by academic peers and associates, and generally the most likely candidate for elimination in the next round of cutbacks. In times of retrenchment, faculty lead the retreat to the institution's central purposes. Thus, instruction survives while student services are the first to be discarded.

Some years ago, the senior author visited a New York City community college that had recently endured one of the first periods of extreme financial constraint that are now commonplace throughout the country. In the first year of austerity, several hundred thousand dollars had to be eliminated from the budget. The college administration asked staff, "What are you willing to give up?" An elevator operator was volunteered here, a counselor or an administrator there. Some services that affected students, such as cafeteria services and bookstore hours, were also cut back. In the second year, cuts were more severe, involving several millions of dollars. The college began to ask fundamental questions: For what do we exist? What is our central purpose? By the third year, it was clear that the central purpose of this institution was instruction. The hardest hit areas in the budget-cutting process were, predictably, counseling and student services. Few faculty members were terminated; many administrators and many student services personnel were terminated. This scenario has probably been repeated many times in states which have faced severe tax cuts.

In tracing the evolution of student services in the community college, we see a series of services which share their roots with traditional higher education. These included, at the very early stage, the typical disciplinary functions under the in loco parentis arrangement. This narrow function grew from a simple dean of men or dean of women to a wider array of services, covering admissions, financial aid, orientation, and many other services which are not well interrelated or integrated. These services never had clear advocacy in the community colleges, and they do not appear now as central to its mission. Finally, these functions, which are taken for granted by student personnel workers, are often the least valued in the financial crisis facing community colleges. Student services have never really come of age in the community college movement. Their current dilemma is still one of identity crisis and survival.

Student Services Classification

One way of understanding student services in community colleges is to classify them into three categories: institutionally based, situationally based, and special interest or developmental services. Institutionally based services are those which provide basic processing and record-keeping services. Regardless of size, location, special clientele, or mission of the college, some basic services must be provided. Situationally based services include health services, student activities, housing, and other services which may be required by the location or special nature of the institution. Special interest or developmental services provide for assistance to such groups as minorities, women, and handicapped students. These services are always in a state of flux since they tend to change with both the social climate and stage of the institution's development.

Institutionally Based Services. Institutionally based services include those services that virtually no college could do without, whether or not it chooses to promote them. And it is striking how few services really are absolutely necessary to the functioning of a community college.

It is possible that a community college could operate with two student services functions: admissions and record keeping. Such a program would not be very elegant, and it might, at first glance, be viewed as limited in scope. However, the prospect of accommodating many of the goals of student service professionals and proponents of growth and development under one service function have greater possibilities than one might first imagine. As information-centered technologies come into place, the possibilities of convenient phone-in registration, accurate student advisement, better articulation, and more humane and individualized treatment of students could occur routinely. The data base from which to note articulation trouble spots is managed by the admissions and registration offices. Why not hold the same offices accountable for advisement and program articulation, which are now left to the randomness of intersegmental articulation conferences, if and when they occur.

Beyond admissions and record keeping, there are not many institutionally based services. If a community college has large numbers of students, some kind of food services probably would be needed. Bookstores, financial aid, and other services might also be included. However, as community colleges become more sophisticated, these services may not be required; they can be contracted. Community colleges have had a long history of contracting food services. Currently, the Maricopa Community Colleges are experimenting with subcontracting all bookstore operations. The numbers of institutionally based services become smaller and smaller when contractual services are part of the community college's options. There would probably be strong objections, but it is even possible that the record-keeping and admissions functions could be commercially contracted.

Situationally Based Services. These include services which are required because of the community college's special location or clientele. Health services, housing, student activities, athletics, and many other services are included here. Institutionally based services can be reduced to admissions and record keeping, but situationally based services are extensive. Arguments can be made as to whether or not to offer any particular service.

An excellent example of a situational service is childcare. Some proponents of this student service program argue that childcare is an indispensable activity tied to the needs of women returning to college, single-parent families, and a variety of clientele. Were it not for childcare services, the option of going to college would not materialize for many students. But childcare can become a bottomless pit. There are probably thousands of students in a large community college system for whom childcare on the campus would be helpful. However, from the standpoint of equity, it can be argued that health care, housing, student activities or athletics may be equally important. These are called situationally based services because the individual college requirements—and the budget—determine priorities.

Special Interest Services. These include special assistance programs for underprepared minorities, re-entry women, the handicapped, and senior adults. This category has done more to shape the current nature of student services than those previously mentioned. The pressure for such special services is often the central reason for their establishment.

An excellent example of a dysfunction in student services, and one potentially correctable by interest group pressures, can be found in the scheduling. Perhaps 80 percent to 90 percent of student services operate from 9:00 A.M. to 3:00 P.M. This assumes that the student body is primarily made up of young daytime students. Nothing could be further from reality. We have long ago moved away from the student body of predominantly eighteen-to-twenty-two-year-olds to a large number of returning, working adults whose average age is between twenty-seven and twenty-eight. The kinds of services provided for the evening student are often quite limited compared to those offered to the daytime student. In this respect, we are still operating community colleges for the convenience of the people who provide the services rather than for the students who use them. A coalition of older evening adult students may well provide impetus for a new schedule of services.

It is doubtful that student services could be based universally on special interest group demands. Yet, this service category promises the widest range of options for community college students. We believe, as many critics of the community colleges argue, that our colleges cannot be all things to all people. Special interest services allow community college leaders to choose the emphasis they wish to have in their programs. Which constituent group should be emphasized at a given community college? A case could probably be made for limiting special developmental services to one or two groups. The institution may have to admit that it has limited its services, but it will also be able to claim that it does one or two things really well. One or two well-done centerpiece programs may have spillover effects on other programs. If programming for handicapped students is carried out exceptionally well, it is bound to affect how instructors look at individualized instruction, how the curriculum is built, and how the features of other services are brought into focus. A concentration on women's re-entry programs might have similar revolutionary effects on the total program in terms of scheduling, peer support groups, and specialized courses in math anxiety and personal financial management.

Student Services Models

How can student services be brought into the mainstream of the college mission? The following models share common elements: the integration of the instructional program with the students services program and the assumption that some special development needs exist for students. A study of these models suggests that many current student services programs should make similar kinds of adaptations. If these adaptations are not occurring, student services, in the classical way that we know them today, will remain unsupported and will eventually perish.

The Miami-Dade Community College. Miami-Dade illustrates a remarkable adaptation of an institution around some existent technologies. We have suggested that a function such as record keeping promises considerable potential for individualization and humane treatment of students. Miami-Dade has developed a program that does just this—and much more. The Response System with Variable Prescriptions, called R.S.V.P., is a computer-based instructional management system that utilizes the computer's remarkable capabilities for memory, storage, and retrieval to develop programs for student services and individualized instruction (Miami-Dade Community College, 1982). It holds considerable promise to designers of alternative student services programs in community colleges. At last, there is some evidence that technology can have liberalizing influences on the often menial tasks of scheduling and mechanically contacting students through personal advisement.

Miami-Dade Community College established R.S.V.P. with the original purpose of helping distant learners in its Open College, but the services have grown to be quite pervasive. It now reaches several thousand students in the huge Miami-Dade system through a sophisticated dialogue system. R.S.V.P. is currently being used in over fifty courses and programs, including basic skills, on-campus classes, college-wide writing projects, health analysis and improvement, and academic advisement. The program has enabled Miami-Dade to communicate on a massive scale with a potential of 40,000 students.

A primary application of R.S.V.P. is its "academic alert and advisement" system, which evaluates the attendance and academic progress of each student at midterm. Faculty rate performance as "satisfactory," "improvement needed," or "non-evaluation." These notices are sent to all faculty members, and each student receives a letter explaining his or her midterm status in some detail. Miami-Dade boasts that the system can generate 26,000 such unique letters. The implementation of the academic alert system at Miami-Dade was initially painful in that several thousand students received notices of academic deficiencies and were subsequently dropped from college. However, as McCabe points out in Chapter Twelve of this volume, most students at Miami-Dade have "endorsed the imposition of higher expectations," and "93 percent have expressed appreciation at receiving personal computerized information."

President McCabe claims that Miami-Dade has responded to the randomness of student placement typical of the urban community college. In the past, at Miami-Dade, "Students didn't know where they stood, whether they were achieving, and, in most instances, what their goals were" (McCabe, 1982). Increasing numbers of poorly prepared students were coming to the college with less and less chance of succeeding in a traditional collegiate environment. What the R.S.V.P. program has done is to provide a variety of interactive information services to the students, assisting them in their personal self-assessment and their development as academic achievers. More important, it has put them on notice as to their progress in achieving their goals and objectives.

Another application of the R.S.V.P. program is a campus-wide information service called "student services information profile," which prior to each term provides basic information to all instructors about the limitations, abilities, disabilities, and academic needs of handicapped students. This information arrives in the form of a surprisingly personalized letter, as the following sample illustrates: "Dear Mrs. Jones: Our records indicate that Charles Doe is enrolled in one or more of your courses. Charles has a back condition that impairs movement somewhat. Charles's treatment includes mild medication, which should not affect his ability to benefit from instruction."

The R.S.V.P. program also gathers information about student health under the "health analysis and improvement" system; it includes such items as blood pressure, heart rate, percent of body fat, and flexibility measures. This aspect of the program involves between fifteen and twenty faculty members and 1,200 to 1,500 students each term.

R.S.V.P. can thus individualize information about the students' progress, health, goals, and missions. It can identify the tasks remaining for students to complete their goals. Interlaced with these valuable profiles is test information and curricular strengths and weaknesses. In short, an entire profile through interactive systems, based on technological developments that heretofore have not been available to colleges and universities, is now in place at Miami-Dade.

At a time of general disenchantment with the quality of education, Miami-Dade's program puts the public on notice, particularly in Florida, that at least one community college is serious about maintaining academic standards. At the same time, it has established the kinds of information support services and followup advisement services that ensure greater chances of success for marginally qualified students.

Many community colleges and some four-year colleges have begun to share the experience of R.S.V.P. Recently, Miami-Dade Community College received an Exxon grant to enhance the already existing systems at Miami-Dade. Under this grant, a project called Camelot has brought together such institutions as the New University of Ulster, the Ontario Educational Consortium, the Maricopa Community Colleges, the Dallas County Community College District, and many others to participate in developmental efforts and research applications for similar kinds of technologies.

R.S.V.P. deserves being watched for the next several semesters. It is an excellent example of a way to integrate instruction with student services, and it assumes that students have individual personal development needs that often present obstacles to the students' academic progress. Whether Miami-Dade will expand the R.S.V.P. program to include other student development services remains to be seen. One thing is fairly certain: this program has launched a major attack on one of the community college's greatest challenges—dealing with the incredible diversity of its students.

The Rio Salado Community College–Motorola Corporation Project. A second program that provides considerable potential as a model for student services is a project involving Rio Salado Community College in Phoenix, Arizona, and the Motorola Corporation. It promises to be a model for integration of student services with the instructional program. It also promises to be one of the major breakthroughs in college-corporation partnerships. Because student services are so integral a part of the Rio Salado project, the college's approach may prove to be a national model for future developments in community college student personnel programs. Among the striking features of this project are that it has achieved close to 100 percent retention of students, and it takes students through a very demanding academic program in a period of one year (normal time for completion for the average community college student would be two or often three or more years).

Rio Salado Community College is a noncampus-based two-year college serving the greater Phoenix area. It uses over 200 community sites and employs radio, television, audio-teleconferencing, and correspondence to reach diverse learners. Its largest program venture is with private industry, and its students include full-time employees in corporations and manufacturing plants. Although Rio Salado serves over 11,000 credit students and offers programs leading to the associate degree, it also serves over 28,000 persons through noncredit programs, including adult basic education programs (English as a second language and general education courses), courses in family living, continuing education for allied health personnel, consumer education public forums, and mobile in-service training. It is a huge operation, reaching almost every segment of the greater Phoenix area; yet it has been in existence less than four years. With full regional accreditation, it has distinguished itself through comprehensive outreach projects involving several hundred different kinds of innovative programs. The college also operates a national public radio FM station, a radio reading service for blind and print-handicapped people, and a nationally known skill center serving the entire county.

Motorola is typical of the large technology firms in Maricopa County and the greater Phoenix area. Like Digital, Honeywell, Intel, Control Data, and numerous other plants, it has centers for the production of electronics equipment and engages in major research and development in the electronics fields. It has become an internationally prominent semiconductor industry, employing several thousand technicians in both its electronics and semiconductor divisions.

The central purpose of the Rio Salado–Motorola project was to take workers, many of them women and minorities, off the assembly line and prepare them for more advanced positions in the semiconductor processing and electronics divisions of the Motorola organization. These workers were selected for potential supervision posts to lead personnel in the burgeoning electronics field.

The first attempts to establish this program were nearly disastrous. The program developers state that it is easy to plan a fifty-two-week program on paper but far more difficult to put it into practice. One of the first experiences was the high degree of stress among the students in the program. The students felt that instructors teaching introductory courses in English, chemistry, algebra, and other demanding academic subjects were unqualified and demanded that they be replaced. After the first few weeks, the students indicated that they felt that the program was some kind of trick or scheme on the part of management that would lead to their failure and agony rather than to a chance for success. They nearly revolted. During the fifth and sixth weeks, the students began to turn on each other. Leaders and instructors noticed a high degree of irritability—much peer pressure, squabbling, and quarreling. A little later in the semester, the program almost blew up in the faces of both the plant's management and the program director. A gifted counselor and advisor, who had worked with the program from its inception, conducted emergency and crisis sessions. The counselor managed to calm the students, the training director, and the college staff. After that, the program was reshaped and began to move forward.

In redesigning the program, the developers saw that their original design did not include enough support services. In the words of one of the program directors, "the complex marginalized lives of assembly line workers, now turned full-time students, have tremendous impact for support services." During the first two weeks of the redesigned program, courses in math anxiety, self-awareness, coping strategies, and team building were added; nevertheless, student frustrations still developed. Surveys were conducted to assess the personal growth of each individual and specialized tutoring was provided.

The competing demands of family and college escalated the stress for many students. Conflict between home and school pressures is seldom manifested in such a dramatic way as it is when the student comes to class with bruises after being beaten by the spouse. This happened frequently in the Motorola project but was magnified by the project's intensity. Because of this intensity, project directors could spot such trouble areas that would have been lost in the anonymity of a normal collegiate environment. Student services such as women's center programs along with small group sessions on family coping skills closely integrated with instructional classes proved a great help. The role of the counselor, who served as a human development specialist, teacher, buffer, translator, and release valve, is just beginning to be realized. The Rio Salado project has only begun to mine the potential contributions of student personnel services. What has been learned, according to the project director, is that "the flow chart is not the person; it is the person in the program who must succeed if the model is to work."

Despite all its problems, there is overwhelming evidence that the persons in this program did succeed. Virtually all of the students who started the program have completed it. In fact, only two students have left the program: one because of relocation and the other because of ill health. Student services can take much of the credit for this extraordinary retention rate.

Currently, the Rio Salado–Motorola project is under evaluation for support from the Fund for Improvement of Postsecondary Education. Although the project is still in its early experimental stages, it promises to demonstrate the full value of integrating individualized, small- and large-group human development elements into the mainstream of the instructional program. Much rhetoric appears in community college literature about the promise of corporate-industry partnerships. Yet few colleges have validated their work in such industry-based programs. The bottom line for the business and industrial community is human productivity. The Rio Salado–Motorola project illustrates that some of the best integration of human development concepts and instructional programs can produce that productivity in an industrial setting.

Besides the two models described here in detail, there are several others that should be noted. Oakton Community College in Illinois, for example, has done some excellent work in integrating the total college program into the student development philosophy of the college. There has also been outstanding leadership in working with vocational programs and career counseling at Oakton, something not found in many community colleges. The Dallas County Community College District, perhaps because of the influence of Don Rippey and others, has made considerable effort in integrating instruction with student services and refers to student personnel administrators, on one campus at least, as student development officers. Currently, Dallas County is going through a systematic appraisal of how student services should respond to the uncertain future, particularly as the changes involved in the information revolution or "electronic age" occur. La Guardia Community College in New York, which attempts to integrate a cooperative work-study feature into much of its academic programming, has some unique student services. Moorpark College in California has developed a well-integrated career advisement and career counseling program.

Corporations may provide further models for student services. In an attempt to "work smarter not harder," corporations are recognizing that objectives of profit must be matched with human needs. The majority of novel corporate efforts (in this behalf) appear in the areas of increasing communication between labor and management and encouraging ownership of corporate decisions. Through participatory management programs and team efforts toward quality, inroads are being made to blend human needs and profit needs. Implicit in this blending is the assumption that quality is productive and humanly rewarding. While some schools of management hold quality as its own reward, productivity is more generally being rewarded with monetary incentives and profit sharing.

Human Development Model. This model assumes that student personnel professionals must be aware of specific problems and processes typically associated with various student populations and attempt to build programs addressing those issues. Effective application of the human development model may require creation of an institution-wide effort that moves fluidly between the instructional base and the student services base at all points of contact in the college. The assumption is that all areas of student services and instruction can become developmentally oriented around the student's natural and special needs. For example, counselors might deal primarily with human development classes while financial aid officers arrange sessions on managing money, and the tutoring arm of the college provides training in test taking and other classroom survival skills. The special services area might be called upon to teach coping skills to handicapped students. Student activities programs might seek to further develop social and leadership skills. The model for this integrated human development approach would require that various divisions of the college conduct activities that are complementary to one another, that interact with one another, and that are based on carefully identified student needs.

Creamer (1980, p. 2) writes that "student development is not merely a term which, because it sounds better than student personnel services, gives significance to student service professionals. It is a concept which focuses on one of the major purposes of higher education." Rogers (1980, p. 10) further argues that student services professionals must approach student development based "upon formal developmental theories rather than intuitive, implicit assumptions about human development."

Human development theories and the subset of student development concepts come from ground-level observations and other empirical data that suggest the processes by which we pass through the human experience. Some theories focus entirely on affective developments, others on cognitive developments. Still others combine both elements to provide unique perspectives on the process of human development. Presumably, these viewpoints provide a means of understanding the student's experience and thus a framework upon which to build a student services program.

Santa Fe Community College in Gainesville, Florida, has developed a process that it believes assists students in examining their life and career goals as a foundation for curricular choices. Students entering Santa Fe are required to participate in the student assessment program where ability levels are determined in reading, writing, and mathematics before initial registration. Academic and counseling personnel have designed a group of courses to assist those students who appear to need additional preparation. This diagnostic element of the program is critical to its overall effectiveness. An occupational counseling component utilizing System of Interactive Guidance and Information (SIGI) materials, a computerized guidance program developed by the Educational Testing Service, is placed at the disposal of the students and advisors. Starting with personal values, the system aids students in career exploration and developing occupational alternatives. Ultimately, these deliberations produce a program of study consistent with the personal goals and occupational objectives of the student. Students are provided with term-by-term progress reports. For those choosing to transfer to one of the universities in the Florida system, additional information is provided with regard to major and institutional requirements at selected universities.

A similar model for academic advisement exists at Prince Georges Community College in Largo, Maryland. Students are directed into the advisement process on the basis of their status as first-time, transfer, veteran, returning, handicapped, and the like. Here, also, attention is given to testing as a basis for beginning course consideration and career exploration. The purpose is to help students clarify their own educational and career objectives and to identify and utilize the college's resources in achieving their goals. While not based on a computerized system, the process does use a variety of formats, including both group and individual sessions. The result affords students quality information and direction for effective progress through their academic programs.

Both the Santa Fe and Prince Georges academic advisement programs meet the criteria which we have suggested as a necessary and sufficient condition for student service programs: (1) they are integrated with the instructional program of the college, and (2) they assume and respond to special developmental needs of the students.

It is not likely that a single theory or set of theories will cover all situations or be applicable in all institutions. Student development theory is far too incomplete at this point to make such claims. As practitioners, we know that programs must often be designed to suit the unique characteristics of our campuses. A long-time observer, Robert Shaffer (1980, p. 311), guides us through the pitfalls: "Others rightfully emphasize the necessity of integrating development activities into the total life of the institution . . . and integration can occur only if based upon a careful, systematic analysis of the specific institutional setting concerned. What approaches work for one institution may not work at another. . . . Miracles will not occur, nor will institutions change over night."

Perhaps the most practical suggestion for the human development model is to create a human development division within a college. Much of the body of human development theory can then be integrated into a variety of activities, including course work, group sessions, information dissemination, counseling, career exploration, and individual research on human problems bearing on developmental needs and the changing stages of the student population. Clearly, we must reverse the trend of delivering student services reactively. Prior planning, assessment, and the broad integration of human development concepts into the curriculum and service delivery processes are advisable. Each college, however, must tailor that integration to fit its own unique setting and characteristics.

Conclusions

Research materials on student services programs in the community colleges are not plentiful. It is clear, however, that community colleges serve an older, more diverse student body with different motivations than those of traditional students. These motivations may be fragile, and changing clientele are quick to vote with their feet if they do not receive the service, instruction, and stimulation that they require. In these difficult fiscal times college administrators and governing boards are voting with their pens and designating student services programs for elimination. This is due to the perception of student services programs as an appendage rather than as an equal partner with instruction. Yet R.S.V.P., Rio Salado–Motorola Project, and several other academic advisement programs demonstrate the tremendous value of student services support systems. When integrated with instruction into the overall mission of community colleges, student services could demonstrate program effectiveness, human resource development, and the human productivity that the corporate world expects of our graduates.

It is imperative that the relationship of student services to the instructional program be clearly defined and enhanced if student services is to survive first round budget cuts that are out of proportion with the cuts for instruction and other functions. Student services personnel need to be more assertive in promoting their viewpoint. They cannot point to the number of full-time equivalent students they produce; however, they can document a number of things. For example, a well-publicized annual report devoted to the activities of the student services division can be quite helpful in demonstrating the value of student services to campus life. Who speaks for student services in the community college at the national level? The answer is no one. Student services personnel need to agree on certain principles and articulate them to the national community college audience.

The Rio Salado–Motorola Project is an excellent example of how student services can, and probably should, fit into the community college of the future. Community college leaders should consider assigning a counselor to business and industry just as counselors have been assigned to the high schools. If the link with industry is not made in conjunction with student services, it will be made in some other manner. A person trained in counseling might be assigned to the cooperative education division or to the community services or continuing education divisions rather than to the student services division. Assigning personnel with the student services' viewpoint to other divisions could do a great deal to emphasize the value of that viewpoint.

We believe that student services have never been needed more than at the present. To be effective, a model must be developed on an institution-by-institution basis to integrate student services with the instructional programs of the college. Hopefully, we have identified some alternative futures in the search for the student services mission.

8

Leading the Educational Program

Arthur M. Cohen

Who plots directions for the educational program? Who considers the potential effects of changes in students, staff, funding, and myriad other influences? If these questions were put to the staff in most colleges, some would respond, "the faculty"; others, "the dean of instruction," or, "the board." The less circumspect would say, "everyone," or, "no one." The true answer depends on the history of the institution and the type of leadership it enjoys.

The analysts who present information on trends in curriculum, demography, and public perception of the colleges are trying to stimulate consideration of what they feel are important issues. Yet they realize that theirs is a precarious exercise. Its success depends upon their audience taking a broad, long-term view of their work, rising above the quotidian. These prophets are not without honor; there are always a few readers who appreciate the literate scholars of education. But the reactions of most educators reveal the uneasy mixture of pride, diffidence, and defensiveness that lies just beneath the surface of a seemingly placid field.

The practitioners' reactions to data offer a case in point. Most of them attend to the verbal, the immediate, and the readily apprehended. They find it difficult to assimilate information stemming from nationwide studies. There is too much missing. What do demographic charts showing static numbers of college-age students have to do with next fall's class schedule? How do declining test scores made by high school graduates relate to tomorrow's class? Most instructors dismiss information coming from statewide or regional studies as irrelevant to them. They want to know how to keep students coming to class, and, once there, how to keep their attention. Administrators seek only those nuggets useful in their own deliberations over fiscal and personnel allocations. The field tends inward; people want information that they can use to solve problems of the day. This characteristic would be acceptable if colleges functioned well as autocracies; no need then for the rank and file to be concerned with overarching matters. But education thrives best when its practitioners act as professionals who integrate what they learn. It does least well when educators deny the data, become angry with those who present them, or dissociate themselves from them.

The process is as follows. First, the denial: "The data (on student learning, for instance) are wrong because in my class it's different." There is a reason for this type of denial. Most instructors are attuned to their own classrooms and are not aware of, not concerned with, don't understand, and don't want to know what is going on across the nation. They focus on individual students, not collectivities. They think of the one student who came into their class reading at a third-grade level, gained two or three grades of achievement in one semester, and eventually transferred and graduated with honors. Most instructors have those types of success stories, and they relish them. That's what allows the instructors to survive in face of the knowledge of how little their students learn *as a group* over the years. That's why they shrink from writing specific objectives, predicting group performance, and giving criterion-based final examinations. They want to remember the individual successes.

The second response often is annoyance: "Even if the data are correct they should not be publicized because they will be used by people who want to destroy the community college, or, more specifically, my program within it." The practitioners fear that reporting accurate data about student retention, academic standards, curriculum outcomes, course completions, and so on, will be turned against them. Instead of using the data as a base for program change and program support, they shortsightedly become angry with the researchers who present them.

The third response is typically dissociation: "Even if the information (about student learning) is correct, it's not our fault. Blame the breakdown in the nuclear family, the lack of respect for authority in society, television viewing, the lower schools that don't teach literacy, the universities that maintain unrealistic expectations—anybody but us." They have numerous excuses, villains, ways of refusing to accept responsibility for their students' failure to read and write, for their own inabilities to teach them.

Fortunately, nearly every college has at least a few astute faculty and administrators who know that they must act also as educational planners. Instead of denying the data, they look to be sure they were correctly collected and analyzed; then they try to see how the implications stemming from them can enhance the college's actions. Anger over the publicity is beneath them. They know they live in a political context where the constructive use of potentially damaging data is the best defense. And they realize that dissociation is short sighted. Of course it would be better if students were literate, but every home has a television set. The students in community colleges are there to be taught; it is idle to wish they were better prepared and more ready to learn.

Still, there is no surfeit of leaders who articulate logical educational plans and pursue them consistently. That lack affects all the programs: career, compensatory, community, and collegiate education alike. Career education can survive the lack of plans; each program within it has its corps of supporters among area employers, and many have their own separate funding channels. Furthermore, colleges have for so long been promoted as essential for training people for technological and semiprofessional jobs that most students and their families probably feel that that is their main purpose. The worst that happens to career education is that it has to suffer occasional accusations: first, that it is an instrument of a capitalistic society helping to perpetuate the system; second, that all students who pass through its programs do not necessarily attain employment in the field for which they were trained. But the proponents of career education tend to disregard those criticisms as niggling attacks by envious outsiders. On the ascendancy since the mid-1960s, career education is in a secure position. This chapter addresses the educational leaders in other fields: compensatory, community, and collegiate education.

Compensatory Education

Compensatory or developmental education is not new to colleges, but its magnitude has increased notably in recent years. Nationwide, one third of the students taking mathematics—60 percent in the large, urban districts—are in classes that teach nothing higher than arithmetic. Around 40 percent of English classes are teaching basic reading, vocabulary, and word usage (Center for the Study of Community Colleges, 1982, p. 1). This enterprise grew massive because of the poor prior preparation of entering students, but it typically has not been fully integrated into the college curriculum. Why? The following criticisms and their corresponding counterarguments were discussed at an Arizona State University conference in 1982.

First Criticism. The community college is the wrong place to do compensatory education. Some have contended that developmental education belongs better in adult schools, in the private sector, or in corporate, on-the-job training programs.

The obvious response is that the community colleges may not be the best place to do compensatory education, but they are stuck with it. Developmental education has become the general education for community colleges of the 1980s, and it continues to grow. Compensatory education's importance should be no surprise. It stems from the changes in the types of students coming to the colleges. In the early part of the nineteenth century, colleges opened for women, and coeducational colleges followed. Thereupon, it became immoral to bar women from collegiate studies. In the latter part of the century the land-grant colleges opened, making it possible for children of the less affluent to go to college. It then became immoral to bar people of modest income. The civil rights movement of the 1950s and

1960s led to the belief that it was immoral to bar members of ethnic minority populations from going to college. More recently, the various financial aid programs have made it immoral to bar the indigent. Most recently, it has become immoral to bar the physically handicapped. And the open access, open door community college finds it unfeasible and, indeed, immoral to bar the ignorant. It has become immoral to deny anyone access to college just because that person cannot read, write, or compute. The colleges' involvement with compensatory education rests on that.

In the 1960s and the 1970s, the community colleges were dedicated primarily to one theme: access. Open the door, get everyone in; build programs for returning women, veterans, drug abusers, displaced homemakers, people with too much time on their hands, people without enough time to learn what they need to know to progress in their specialized area of work. The colleges built programs to attract people from every corner of the community. And the enrollments swelled. Now that everyone who can reasonably be enticed to come to the institution has enrolled, they must be taught. And that suggests literacy development.

Second Criticism. Compensatory education costs too much. How many times should the public have to pay to teach the same person how to read? The argument is that compensatory education yields a low benefit for a high cost, that the taxpayers will not be willing to pay for the same type of instruction over and over.

Many community college leaders have responded that it costs less to teach developmental education in community colleges than in universities and other institutions. It is time they stopped talking about the economies of the community college versus the university. It makes them sound like a restaurant owner who says, "Our food is not good, but it's cheap." That is not a very apt way of advertising. Nonetheless, there are many ways of making developmental education better without spending more. The practitioners of instruction, faculty and administrators alike, have yet to understand that the use of paraprofessional aides can greatly enhance developmental education—as, indeed all other types of education—while holding costs down. Using senior citizens, other lay people, and advanced students as aides to the faculty and tutors to the students who need assistance can be quite salutary. They can assist in numerous ways, and they will work for a pittance. Yet, few college staff members have understood or want to understand how to take advantage of this great pool of available economical assistance. The mores of the educators seem to mitigate their understanding that successful teaching does not necessarily depend on a $30,000-a-year professional person working on a one-to-one basis with a student.

Third Criticism. Because the academic faculty do not want or know how to teach literacy, developmental education should be operated as a separate department.

That is wrong. The community colleges are so deeply involved in developmental education that it must involve the total faculty. Every faculty member is affected. In the open access policy of the community college the only programs that can control entry are those that are in high demand, such as the high technology and the allied health programs. They can afford to be selective and can demand literacy. None of the other programs enjoy that prerogative. In all other curriculums the students must be taught, whether or not they can read and write at the outset. Separate developmental studies programs or departments only serve to widen a gulf that already exists between faculty with high pretensions (those who neither know how nor want to teach literacy) and those who are totally involved with developmental education. A separate developmental studies department also suggests tracking, a concept that has adverse connotations of its own.

Every program and every department should have a developmental education component within it: either separate courses within the department, or, better, literacy in every course. Nationwide, less than 5 percent of community college students complete two years and transfer to the university. Fewer than 10 percent are enrolled in courses for which there is a prerequisite (Cohen, 1979). The entire institution has become a combination of introductory courses and developmental studies. It is in danger of losing the sophomore year. Separate developmental studies departments serve only to accelerate that trend. Developmental education should be integrated into every course.

Fourth Criticism. There is insufficient articulation with the secondary schools. That is a justified criticism. When the community college was young, grown out of secondary school districts in many states, many of its instructors taught in the high school in the daytime and in the community college at night. Most of the full-time community college instructors were former secondary school teachers. Now, that connection has been weakened. The community colleges demanded the right to become a part of higher education and, as they did, they tended to turn their backs on the secondary schools. Since so few community college students complete two years and go to the university but practically all of them come from neighboring secondary schools, the community colleges are facing the wrong way.

Educational leaders in some states are trying to rebuild the links between higher education and the secondary schools. California public colleges and universities issued a joint statement in 1981 contending that college preparation programs (grades 9 through 12) should include a minimum of four years of English and a minimum of three years of mathematics. A report from New Jersey noted, "The level of proficiency required to complete three years of high school English and math is considerably lower than the proficiency expected of entering freshmen in the institutions of this state" (Edge, 1979). And the president of Miami-Dade Community College collected data on the preparation level of entering students and presented those data to the secondary schools in his area.

Fifth Criticism. The faculty don't know how to teach literacy. That criticism may be warranted generally, but there is much variation among instructors. Surely, few instructors enjoy teaching students who do not know how to read and write; most want bright, capable, literate individuals eager to learn the most specialized bits of subject matter. But those students are not forthcoming.

This suggests a role for the developmental educators. They

should treat the faculty in the collegiate programs as their students. Instead of isolating themselves in a separate department to which the collegiate faculty happily send their poorer students, they should work directly with that faculty. That is one of the reasons for integrating developmental studies within the academic departments; it brings the developmental educator into association with the collegiate faculty. It allows the developmental educator to become an educator of instructors.

Sixth Criticism. There is too much experimentation and too few results. That is a justifiable criticism. We know what types of programs work. Every college president can point to a special program where a few dozen students are getting a high-intensity experience, a program in which a few students are learning to read so well that they are moving up three grade levels in one semester. But those programs are not feasibly extended to the population at large. A high faculty/student ratio, special additional funds, a high level of involvement for support people, and small groups of students yield wondrous results. But that is not nearly enough. Developmental education must be woven into the fabric of the institution.

Seventh Criticism. We ask too little. That may sound strange, but few teachers use readers or paraprofessional aides to assist in reacting to students' writing; they merely assign fewer papers.

Writing is a skill learned through practice, just as speaking is a skill learned through practice. We become literate by reading and writing, whether by joy or coercion or some combination of both. Literacy is developed by doing it; people cannot learn to write unless they sit down and write. Most of the problems in literacy development that community colleges face, or at least the portions of those problems that the schools have the power to mitigate, can be traced to declining demands. The schools do not demand as much reading and writing as they did a generation ago. Less practice yields poorer results.

Eighth Criticism. There are inconsistent standards in the classrooms. This criticism is certainly warranted. Different demands are placed on students in different fields and in different classes in the same field. An alert student can track a path through college without ever being asked to write a paper.

Surveys have found tremendous variation in reading and writing requirements, not only between fields, but also between instructors in the same field. There may be as much variation between instructors teaching the same types of courses in the same discipline as there is between disciplines. As long as students can find courses that do not demand writing, it remains difficult to effect literacy development in the institution.

Ninth Criticism. Placement and diagnostic tests are not valid. The tests are usually seen as culturally biased and are not relevant except to English and mathematics.

These objections can be countered. Every test of anything is culturally biased; the entire school system is culturally biased. Of course, the tests are not relevant to courses other than English and math because few people know what instructors in those other courses expect. It is not valid to ask applicants to take a reading test if they can earn a diploma by taking courses in which they just have to watch films. Which tests should be used? And when? Who should administer them?

Miami-Dade Community College has a procedure whereby any student who enrolls for more than three classes at once or in sequence and any student who enrolls for a class in English or mathematics is sent to the testing center to take a placement examination in English and mathematics (Kelly, 1981). On the basis of the results, the student is placed into certain sections of those courses. But this depends on a sophisticated student monitoring system, which few institutions have. Students may go along taking course after course without ever having been tested. Only when they sign up for an English or mathematics class does the testing procedure come into effect. And even then, it may be a homemade test devised by the members of that department. Nonetheless, more testing is better than less in the current climate.

Tenth Criticism. Support services are not worth what they cost. Counseling, tutorials, learning laboratories, and other types of student learning areas that have been built outside formal classrooms have been accused of being too costly for what they provide. That may be so, but there is good reason for it. The reason is that classroom instructors have tended to have little affiliation with the supportive activities. The learning laboratory is usually managed by a learning resource director. The tutorial center may be managed by some other group. There is little association between course content and ancillary services. Few instructors work with support people.

That suggests another role for developmental educators. They must bring support activities and instructors together, showing the instructors how they can use the support services as a way of bolstering their instruction. The instructors need to be helped to integrate the work they are doing in the classroom with the services available. They themselves need to feel confident in their use of support services.

To conclude, compensatory education is now part of the reality of community colleges. The students entering in the coming years are not going to be better prepared. But the slide away from the higher learning may have gone as far as it can go for a while. Various demands for increased linearity in curriculum and student placement are being made. Sophomore-level achievement tests are being introduced in several states. And at least a few educators have realized that if the colleges are to maintain their transfer function, developmental education must be built into it.

The solution is not to undertake misguided action. For example, it is not feasible to limit the number of courses an employed student may take; more than 70 percent of students work now (Friedlander, 1981). Nor is it feasible to keep students out of the collegiate courses until they prove they can read; too few students can read at the level that their instructors would prefer. But support services can be mandated, and tutorials and learning laboratory activities can be integrated with classroom instruction. Every instructor can demand reading and writing in every classroom. Exit tests can be offered so that the colleges can demonstrate what their programs have actually done, whether or not the students transfer. Literacy development can become the community colleges' strength.

Community Education

Community education presents a set of different problems. First, what is it? Like most community college programs, its roots are in senior institutions. University extension courses, agricultural experiment stations, and professors' consultancies and research concerned with extramural problems all suggest service to the community. In most universities those activities were seen as important functions. But organizationally they developed apart from the degree and credit programs. They now tend to be housed, funded, and staffed in separate divisions.

In the community colleges, community services developed similarly but in a much more limited fashion. Their instructors typically were not researchers, and few acted as consultants on community projects. Agricultural or other direct service activities were at a minimum. The major similarity was in the short noncredit courses offered in university extension fashion. These too tended to be funded and staffed separately.

Thus the community education dimension of community colleges centered on unconnected courses, events, and short-term programs. Its guiding principle was that any activity that any local community group wanted was appropriate. It was defined by exclusion: community service was any activity not included in the traditional transfer and occupational programs.

By 1980 this definition of community services had fallen into disrepute, primarily due to problems of funding and image. Community colleges in many states found their local funding base severely reduced. It is that base that was being used to pay for recreational and cultural activities. State-level funding formulas became more restrictive, excluding a sizable complement of noncredit courses or activities that fell outside the traditional curriculum. In 1982, for instance, when the California Community College Board of Governors issued a list of courses that would no longer be eligible for state reimbursement, Coastline Community College, an institution centering on community services, had to eliminate 30 percent of its class sections (Luskin, 1982).

The cutbacks in funding rekindled attempts to redefine community services. But first it was necessary to put the old definition to rest. Richardson and Leslie (1980) noted that in periods of reduced support for education, it would be difficult for colleges to maintain hobby and recreational programs. Breneman and Nelson (1981) explained how state-level funding typically put programs designed for the good of society ahead of those directed toward individual interests. Parnell (1982) challenged the personal interest activities because they were damaging the colleges' image. He felt that the public relations costs of belly dancing, poodle grooming, and macrame were more than the community colleges could afford. Even when those activities were fully supported by participants, the public perceived them as evidence that the community college was not a serious educational institution. He was willing to "bequeath" them "to the local YMCA, local YWCA, senior citizens' center, or other community service organizations not faced with projecting the same kind of image that colleges must maintain for continued legislative and general public support" (Parnell, 1982, p. 4).

If community services can no longer be justified as useful to individuals, how can they be redefined? Perhaps because they anticipated lack of support for unconnected activities, some proponents of community education began promoting it as community development. To them the community college could enhance a sense of community, assist in solving community problems, and, in general, uplift the social, political, and economic climate of its region. It would do this by offering workshops, consultantships, and surveys to its local community. The activities would include short courses for target groups, such as employees of certain industries, forums on local social problems and on national and international affairs, and consumer education.

The term *community-based education* also gained currency. It is somewhat of an amalgamation of the traditional community services concept with the newer idea of community development. Under community-based education, the local citizenry are encouraged to advise the institution on issues that should be addressed; the college planners arrange the forums and short courses. Both the advisory groups and the institutional leaders attempt to stimulate other community agencies also to address the identified problems. Courses and seminars may be offered by the college alone or in conjunction with other community groups.

Community development and activities planned with and

on behalf of the local community have made some progress. The thread holding them together is that they represent a break with college-credit, discipline-based educational forms. But educational institutions are slow to change, and community education is far from being a central position among community college functions. Atwell, Vaughan, and Sullins (1982) addressed the reasons for its failure to achieve prominence and found five: too few college staff members who understand the concept, sizable enrollments which give the illusion of success, failure of coordinated leadership on individual campuses, lack of a sound funding base, and diverse messages coming from national leaders. They concluded that until the disparate activities conducted in the name of community education were linked together into a program with consistent long-term goals, community education would not achieve the prominence it deserved.

Can community education be coordinated into a program with long-term goals? One problem with this idea is that as soon as community education is defined and put into a program, it risks being co-opted by the traditional career and collegiate education programs. If one of the goals is that community education enhance the work skills of the populace, even those skills that fit them particularly for local industries, the career education group is likely to take it over and make it one of their curricula. If one of the goals is to enhance people's knowledge of local history or ecology, the academic faculty can make that part of their offerings in science, social science, and the humanities. Once brought to public view, a consistent program of community education becomes only another part of the career and collegiate curricula. That may be its greatest contribution.

Apart from attempting to coordinate a program with consistent, long-term goals, community education has other problems. It poses a threat to full-time instructors. Community service programs historically have been developed without involving the regular faculty; the community service directors merely arrange for lay people or part-time instructors to lead the activities. Where the community service directors have been sufficiently astute to realize that involving the regular instructors in their programs is a way of gaining college-wide support, the in-

structors have taken part in the events. But too often the directors have held their programs apart. Because of their unions and
new-found political power, the regular faculty can no longer be
ignored by anyone who wants to develop a viable community
education program.

New types of funding patterns will also have to be developed if community education is to thrive. When community services compete with career and collegiate programs, they usually
lose. The idea of supporting those courses that offer credit
toward academic degrees or occupational certificates is too
powerful for a community service director to overcome. Community education might thrive if the community service division could be funded programmatically; for years community
colleges in California funded their community services in large
measure through the imposition of a special 5-cent tax override
earmarked for that purpose, but by the end of 1970s that tax
was no longer available to them. Some states have made progress in funding community services through block grants, but in
an era of tight money for education it may be difficult to make
additional progress.

Institutional leadership on behalf of community services
is not widespread. Some community college leaders have taken
on service to the community as their personal mission and built
strong community education programs outside the traditional
curricula. But few others have been willing to become so identified with a single function. Most prefer to remain—or at least
give the appearance of remaining—even-handed in their treatment of all the functions.

Community education proponents who see their services
as community development face even greater problems. The
community colleges have never done well in presenting evidence
of individual students' learning. It would be even more difficult
for them to demonstrate their success in uplifting entire communities. The most partisan advocate of community development should recognize the difficulty in providing that type of
evidence. Community development as a goal also brings community colleges into competition with other community agencies
whose directors may not take kindly to the intrusion. The com-

munity colleges are schools, not social welfare agencies. The gap between the public perception of them as schools and as agencies of community uplift is too great for them to overcome in the near future. The move from local to state funding alone should be sufficient to discourage the advocates of community development. As long as community services are seen as benefiting individuals instead of the broader society they will not enjoy widespread support in state capitals.

The community colleges have been moving rapidly to put their community services on a pay-as-you-go basis with the costs being borne by the consumers. Should that trend continue, community services may well remain adjunctive. At most, they would develop as university extension divisions have, completely separate from the degree-credit programs. Some community services directors have attempted to build separate divisions; others have taken a different approach and attempted to fund their programs through contracts with local industries. In the latter case, the community education division has become a holding company for service contracts with private employers and governmental agencies.

Parnell (1982, p. 5) has said that community services should deal with community problems, not community entertainment and trivia. He has challenged the colleges to provide information about "toxic waste disposal, energy conservation, economic survival, improving intergroup human relations." According to him, the colleges might thereby connect community services with the traditional college disciplines and curriculum, thus involving the regular full-time faculty in presenting such programs. Parnell is not the first to articulate such an idea; as community services evolved into community education, college leaders such as Harlacher and Gollattscheck (1978) saw the concept shifting from personal to social issues.

Community education seems poised to go in either, perhaps both, of two directions. One is toward a separate division funded, staffed, and operated apart from regular college programs. The model for such a separation is afforded by the university extension divisions that offer cultural, recreational, and short-term occupational programs and activities on a self-sus-

taining basis. If the institutions that build such divisions promote them properly, they can readily overcome the charge that
taxpayer funds are being squandered on activities of little value
except to the people who participate in them. The University of
California at Los Angeles (UCLA) Extension catalogue for fall
1982 offered 220 pages of courses in business, the arts, the humanities, education, and the sciences, among others, all on a
self-sustaining basis. Carefully noted on the inside front cover
was the statement, "Not printed at state expense. UCLA Extension receives no state tax monies whatever. Its program of continuing education is supported entirely from student enrollment
fees."

Another promising route for community education is for
the community services division to be collapsed entirely and re-
constituted as a different arm of the college. The new division
would offer no courses or activities. Instead, a team of community education specialists comprised of administrators and faculty on temporary assignment would act as advisors to the career
and collegiate programs. They would help the faculty in those
programs organize events such as exhibits, forums, recitals, and
lecture series. They would organize community surveys and
commission social science students and instructors to conduct
them. They would encourage instructors in the sciences to include issues pertaining to local environmental concerns in their
courses. They would arrange for assessments of occupational
trends in the community and assist career educators in organizing programs to accommodate them. They would help the collegiate faculty to build general education programs for local citizenry cohort by cohort. In sum, they would be facilitators,
organizers, and leaders bridging the gap between community
education and the career and collegiate degree-credit programs.
Their work would supplant that of the institutional research directors. They would act on behalf of the instructional program,
integrating their activities with the traditional functions, helping
modify those functions so that they became more attuned to
concepts of community education. To the extent they were successful, the entire college would become a community service.

Collegiate Education

Collegiate education is the term used for all courses and programs for which academic degree credit is offered. When the community colleges began, most of their curriculum was college credit. But this proportion has diminished steadily in recent years. Most of the rhetoric and a large part of the reality of the community college in recent years has been dedicated to compensatory noncredit education, career education, and service to the community.

How much has collegiate education suffered? It is not difficult to trace the fate of the collegiate function because it is embedded in the associate degree program, and figures on numbers of degrees awarded are collected routinely. During the decade of the 1970s the number of associate degrees conferred changed hardly at all: from 145,473 in 1970-71 to 152,169 in 1979-80 (Cohen and Brawer, 1982, p. 203). Yet community college enrollments doubled during those same years. Thus the number of students completing the transfer programs declined notably as a percentage of total enrollments.

The reasons for this decline are also not difficult to trace. The people born during the post–World War II baby boom came of college age in the 1960s and clamored for access to higher education. Because the universities could not take all those students the community colleges expanded rapidly to accommodate them. Since a sizable proportion of the students had aspirations for the baccalaureate, they inflated the transfer program figures.

A second phenomenon of the mid-1960s was that the purpose of going to college became inverted. In earlier generations, young people who wanted to go to work apprenticed to tradesmen or took entry-level jobs in business; those who wanted to study the liberal arts went to college. That pattern turned around so that those who sought jobs went to school and demanded that the institution prepare them to earn a living. Accordingly, career education grew dramatically during the 1960s and 1970s as educators and students alike became convinced that unless there was a job waiting at the end of the program, the education was wasted. Conversely, many of those who wanted to study the liberal arts began doing so on their own in university extension divisions, adult schools, and through community college community service programs.

Another influence on the transfer program began in the 1960s when the first generation of young people reared from infancy on television entered the colleges. The collegiate function had been based on the apprehension of texts. But this new group's main method of information reception was through nonprint media, and they ascribed little value to reading and writing. Although these students have been in the institutions for a generation, few instructors in the transfer programs have learned how to educate them.

The transfer program suffered also from the decline in academic studies in the nation's high schools. During the 1960s and 1970s, the requirements for high school graduation changed so that students took considerably less English, history, mathematics, science, and foreign languages. Boyer (1980) documented that trend, showing how the academic courses had been replaced by driver education, personal interest courses, and reduced time spent in school.

Reduced high school graduation requirements were followed in the colleges by reduced academic graduation requirements and grade inflation. Blackburn and others (1976) detailed the reduction in academic requirements and found that although the reduction in two-year colleges was not as severe as that in four-year institutions, it still was marked. Numerous community colleges made their own contribution to grade inflation in higher education during that period by allowing students the option of withdrawing from classes without penalty at any time up until the last week of the term.

As a consequence of this collection of influences, the curriculum in the academic transfer programs flattened out. Instead of a linear sequence with students starting with introductory courses and progressing to advanced courses, it tended to take lateral form. By the beginning of the 1980s, the catalogues still displayed a complete array of course prerequisites and graduation expectations, but many students were attending the colleges as though there were no requirements. Except for the students in occupational programs that had selective entry and licensure requirements, 90 percent of the enrollment was in courses for which there was no prerequisite or in which the prerequisite was not enforced. Introductory courses and courses that were not part of any sequence occupied the major portion of the academic program.

Should community college planners be concerned with the collegiate function? Many would say that it is archaic, that students want jobs, not the higher learning. They point to the part-timers who have swelled the enrollment figures in their quest for skills leading to immediate employment or upgrading within jobs they already hold. They claim that the institution has become an adult education center where sequenced curriculum is not properly a consideration. To them the biggest problem is how to convince the legislators and the public that this transformation in institutional purpose has actually occurred so that new funding patterns can be devised to accommodate it.

However, the transfer program, the collegiate function, the academic dimension of the community college cannot be written off casually. A sizable portion of the public still sees transfer education as the college's primary function; a Gallup Poll in 1977 found nearly half the people interviewed identifying transfer studies as the main mission (*A Gallup Study . . . ,* 1981). Nor can funding formulas be overturned easily. As educators in many states have learned to their dismay, legislators still accord the highest priority to occupational and transfer studies.

Certain other factors point also to continuation of the academic program. The community colleges were never successful in attracting sizable numbers of serious, literate scholars with a commitment to learning. They offered academic studies from the start, but as their clients changed they changed their mission to fit the proclivities of the new students. Still, the colleges represented the point of first entry to higher education for many people who would not otherwise go to college. That is the true meaning of expanded access: access for the underprivileged.

Were the colleges to abandon the collegiate function, an entire social stratum would be ill-served. That decision should not be made lightly.

Besides, who can say with certainty that the collegiate function is outmoded? Historically, obtaining a college degree represented a form of accomplishment. It showed that the person had persisted through a course of study of his or her own volition, had been exposed to the major ideas and concepts undergirding our society, had learned to communicate passably well with others similarly trained. The highest status, highest paying jobs in our society still tend to go to the college educated, especially to those who have *not* been through a program preparing them for work in a specific occupation. True, the more specific the skill, the easier to teach it, but the more specific the skill, the less it is applicable outside particular situations and the more rapidly it becomes obsolete. And it is not sufficient to say that students learning specific skills acquire general concepts along the way; Gresham's Law applied to education holds that the specific training crowds out the general education.

The major difficulty in the academic transfer programs is that they have not been reconceptualized to fit the changes of the past two decades. When faced with students who were not the independent, self-directed learners they fondly—and perhaps inaccurately—remembered, the educators have been too ready to say, "Well, we cannot teach higher order concepts because the students cannot grasp them; therefore we will reduce the education to a few specifics that we can teach. The students cannot write because they were not taught to write in the lower schools; therefore we will not ask them to write. Since they tend not to read, we will demand less reading from them. We will fit the education to the 'needs' of the learner." Numerous studies, including several done at the Center for the Study of Community Colleges in Los Angeles (Cohen and Brawer, 1982, pp. 153-157) and at Arizona State University (Richardson, Fisk, and Okun, 1983) have demonstrated these proclivities.

Education demands time spent on tasks; short-cycle experiences do not help students learn to conceptualize. Education is linear—sequential; it does not always proceed in a straight line from lesser- to higher-order concepts, but it does demand aggregation. Education takes time; reduced demands for time spent on tasks in the lower schools were accompanied by reduced learning there. Reducing education to that which can be learned in a single session reduces it to a series of rapidly obsolete skills. The excuse that students will not show up for classes taught in sequence or will withdraw from school if too many demands are placed upon them or will not write papers and perform other tasks that require them to bring together knowledge from several areas, is just that—an excuse to show progress by teaching the trivial. There is much evidence to show that greater expectations, higher demands, and carefully tailored support services yield considerably greater results.

The problem of the trivial driving out the general is not peculiar to higher learning. Many employers have reacted to the same phenomenon. The goals of the collegiate function are often stated as helping students to gain a cultural perspective, understand their heritage, gain better interpersonal relations, learn critical thinking, and learn to communicate. These were the general abilities that employers expected students to present when they had completed secondary school, the reasons why the high school diploma was a precondition of job application. The diploma has lost its credibility, and many employers now want college degrees from entry-level applicants. Such employers expect more than specific skills from their workers.

The community colleges have made several misguided changes in their effort to be accepted by employers and to be relevant to students. They have allowed the specifics of remedial and occupational education to drive out the general of the liberal arts. Many leaders felt they were doing a service by making it easier for students to obtain a certificate or credential. Yet that was destructive to curricular sequence. When students can drop in and out of classes, withdraw at any time with no penalty, take classes off campus at places and times of their own choosing, sign up for almost any course without fulfilling prerequisites, then the trivial has crowded out the educative dimension.

The case for the collegiate function rests not on nostalgia

for the time when upper-class gentlemen and ladies went to college to learn manners. It is based on a belief that an exclusive emphasis on specifics offers little to students who would make their way in the world. Employers will not be satisfied with people who are minimally able to communicate, think, and understand. Young people who are awarded credentials that have lost their value have not been well served.

It is objected that students don't know how to study; they can't learn; they aren't able. Can the colleges change the students' approach to education? How much is within their control? They cannot change the students' pattern of television watching. They cannot change the reasons why students come to school. However, they can effect changes in the courses students take, the sequences in which they take them, and the requirements within the courses. They can increase the demands they make upon students. They do not have to continue allowing students to drop in and out of the institution haphazardly. They do not have to emphasize the trivial.

The term *college level* is often used as a way of differentiating between remedial education and higher learning. The term is not precise; its meaning fluctuates. It is probably best defined as being the average of the demands placed on students in all sections of all courses of that type in all community colleges. It can be assessed by asking instructors questions regarding course requirements, grading standards, texts in use, number of pages students are required to read, and so on. It is related to content only insofar as such content leads students to higher levels of literacy and reflection, better understanding of alternatives, increased awareness of ethical issues, and greater realization of past and present time. A course in a nursing program may be college level whereas a course in United States history may not. It depends upon the demands it makes; it depends upon the instructor's expectations.

The collegiate function faces a long period of difficult times. Tradition, public perception, and the faculty who teach the academic courses ensure that it will not readily disappear. Operating against it are student demands for quick access to jobs, poor academic preparation of entering students, and the belief of college leaders that their institution serves its community best when it offers up a wide variety of unconnected events.

The collegiate function will survive because of inertia, but if it is to thrive, the liberal arts will have to be reconceptualized to fit the reality of the community college. Can the arts be taught without expecting students to read or demanding that they write? Can the arts be taught to students who shun any activity that does not promise to connect them quickly with a job? Can the arts be merged with general education so that a unique community college collegiate experience is effected? The curriculum planners grope for ways of doing it.

Between now and the time when the necessary reconceptualization emerges, several well-meaning and, in some cases, modestly effective attempts are being made to patch over the problems. One is to reinstate selective admissions into college-level courses. Institutions that have done this have been forced to tailor special admissions tests for their clients and to build extensive developmental education programs. In other colleges, students are allowed to enroll in collegiate courses but are required to participate in an extensive array of concurrent instructional support activities including tutorials, counseling, and media-based programs. Some community college systems have moved so markedly in the direction of occupational and adult basic education that they have let the collegiate function wash out of the institution entirely. All those options are feasible and each has its supporters. Each can be and is being done in the context of the contemporary college.

Integrating the collegiate function with community education shows promise, at least in principle. The college that has a sizable cohort of students working on community problems while attending collegiate courses may be on the way to the needed reconceptualization of the collegiate function. The colleges' community base demands that its students and faculty be in close contact with local issues; its role in higher education demands that its courses maintain academic rigor. And, again, academic rigor depends more on the demands for literacy placed on the students than it does on the course content. For this reason the course materials, including textbooks, will have to be

prepared by the faculty within the community college themselves. And much data will have to be gathered to show that the
courses are academically respectable even though the content
differs from that presented in the lower division of senior institutions.

Leadership

Compensatory education needs to be merged with degree-
credit courses; community services should be split into a totally
separate division; the collegiate function must be bolstered with
a comprehensive array of especially designed support services.
There are plenty of challenges for forward-looking presidents,
deans, program coordinators, and division chairpersons. Will
they do it? Possibly, because they have been forced to shift focus. During the era of growth, the time when most current administrators assumed their responsibilities, the introduction of
new programs was applauded. It was easy for administrators to
say they were serving new clients, hence increasing their institution's value to the community. Few seemed to realize that each
new program, once institutionalized, would become a source of
rigidity that would stand to block future change. Even though
few of the new programs became written into law, they did
bring with them their complement of staff, hence supporters.
Few community college leaders realized that opening access to
people with decidedly undistinguished prior school records
would eventually lessen their college's value for better students.
They were unprepared for the decline in preparation in the
secondary schools. They ignored the demographics which could
have warned them that when the people born in the late 1940s
and early 1950s had passed through their colleges, there would
be a smaller pool of well-qualified students who would tend to
opt for senior institutions.

Leaders need vision. As one example, when growth was
the sine qua non of the community college, the questions most
commonly asked were how to staff the institution properly,
how to recruit students from among populations not otherwise
being served, and how to gain approval for new programs. The

literature was filled with plans for staff development, new forms of financing, and new program descriptions. Leaders who subscribed to growth attempted to pull their institutions toward broader patterns of service including adult education, education for members of minority groups, education to serve the community's industries. They gladly took on all services, justifying them with the claim that the "people's college" should attempt to enroll all the people.

More recently the era of declining resources has forced a redefinition of institutional purpose. The question now is not how to add but how to drop programs, how to eliminate curriculums and services. The question is no longer a new program versus no program; it is which program to keep, which one to drop.

In state after state, cutbacks in funding force the choices. In enrollments, which categories of students get priority? Transfer students? The poorly prepared? Students preparing for entry-level jobs? Those who seek long-term careers? Who decides, the institutional managers or the state-level agents? Who takes hold and leads the college into the new era? Who abdicates responsibility? It is considerably more rewarding to decide which programs to add than to make choices about which ones to drop.

The change from an era of growth to one of shrinkage has also changed the pace at which decisions are made. During the time of growth, the programs shifted in relation to the clients. People seeking immediate job-entry skills, transfer education, or basic literacy training were served with new programs or modifications of existing programs. Rapid growth made it relatively easy to install new programs; a college that doubled its population in a span of a few years found it simple to add a roster of new services. The change also depended somewhat on the strength of the informal, intercollege networks that bound the staff to other institutions. If the educators were in frequent contact with their counterparts in other institutions that were also growing and changing, a climate of rapid modification could be fostered.

Forced choices demand a different set of behaviors. The

rationale for dropping a program is not a mirror image of the arguments for introducing it in the first place. Creating a new program could always be justified by saying that the institution was offering a new service to meet demands that were not otherwise being satisfied. Those demands may still be present when the program must be cut, but a different set of questions must be answered as programs are compared with each other, not against the criteria of lack of service to a certain constituency.

Think of the questions that must be asked when a manager must decide on which programs should be maintained. Which is most effective for its clients—that is, most verifiably educative? Which is least readily available elsewhere for the people it serves? Which has a staff that is most easily reassigned? Which is politically most attractive? Which is most distinguished and contributes most to the image that the college should maintain? Which is most supportive of or related to other college programs? Which has the best future prospects? Which is currently most vital? Which can best be justified as being socially useful? Good questions all, and all must be considered.

The context of decision making shifts as well. When programs were introduced, few of the staff members involved in other programs were concerned. New programs usually meant new facilities, new staff, new funding. If the managers could locate the resources, the existing staff rarely commented adversely on its introduction. However, when a program is to be eliminated, intrainstitutional considerations become paramount. Whose job will be affected? Whose students will be withdrawn? What will the absence of a program mean to other programs of its type? Does the reduction in one program presage cuts in similar programs? Staff members tend to be considerably more skittish, hence more likely to voice their concerns, when reductions are being made. A parallel may be drawn with nations that in a time of recession seek trade barriers to protect their own industries and exports.

The leader who would manage the curriculum has to understand the directions that curriculum is taking, the forces propelling it. He or she must take a position and move the institution toward it. The astute leader knows that the institution must not be left to drift haphazardly. Early in the 1980s it was obvious that compensatory education was on the rise, that community education was declining, and that the collegiate function was struggling to maintain itself. But decisions made in each college affect the speed with which those changes occur.

Groups who line up in support for one or another of the curriculum forms are easy to find. Faculty members want stricter prerequisites for their classes. Lifelong learning advocates want an institution that offers short courses, easily entered by anyone. Business leaders want students prepared to work effectively. True leaders understand that all groups must be accommodated, but they do not shrink from taking the institution in the direction of maximum service.

The leader who would strengthen compensatory education would acknowledge its place in the college, see that it is not operated within a separate department but is integrated with the career and collegiate functions, send frequent messages to the secondary schools regarding college-entry expectations, and build and use a testing program that matches the realities of the instruction program.

The leader who would strengthen community education would separate the community service division so that it operated at arms-length from the regular curriculum, give over most of the recreational portions of the program to other agencies, and establish a team of community education specialists who could turn the attention of faculty and students in the academic program to local, national, and international issues.

The leader who would strengthen the collegiate function would pull it back to linearity by offering fewer courses that could be taken to fulfill graduation requirements, enforce prerequisites and probation standards, articulate curriculum with the secondary schools, encourage consistent objectives across sections of the same courses, and demand literacy development as a goal of every course.

There is quite enough to capture the attention of the administrators and faculty alike. Institutional managers who insist that their hands are tied by externally derived rules can be safely ignored. Educational leaders can take the community colleges into forms of service frequently imagined but rarely realized.

9

Building Commitment to the Institution

Richard C. Richardson, Jr.
William R. Rhodes

The decade of the eighties will be stressful for postsecondary education. Declining enrollments, changing clientele, reduced resources, and regulations imposed by external agencies accompany growing concerns about quality. Community colleges will not escape public pressures for accountability.

Pressures for improved quality in the midst of austerity are occurring at a time when change has become more difficult for community colleges to achieve. Internally, full-time faculty have grown older, more secure, and financially more comfortable. Increasingly, they realize their power in the classroom, in the courts, in organized employee associations, and in the growing acceptance of their legitimate professional role in American higher education. Faculty have exerted their power to improve wages, benefits, job security, and working conditions. At the same time, they have failed to assert their professional interests in curricular and instructional reform.

There is evidence to suggest that community college faculty are becoming alienated from administration, from institutional goals, and from one another. The distrust inherent in the differing roles of faculty and administrators has been further aggravated by the rapid growth in size and complexity of institutions with its subsequent attenuation of communication. Many faculty members have chosen to ignore, and some have chosen to resist, institutional goals imposed by administrators who show little sensitivity to faculty concerns. An administratively dominated decision-making process has produced a heterogeneous mix of transfer, vocational, occupational, and developmental courses loosely organized around the availability of part-time faculty. Differing values and philosophical orientations were manageable during years of adequate resources and growth. In the current environment, the antagonism of differing values may give way to open conflict resulting from perceived threats to job security.

Middle-level administrators suffer from disillusionment and skepticism similar to that of the faculty. Many came from the faculty, continue to interact professionally and socially with faculty, share many of the same values as faculty, and are often frustrated by the decisions of top administrators. The suggestion that faculty and middle-level administrators share an alienation from institutional priorities is supported by the results of a recent study of a major, urban, multiunit community college district (Richardson and others, 1982). The institutional priorities, as identified by ranking district administrators, included new clientele, developmental education, student retention, and occupational education. The responses of both faculty and middle-level administrators indicated relatively low commitment to these priorities.

Faculty may feel overworked in the classroom, but middle-level administrators are faced with a daily grind devoted towards holding their own, making as few mistakes as possible, and dealing with the inevitable trauma of taking the responsibility for tough decisions. While faculty have been beneficiaries of the collective bargaining process, middle-level administrators have lost prestige and authority. They have less job security than faculty and may feel particularly vulnerable in the climate of uncertainty generated by confusion about mission and purpose, as well as by the impending financial crunch.

Some contemporary community colleges may be likened to a large "Rube Goldberg" machine with its miscellaneous parts pieced together as follows: The president has responsibility for controlling direction and speed through a set of levers that are moved in various directions to cause the machine to speed up, slow down, change direction, or produce a new product. The machine is powered by a vast treadmill, on which faculty walk at a steady pace. Some walk a little faster than others; occasionally some complain or exhort the treadmill to go faster or slower or to change direction. Most simply ignore their colleagues, put in their time on the treadmill, collect their pay, and then disappear until their next turn.

Administrators, influenced by external pressures or by their own aspirations, grasp levers with both hands and pull with all their might. The levers move, accompanied by a great cacophonous noise and the external appearance of change. The wind whistles, bells clang, shouts of self-praise are heard, and public information missiles are launched. The machine shakes and occasionally parts fall off; unlike when the machine was new, no parts are added. The entire effect is one of speed and motion accompanied by a changing landscape on a huge circular screen. The screen rotates slowly so that by the time it makes a complete turn, most people are unaware they have seen the same landscape before. Inside the machine, faculty, hardly aware of the clatter and roar outside, continue to plod along on the treadmill.

Students feed into one end of the machine and emerge from openings randomly distributed over the surface. The students stay for differing lengths of time: Some emerge from an opening, look around briefly and then re-enter; others simply go away. Some wear caps and gowns when they come out, and others carry pieces of paper, but most look like they did when they entered.

The administrator who runs the machine beckons to people passing by and extols its virtues. They ask what will happen if they enter and are told, "whatever you want." Of course, many do not really know what they want, which is just as well since many come out not knowing what they have. But things have changed: The machine has become expensive to maintain and operate, and the people who pay for it want to know what it does.

The president is frustrated by the demands of lay people

who do not realize the complexity of his job, by the lack of appreciation for past achievements, and by the fact that the machine no longer seems responsive to its levers. Sometimes the president suspects that the levers are no longer connected to the engine—at least, not in any reliable way. The blame for the corrosion in the linkage is placed on faculty and their lack of obedience, professional responsibility, and commitment.

The president is right in suggesting that the problem lies with professional responsibility and commitment. What he may not realize is that these qualities can be restored by involving faculty in the process which determines the primary functions of the machine. This process is the internal governance mechanism.

Governance

Corson (1960, p. 13) first applied the term *governance* to higher education. He defined it as "the process or act with which scholars, students, teachers, administrators and trustees associated together in a college or university establish and carry out rules and regulations that minimize conflict, facilitate their collaboration and preserve essential individual freedom." Corson's definition is broad and reflects the traditional ideal view of the university as a community of scholars (and scholars in training) with common interests and common values. Monroe (1977, p. 303) defined governance as "a comprehensive term to describe all aspects of the control and direction of the college ... it includes both the policy making mechanisms and the agencies through which the policies are executed and administered." Neither of these definitions makes a distinction between higher-level and day-to-day management decisions.

Millett (1980) accepted the close interrelationship between governance and administration (taken here to mean management) but advocated a sharp distinction between the two. He stated that "governance is decision-making about purposes, policies, programs and resources" (p. 147). Governance decisions impact organizational values and have long-term effects. Management is work planning and work performance. By Millett's definition, the adoption of a policy of affirmative action is an act of governance; the application of this policy to hiring is an act of management.

Millett's distinction is appropriate to our discussion. We define governance as those institutional arrangements, both structural and procedural, for addressing major problems and making decisions that affect institutional mission, resource allocation and the roles of internal constituencies and subgroups. The results of governance are decisions that shape the future of the institution.

The traditional view of academic governance has its foundation in the early twentieth-century movement through which faculty used growing prestige and power to gain access to the decision-making process. Kemmerer (1978) recognized the foundation of the American Association of University Professors (AAUP) in 1915 as the first important symbol of a dual system of governance. Corson's definition of governance (1960) reflects the ideal of this collegial process. However, the most unequivocal statements advocating shared authority came in the 1960s from several influential organizations in higher education.

In 1966, a joint statement issued by the AAUP, American Council on Education (ACE), and the Association of Governing Boards (AGB) strongly supported the interdependence and sharing of authority among governing boards, administrators, faculty, students, and support staff. Although the method of shared authority was not specified, the statement clearly indicated that the initiating responsibility and relative voice in decision making of each group should depend on the "matter at hand." This concept of shared authority was further elaborated in a joint statement from the American Association for Higher Education (AAHE) and the National Education Association (for a review of the major points of these two statements, see Mortimer and McConnell, 1978).

These statements advocating shared authority came at the height of faculty power in American colleges and universities. Shortly thereafter, government research monies began to decline, student activists demanded relevance in the curriculum, growth in enrollments peaked, and a period of uncertainty followed. In practice, the ideal of shared authority seems to have been realized in only a few of the top-tier research universities and more prestigious private colleges (Baldridge, Curtiss, and Riley, 1977).

The typical two-year public community college was established and has been maintained as a bureaucracy. Bers (1980) pointed out that many community colleges meet most of the criteria to be called local governments—that is, they are publicly financed, serve the residents of the local community, and are governed by lay officials. Typically, the powers and responsibilities of the governing board, and occasionally of the chief administrator, are spelled out in state legislation or in the rules and policies of a government agency or lay board. The local board, operating within statutory guidelines and government regulations, serves as the major policy-making body. The chief administrator has the authority by statute or by delegation to manage the institution and implement the policies established by the board. The president's expertise and responsibility for the daily functioning of the institution usually have permitted him or her significant influence over decisions of the governing board.

The tendency toward bureaucratic structure has been accompanied by forces that further encourage an authoritarian management style. The most important of these forces include the following:

1. Community colleges have had strong ties to the public school system. Many states have followed the California plan for inclusion of community colleges in the public school system. In those states that adopted different organizational arrangements, most of the early administrators and faculty came out of the public school system.
2. There has been a substantial imbalance in prestige between top-level administrators and faculty. Presidents, and usually deans, have been career professionals, often with academic credentials that have enhanced their legal authority. In addition, salaries, status, opportunities for recognition, and sense of achievement have been greater for presidents

than for faculty members. Relatively few faculty have had terminal degrees, and classroom teaching has comprised their primary responsibility. Unlike faculty in the four-year colleges and universities, they were relatively unaffected by the post-Sputnik boom resulting in research monies and prestige.

3. Community college faculty have exhibited little interest in shared authority, collegiality, and academic freedom. Their training and experience has not resulted in strong allegience to these traditional values of higher education.

4. The 1950s and 1960s were periods of rapid growth. Presidents had the resources to add new programs without concern for the approval or cooperation of existing faculty.

5. In the few instances where the faculty's voice was encouraged through senates, all-college councils, and committees, both administrators and faculty, who were usually inexperienced in the participation process, found the shared approach slow and inefficient.

By the early 1970s, the characteristics of community colleges had changed dramatically, but presidents continued to employ the informal consultative methods that had been successful in younger institutions with their smaller faculties who shared enthusiasm for the institutional mission. Many presidents seemed unaware of the magnitude and consequences of these changes.

As employee dissatisfaction became evident, alternatives were sought. Research in complex organizations had demonstrated the effectiveness of participation as a means of motivating employees and of increasing job satisfaction. In addition, in studies completed by the AAHE and the AAUP, the absence of opportunity to participate in decision making was frequently cited as a cause of dissatisfaction by faculty members.

Frequently the response chosen by community college administrators was to adopt the committee-senate structure long prevalent in four-year colleges and universities. Most two-year college administrators lacked experience with and commitment to such arrangements. Often, the responsibilities of senates and committees were unclear and ambiguous. As a result, committees deliberated in areas of overlapping jurisdictions and then reported to senates where the work was often repeated. When a recommendation finally emerged, the president accepted or rejected it as he saw fit. The system was inefficient, slow, and easy to manipulate by withholding information. The resulting decisions were often unsatisfactory or impractical, and the president's rejection was perceived as lack of trust or concern for faculty voice.

The successor to the committee-senate arrangement has often been a faculty union. In states where collective bargaining is prohibited, dissident faculty groups form and seek to exert influence through direct contact with board members. Occasionally, faculty groups have been successful in promoting the election of trustees favorably disposed to their viewpoints. The adversarial relationship resulting from bargaining for wages and benefits has affected relationships between administration and faculty in other areas, including educational activities. However, in this case, faculty have chosen to ignore the situation rather than to exert pressure to influence academic decision making.

The present pressures for faculty participation in governance stem from a far more potent need than the realization of the ideal of collegiality and shared authority. Effective participation in governance, a process that develops, enhances, and sustains commitment to organizational priorities, can be a powerful tool for organizational change. It may be the only effective tool left to community college administrators.

Commitment

Committed employees identify strongly with, are loyal to, and are willing to work hard for their organization. It is not difficult to convince administrators that these are desirable characteristics for employees, especially when those employees are secure in their positions and have a great deal of personal autonomy and control over their daily activities. It is difficult to convince administrators that they should employ the skills and management techniques necessary to secure employee commitment.

Steers (1977) suggests that employee commitment is a

function of what March and Simon (1958) call the "exchange process." An employee brings certain needs and skills to the organization. If the organization meets those needs and utilizes those skills, the employee will become committed. Both the individuals and the organization are beneficiaries of this relationship. If the organization fails to meet these needs, the employee remains uncommitted and ineffective. Employee needs are not limited to such tangible benefits as salaries and fringe benefits. They also include such intangibles as status, participation, and sense of achievement. In fact, social psychologists have suggested that intangible rewards may be far more valuable than most of us imagine.

Salancik (1977; 1979) views commitment from the perspective of social psychology. From this point of view, commitment results from a process in which an individual's attitudes are changed to make them consistent with his or her overt behavior. The extent to which employee attitudes can be altered depends upon: (1) consistency between behaviors expected of them by the organization and their preexisting beliefs; (2) the perceived conditions under which the behaviors are expected; and (3) the frequency of such behaviors. An increase in commitment to organizational priorities will result when employees participate in public behavior that is supportive of these priorities. The more public and the more frequent the behavior, the greater the adjustment of the employee's belief system. Salancik discusses the potential applications of this behavioral view of commitment in management practice. A manager can effectively induce employee commitment to an organization by engaging in or supporting behavior that contributes to the achievement of organizational goals.

Whether we view commitment as the result of an exchange process or as the result of an innate tendency to adjust attitude to be consistent with behavior, the strategies for gaining employee commitment will be the same. Participation in the decision-making process can develop loyalty, a sense of responsibility, and active support of organizational goals.

Institutional governance is a process that may result in change, renewal, and revitalization. A commitment-building, participative decision-making process can be the primary means for encouraging staff to accept the philosophy and values which undergird the concept of the open door, comprehensive community college. A successful governance program should persuade transfer-oriented faculty to give greater support to developmental and vocational programs, outreach programs, and programs for the adult learner. Occupational, vocational, and technical faculty should become more supportive of the need and role of general education courses in career and job-oriented programs. Developmental education faculty ought to become more inclined to teach the skills and basic knowledge necessary for entry into the collegiate-level courses taught by their colleagues. And all faculty should work to reduce attrition and slow, if not halt, the movement of the revolving door.

There are three prerequisites for the achievement of an effective governance process that builds commitment.

1. Leadership Quality. Michael Maccoby identified the qualities needed by education leaders in the 1980s in a paper delivered at the 1979 meeting of the American Association for Higher Education. He suggested that such leaders will share rather than hoard the functions of leadership, but that they will also be competent and willing to fight on matters of principle. Both masters and students of the organizations they lead, they will understand the relationship of the parts to the whole of the system and realize that one part cannot be altered without making allowances for the impact on all other parts. These new leaders will know that "leaders must participate with those they lead in defining problems and finding solutions. They cannot stand aloof from the process judging its consequences, like a 'perverse Solomon.' " Maccoby suggests that there is no shortage of leaders who maintain outmoded management styles or who lack the competencies to manage complex organizations. The place for most community colleges to start with staff development is not with faculty or even with middle management. Until key administrators, especially the president, learn how to bring out the best in people through creating an environment conducive to growth, staff development or governance activities can only be counterproductive.

Faculty will not be fooled by a president who claims allegiance to the collegial process, encourages them to take the time and make the effort to participate, and then prolongs the process until they endorse predetermined solutions. Such behavior will serve to reinforce faculty skepticism about the motives and credibility of administrators. Employee commitment is gained through a process of human interaction that involves trust and mutual respect among all parties; it is not gained through the contrivances of a president who uses a shallow knowledge of management theory to create a facade of personal involvement.

2. *Adequate Faculty Support.* If members of an organization are expected to grow and change, they must be provided with opportunities to participate in deciding what is to be done, as well as how it is to be done. Current practice in most community colleges casts administrators in the role of decision makers and faculty in the role of implementors. While neither group is very effective in its respective role, some faculty are as satisfied with this arrangement as administrators since it reduces their commitment to that of simply meeting scheduled classes. Implementing a successful governance process will require a realistic view of faculty motives, value systems, and concerns. Faculty realize that acquiring the expertise necessary to make a significant contribution to the governance process is time consuming and difficult. They will not be anxious to participate in governance unless the time and knowledge necessary to make such participation meaningful are provided by administrative action. Motivating faculty to participate in governance and teaching them how to do so will not be easy and will require administrative concessions in terms of adjustments in work load.

3. *Growth-Enhancing Environment.* Governance is not limited to planning for the implementation of decisions that have already been made. It is a process in which decisions about programs, curriculum, and associated priorities are made. It includes or is followed by planning and development of strategies for implementation of the solutions determined by the governance process. In addition, the problems or issues being addressed must seem worthwhile for the long-term health of the

institution. Relegating minor, insignificant, unsolvable, or pseudoproblems to the governance process will result in loss of credibility in the system. Faculty commitment to solutions for insignificant problems is of little value.

The perception of the significance of the issues addressed by participants will be greatly enhanced by the behavior of the administration. The president must show a genuine concern for the issue at hand, facilitate the decision-making process whenever necessary (encourage participants to take tough stands or guide the participants past serious stumbling blocks), and throw his or her weight and prestige behind the outcomes. The more public and the more tangible the signs of administrative commitment, the better. Allocating money to support committee activities is an explicit sign of commitment to the governance process and to the issue at hand. Giving participants the right to determine how that money is spent will further cement that commitment.

A successful governance process does not appear to be dependent upon a particular model of organizational structure. In fact, the limited number of empirical studies suggest that successful participatory governance is a function of the attitudes of those who are involved.

Participation may involve nothing more than frequent informal discussions between administrators and faculty through which ideas are exchanged and decisions tested before they are finalized and made operational. In smaller colleges informal methods of consultation have proven effective when faculty have perceived that their input and concerns are taken seriously by the administration. In larger organizations, more complex arrangements are required. The literature abounds with descriptions of arrangements that have been made to work in one setting or another (see for example: Richardson, Blocker, and Bender, 1972; Richardson, 1975; Carhart and Collins, 1977; Romine, 1981). Important characteristics of systems that have worked include significant and well-defined responsibilities for participants, clear lines of authority, avoidance of redundance, and adequate work load adjustments for participants.

The Richfield Study

Some insight into the methodology employed in successful organizational change, conflict resolution, and commitment building can be gained from the findings of a recent three-year study (Richardson and others, 1982) of a large, urban, multicampus district given the pseudonym Richfield. For the Richfield District, financial constraints, first in the form of declining percentages of state support of the operating budget and later in the form of a legislatively mandated limit on the increases in property taxes, were pervasive considerations in the decisionmaking process. In addition, a changing and more diverse student clientele, developed partly in response to an administrative decision to engage in aggressive recruiting activities, placed pressure on educational programs and services designed around the needs of an earlier clientele who were full-time, baccalaureate-oriented students from a white, nonhispanic background.

Administrators in the Richfield District were able to stimulate needed changes in the educational program. Changes included more emphasis on remedial education and a redefinition of its purposes, increased effort to improve student retention, and significant expansion and improvement of career education programs. The strategies used to promote change were: planning, resource allocation, reorganization, staffing changes, staff development, evaluation, and participation in decision making. The process involved defining goals, setting priorities, and allocating resources to achieve these priorities. While many groups had input into this process, the power to implement decisions remained with the chief executive and his cabinet providing a fail-safe mechanism for directing the change process.

Initial strategies for change were directed at organization and staffing. These included the establishment of a college-without-walls, the implementation of an extensive student recruiting process, and the appointment of many outsiders to key district positions. These innovations substantially altered the traditional orientation towards transfer education; however, they also caused significant conflict, much of which focused on the chief executive and his new appointments.

Subsequent strategies emphasized planning, allocation of discretionary resources, and participation in decision making. These strategies, strongly supported by staff and instructional development, were directed toward reducing the level of conflict by slowing the pace of change and establishing a wider range of goals more representative of the values of district staff.

Administrators and faculty in the Richfield District brought different values to the change process. Administrators were growth oriented. A significant indicator of success, for them, was an increase in the numbers of full-time student equivalents. Growth also resulted in budget increases, bringing the flexibility to initiate new services. Faculty, by contrast, were concerned about the impact of additional growth on already crowded facilities and the consequences of increasing clientele diversity on their ability to teach effectively and to experience success as they defined it. Administrators prized innovation and problem solving as appropriate responses to what they perceived as a need to change the educational program and services in order to make them more responsive to the external community. Faculty resisted administratively directed innovation and belittled the use of outside experts brought in to tell them how to improve or change. Administrators were concerned with numbers; faculty were concerned with process. Administrators believed that every adult not being served by some other type of institution was an appropriate focus for community college recruitment. Faculty preferred to restrict their efforts to students who exhibited the characteristics they regarded as essential for success in the college transfer or career programs.

The planning and resource allocation processes became the central means for accomplishing change. Discretionary funds were used to free those faculty members who were willing to pursue institutional priorities from the constraints of their heavy teaching loads. Staff development activities supported the pursuit of administrative priorities, and instructional development personnel assisted in changing traditional classroom practices.

Perhaps the most important contribution of both the planning process and staff development activities was to change faculty perceptions of acceptable and valued behavior. Because administrators controlled the process of disseminating information and gave significant publicity to the outcomes of the planning and staff development activities, there was little doubt in anyone's mind as to what the priorities actually were. This approach left the faculty with a limited number of options. They could choose to commit themselves to the achievement of administratively defined priorities and, by so doing, qualify for the rewards that were made available in the form of released time, supplementary pay, and perhaps, an administrative appointment. Alternatively, they could choose to resist institutional priorities or to transfer their energies to personal involvements outside the institution. The threat of sanctions was minimal given the high job security of the faculty.

A majority of the faculty remained uncommitted to district priorities; however, the planning process employed and the support afforded by staff development appeared to be instrumental in keeping resistance to manageable levels. As a result, those faculty and administrators who chose to work towards change were reasonably successful.

We concluded, as a result of more than three years of intensive observation of the Richfield District, as well as several related empirical studies presented in more detail in our final report, *Literacy Development in Community Colleges* (1982, soon to be available through ERIC Clearinghouse for Junior Colleges), that administrators can change the educational program by judicious use of the resources available to them. The governance procedures used effectively by Richfield administrators included the following steps:

1. A one-day assembly involving broad representation from district constituencies, including faculty and middle-level administrators, was scheduled each spring. At these assemblies, reports were given on progress in meeting district goals during the past year, and participants worked in small teams to consider priorities for the following year and beyond. All key district administrators, as well as several board members, attended the assemblies and were distributed among the various working teams.

2. A district plan listing the goals identified through the assembly was made. It included comments about implementation and responsibilities.
3. Each college in the Richfield District was expected to develop its own plan for addressing priorities identified at the annual assembly.
4. Implementation of district goals was controlled and monitored through an administrative council and the actions of key administrators. The most important strategies used to achieve high priorities (the assembly identified more goals than could reasonably be addressed in any given year with available resources) included making discretionary funds available to faculty and administrators willing to pursue high-priority goals and used district task forces to plan areas of special concern in detail.
5. During the period of the study, district task forces were established in the areas of developmental education and career education. An initial allocation of $200,000 for discretionary projects was soon increased to $400,000. A district committee evaluated proposals submitted for these funds against criteria developed from the assemblies.
6. Staff development activities were scheduled to support the priorities. Since attendance was voluntary, many faculty (especially those perceived to need such support most) did not attend. Despite their absence staff development emerged as an important variable in achieving change. Staff development activities furnished social support and new skills to those willing to commit themselves to change; the emphasis placed on these activities by administrators, as well as the publicity they received, seemed to reduce the amount of resistance from faculty who were unwilling to support the priorities, thus creating conditions that could facilitate institutional change.

Conclusion

There has been much written about the difficulties of achieving change in educational organizations. A recent article by Perrow (1982) goes so far as to suggest that organizations in

general are incapable of identifying and pursuing goals, that
their leaders rationalize that whatever is happening at the moment is right for the organization. Certainly, community colleges have received their share of criticism as they have pursued
the "all things to all people" philosophy.

If administrators want to change educational programs
and services, they need to convince faculty that existing practices are inadequate and that proposed changes merit faculty
commitment. The mechanism for accomplishing changes in the
attitudes and behavior of faculty is the governance process. Research has shown that increasing the commitment of organizational members requires their active participation in decision
processes. At the same time, experiences with participative
forms of governance in the early seventies have demonstrated
that it is extremely difficult to make these forms work and that
their use may produce undesirable as well as desirable results.

Many administrators have concluded that they would prefer to work with a faculty union because the rules are clearly
defined. Unfortunately, there is no provision within collective
bargaining agreements that deals with commitment or need for
changes in behaviors or attitudes. Negotiating new contracts involves only a few leaders who become responsible for selling
their membership on the desirability of whatever compromises
have been struck by the opposing teams. Most commonly, arguments aimed at securing support for a ratification vote dwell
upon the advantages of the new agreement in terms of concessions won rather than expectations for changes in member behavior. This arrangement may be satisfactory for those who are
content to pull levers and watch the rotating screen; however,
those who are interested in what happens to the students in the
depths of the machine may wish to consider such methods as
those employed by the Richfield District.

Community college administrators in the eighties will
need to achieve change without benefit of growth. Grounds,
buildings, capital equipment, and human resources must be
adapted to carry out existing programs more efficiently or to
implement new programs. Faculty have substantial job security
and personal autonomy. In many institutions they have been

alienated by the constantly changing mission of the community college, by a heavy teaching load with underprepared and un-enthusiastic students, and by other subgroups of faculty who threaten values and personal security. Under these circum-stances, successful institutional change must come through changes in faculty behavior and attitudes rather than through employment of new faculty.

Faculty participation in an effective governance process can build professionalism and commitment. A governance pro-cess that builds commitment should be concerned with making important decisions—not simply with planning for or gaining acceptance of decisions that have already been made. An effec-tive governance process does not depend on the organizational structure through which it operates as much as it does upon the quality of leadership provided by administration. Governance structures may fail because of complexity or unsuitability in a particular environment, but this does not mean that the process of participation in decision making is not viable. Effective par-ticipation requires that participants be committed to the pro-cess, acquire necessary skills and knowledge, and view the process as credible.

Staff development should be redirected from its bureau-cratic role of supporting predetermined decisions to a new role as a facilitator of organizational renewal. Planning, resource allocation, and other decision-making procedures should be-come primary vehicles of staff development. Staff development can support the commitment-building process by providing op-portunities for participation in the identification of problems and solutions, as well as for learning the competencies needed to implement solutions. The reward structure must be revised so that those who are asked to participate receive adequate re-leased time, recognition, and a sense of personal achievement. Barriers to change, whether personal or institutional, that were created by past practices must be recognized and overcome. The governance process must provide time for participants to be-come effective problem solvers, planners, and agents of change.

For the chief administrator a shared governance process offers the opportunity to become a leader. High status, high pay, and power derived from rank are not the stuff of which leadership is made. Leaders are people who move organizations because of their personal credibility and the commitment they develop among those they lead. The commitment to be gained from faculty, the development of a sense of professional responsibility, and the wealth of enthusiasm and talent that faculty can bring to the implementation of institutional priorities and the search for excellence is priceless.

10

Population Trends and Need for Diversity

J. Wade Gilley

Since World War II, college and university enrollments in the United States have virtually exploded—increasing some fourfold while the total population increased by one-eighth that amount or some 50 percent (American Council on Education, 1982a). This surge was led by the full development of a relatively new institution—the community college. Table 10.1 dramatically illustrates what has happened to college enrollments in the nation between 1950 and 1980 compared to the growth of the general population. The figures on two-year college growth are even more impressive.

Table 10.1. U.S. Population and College Enrollments: 1950–1980.

	1950	1980	Percent Increase
U.S. population	152,271,000	226,505,000	48.7
U.S. college enrollments	2,296,592	12,088,200	426
Two-year college enrollments	217,572	4,487,928	1962

Source: American Council on Education, 1982a, pp. 1, 58, 74.

The growth of college enrollments and the diverse system of higher education that has formed in response to it has been a result of demographics and the stimulation of student demand by federal policies rather than a result of leadership from the higher education community or the demands of society. If this

205

thesis is valid, equivalent forces, now forming independently of colleges and universities, will shape American higher education in the twenty-first century. The challenge of the 1980s is to identify and shape a response to those forces.

A relatively new way of thinking about economics, known as "public choice," contends that public policy makers influence the course of the nation's economy by their decisions. The adherents of this line of thought have concluded that economic theory can be used to predict the actions of officials in the public arena, including politicians and bureaucrats (Buchanan and Tullock, 1962). Without question, economics and public policy have been intertwined and mutually influencing throughout American history.

If this theory is applied to a subsystem of society such as public higher education, it follows that economic forces, including demographics, are primarily responsible for the growth of colleges and universities during the postwar period and that public policy economic decisions are an equally important force. With the nation shifting toward more conservative economic principles and practices, the implications for the nation's higher education system are significant: the trend toward limited government will seriously challenge college and university leaders in the years ahead.

Practically every college student, and for that matter every American, has some familiarity with the terms *supply* and *demand* as they relate to economics. Further, it is common knowledge that the federal government has been tinkering with the economic system of the country by stimulating demand since President Franklin D. Roosevelt began "priming the pump" some fifty years ago. In economics the consumer who uses goods and services is central to any theory, government policy, or practice. The number of potential consumers, and thus demographics, is important to the functioning of the economy.

Since 1932 federal policy has followed the theory that government can and should improve the economy by stimulating demand. It has done this both by increasing the money supply (through the Federal Reserve Board) and by deficit spending. Partially because of cheap imported raw materials and a growing population, economic policies emphasizing demand resulted in real growth for several decades. Now federal policy, after several years of inflationary problems, seems to be shifting to an emphasis on supply, and even the most liberal congressmen are bemoaning the federal budget deficit. The emerging philosophy seems to be that government policy should encourage excess supply and allow this excess to influence demand. This approach has implications for both revenues and spending patterns of government.

At the same time that it was stimulating demand in the economy, the federal government was gradually adding public programs which stimulated demand for many social programs, including education. As it has turned out, the states have had the major responsibility for supplying a wide variety of programs over the long term; state leaders are now questioning that role and are actively pursuing the "new federalism," though a somewhat different model from that proposed by President Reagan. All of this will have significant ramifications for higher education in America: States have been supplying college programs to meet the demand of students in something of a free market situation but are now talking about supplying programs in the interest of the corporate state, those that support economic development rather than those desired by the individual.

The federal government has stimulated demand for social programs not only in the name of equity but also in the name of national defense. This stimulation of demand for government services has been accomplished primarily by the use of financial incentives. For example, individual home ownership has been encouraged by federal policies such as income tax deductions of interest and mortgages guaranteed by the federal government. The interstate highway system was constructed by making it very attractive for states to buy into a 90 to 10 state to federal financing ratio. This program, like so many others, leaves the states with the responsibility for the cost of maintenance, which now far exceeds the original costs of the federal government. In many national programs similar to these, the nation is now facing a crisis at least partially because of earlier policies. For instance, in the case of housing the United States now finds itself with an extraordinary amount of the nation's wealth tied up in one-family homes, many of them constructed for an average family size of 3.67 persons but actually occupied by some 2.8 persons in 40 years (American Council on Education, 1982a, p. 12).

Likewise, over the past three decades the nation has stimulated demand for educational programs by passing laws (special educational requirements) and providing seed money or financial incentives for Americans to take part in state-operated and -financed programs such as higher education. Simply stated, in higher education as in other programs, the national government has been stimulating student demands and leaving it to the states to respond to these demands.

Economics and Enrollments

The idea that economic forces, including demographics and federal stimulating of demand, have been primary factors in the growth of college enrollments over the last thirty-five years deserves a more detailed analysis. The forces behind increased enrollments for these past three and a half decades have included demographics, societal factors, and finances.

Demographics. Demographics, or the study of population, has demonstrated that the number of births in the nation, which increased from 2.6 million in 1940 to 4.3 million in 1976 (American Council on Education, 1982a, p. 13), has influenced and will continue to influence enrollments in public schools as well as colleges and universities. The significance of this force has been well recognized within the educational community. In addition, the post-World War II migration from the country to the city, only recently reversed, set in motion many forces, including economic ones, which had a significant impact on the size and shape of colleges and enrollments.

Societal Factors. The change in America's basic economy after World War II created new jobs in ever-increasing numbers. The requirements of these technical jobs meant that more Americans would need to continue their education beyond high school. This change in the economy was a primary force in the development of community colleges with their vocational and technical programs. The changing economy further served to reinforce a long-held American belief that education is the path to economic success and self-fulfillment. More parents expected their children to go to college and at the same time expected the state to provide the necessary programs and places.

The mass migration which carried millions of Americans from the farms and towns to the cities for more than twenty-five years after World War II created a reaction in rural America. Schemes were designed to attract new industries to rural areas to keep young people at home. It became apparent in most communities that industrial development would require technically trained people; thus a force for the creation of local community colleges with technical training components emerged. The number of public two-year colleges increased from 405 in 1961 to 850 in 1970, with most being community and technical colleges and many being located in rural areas (Monroe, 1972). These local institutions created opportunities which had been unavailable to rural populations; many Americans discovered that they could now stay at home and go to college on either a full- or part-time basis.

Further, as America began to shed its pre-World War II racial segregation policies, the nation realized that equal opportunity now required positive action to bring racial minorities into the mainstream of American life. Affirmative action programs were designed to provide new opportunities for minorities, particularly Blacks. Minorities have not yet achieved full parity in the nation's higher education system, but increased opportunities for minorities contributed significantly to enrollment growth in America's colleges and universities—especially in community colleges.

Finances. Low- or no-cost community colleges (and urban universities) were touted during the 1960s and 1970s as being essential to provide educational opportunities for nontraditional students. The creation or expansion of commuter institutions in convenient locations with a comprehensive array of low-cost programs had a positive impact on enrollment growth.

Federal student financial aid programs have also been a key factor in increasing enrollments. Congress began helping students financially after World War II with the first GI Bill, which stimulated returning veterans (who represented four to five years of pent-up demand) to pursue a college education. The World War II and Korean War GI Bills were followed by the National Student Defense Loan Program in the late 1950s, which was initiated in the name of national defense. The education opportunity programs of the 1960s and the early 1970s were initiated in the name of equity, and the Middle Income Education Act of 1978 was implemented in the name of fairness to the middle class. These programs stimulated higher education enrollments. Most educators still believe that this stimulation was and is good public policy.

Public Policies

It is possible to test the theory that demographic and federal stimulation of demand were the primary driving forces behind increased higher education enrollments by looking at population, enrollment, and other data. It is possible to test other economic theories regarding enrollments—such as the effect of unemployment—in the same manner.

Most investigators acknowledge the influence of demographics on enrollments in colleges as well as secondary schools. However, the trends demonstrated in Figure 10.1 provide some additional insights into college enrollment trends. This figure contrasts the number of seventeen-year-olds in the general population with the number of high school graduates and the number of first-time college students over the last three decades. There is a definite correlation between the rate of increase from decade to decade. However, it is also clear that other factors are at work, especially in the 1970s. As public policies impact in time frames shorter than one decade, it is necessary to look closer at specific and shorter periods to attempt to correlate the dynamics of enrollments with specific public policies.

Figure 10.2 reveals some interesting dynamics during the World War II period and shortly thereafter. As most Americans

Figure 10.1. Populations by Decade: 1950-1979.

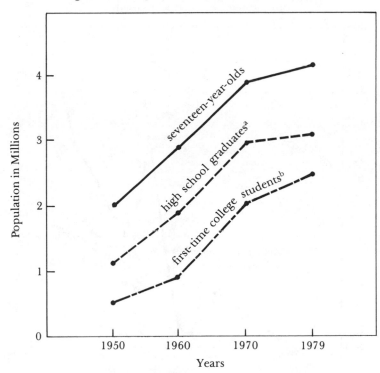

[a]U.S. National Center for Education Statistics, 1982a, p. 67.
[b]American Council on Education, 1982a, p. 198.

are aware, many young men went into the armed services from 1942 to 1944 and thus were not available to go to college. After the war, enrollments increased and the first GI Bill provided financial incentives for veterans to attend college. Figure 10.2 shows a dynamic increase in bachelor's degrees awarded through 1952—432,000, compared to only 186,000 in 1940—with no significant changes in the number of high school graduates. Does this reflect a stimulation by federal policies? Or is it simply a reflection of pent-up demand released in the postwar years? To examine the latter possibility, the number of bachelor's degrees awarded from 1942 to 1952 were calculated and this figure was compared with a hypothetical degree production assuming no war and a modest but progressive increase in col-

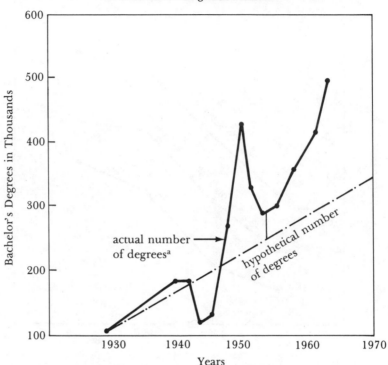

Figure 10.2. Actual and Hypothetical Numbers
of Bachelor's Degrees Awarded.

aU.S. National Center for Education Statistics, 1982a, p. 132.

lege attendance. The real production of college degrees during
this period was approximately 2,586,000. The hypothetical
number of degrees produced would have been some 2,130,000.
Some 456,000 more bachelor's degrees were produced than
would normally have been expected if one considers only demographics and changes in society, such as increased college attendance rates.

Something happened during or just after the war stimulating college enrollments (and eventually degrees) that only
lasted for a short period. It is possible to speculate about the
impact of the war on the veterans themselves—no doubt they
were a more determined lot after 1945—but would the result
have been as great without the financial incentives provided by

the federal government? The data presented here reinforce the conventional wisdom that the GI Bill stimulated enrollments, and that student financial aid programs do have a positive effect on college enrollments.

Next, it might be useful to assess the impact on enrollments of two specific federal initiatives: the Higher Education Amendments of 1972 and the Middle Income Education Act of 1978. Figure 10.3 represents the total number of students per

Figure 10.3. Enrollments of Eighteen-to-Twenty-Four-Year-Olds.

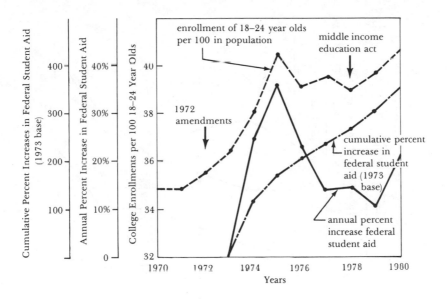

a U.S. National Center for Education Statistics, 1982a, p. 90.
b U.S. National Center for Education Statistics, 1982b, p. 164.

100 eighteen-to-twenty-four-year-olds in the population and the percent increase in expenditures for student aid on a year-by-year basis from 1973 to 1980. What is evident here is that student aid influences enrollments in a positive way. For example, the college attendance rate accelerates rather quickly after a

federal initiative and then stabilizes at a higher level after the
full effect of the new program. Further, the data for 1975 (Figure 10.3) show that a significant increase in appropriations for
an ongoing program seems to have a positive influence on enrollments.

There are those who argue that the significant enrollment
increase in 1975 was due to the high unemployment rate that
year. Figure 10.4 provides some interesting insights into this

Figure 10.4. Student Aid Recipients and Unemployment, 1970–1975.

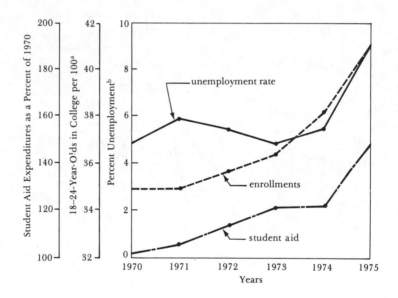

[a]U.S. National Center for Education Statistics, 1982a, pp. 90,
150–151.
[b]American Council on Education, 1982a, p. 34.

theory. College and university participation rates per 100
eighteen-to-twenty-four-year olds, unemployment rates, and the
accumulative percentage increase in student aid (with 1969
being a base year) are presented year by year from 1970 to 1975.
It is readily apparent that attendance rates are more closely cor-

related with increases in student aid expenditures than with unemployment rates. For example, between 1970 and 1971 unemployment rates went up while enrollment rates slipped slightly; between 1971 and 1972 enrollment rates went up, but unemployment dropped. In these years (1970–1975) unemployment and enrollments do not correlate well, if at all.

The conclusions drawn from the analyses presented here are that (1) federal policies, particularly financial incentives, stimulate student demand for college programs, and (2) unemployment seems to have little short- or long-term influence on college enrollments, especially if unemployment rates are in the ranges of 3 to 8.5 percent. (A major depression could have some significant short- and long-term impacts on institutions of higher education, but data from the 1920s and 1930s are inadequate to speculate on the impact of such an event.)

Leadership

It is not possible or even practical here to enter into an extensive review of higher education leadership during the postwar period. However, without question, many activities of leaders have been important to the higher education developments of the past thirty-five years, and an overview can be instructive.

There are three important characteristics of the American system of higher education. First, size: no other country in the history of the world has attempted to develop a postsecondary educational system that provides a place and program for any citizen who has the interest and ability to pursue it. This has resulted in a very large system by any standard. Second, diversity: The very diverse yet definable system of two- and four-year, public and private, residential and commuter, liberal arts and vocational, and open door and restrictive institutions puts American higher education in a world class by itself. Third, the symbiotic relationship that the system has enjoyed with the developing American economy and society makes it unique.

The decentralized system of government and life which characterizes the United States has provided considerable inertia to radical restructuring of institutions as times and conditions change; it is easier to create new institutions. This has been manifested in the progressive development of liberal arts colleges, public universities, land-grant universities, normal schools, urban institutions and, finally, community colleges as the needs of society and the economy have grown and changed over the years. This is one of the reasons why private liberal arts colleges represent the smallest of these subsystems, while community colleges, the youngest, are the largest—both in number of institutions and in enrollments. Different institutions were developed at different points in America's development and reflect the size and needs of the nation at the time that they came into being. For example, land-grant institutions were established to offer training in the agricultural and mechanical arts when the nation was entering the industrial age because liberal arts colleges were not willing or able to do the job; normal schools were developed to train teachers as the nation got serious about public education and no existing institution was willing to train the teachers needed; and community colleges later became commonplace, partially in response to a growing need for technological education not provided by existing institutions.

Higher education leaders in most institutions have provided the leadership necessary to adjust, without radically transforming, institutional missions to respond to the pressures of a changing society. For example, many church-founded colleges in recent decades have become market oriented. This does not mean, however, that their basic mission has changed. If one considers the symbiotic relationship between higher education and the economy, it is possible to speculate that a combination of outside pressures and internal leadership are responsible for the continuing adjustment and subsequent contribution of education to the economy. Business and political leaders have played important roles in shaping the curriculum and the system by continually challenging it to meet the economic needs of society.

The topics as outlined in *Leadership for Higher Education: The Campus View* (Heyns, 1977) provide a rough outline for discussion of certain leadership activities and their influence on the development of the size and shape of American higher education since World War II. One can classify the activities of college and university leaders identified by Heyns into three groups in terms of their impact on the basic character of American higher education: noninfluential, minimally influential, and influential.

Noninfluential. Few, if any, of the efforts to tinker with the curriculum or use education technology have had significant influence. Educators can take a little overall credit for increased participation of minorities or women in higher education (although there is nothing in the literature of higher education to support such a claim). Movements like consumerism, planning for retrenchment, finding alternatives to tenure, or responding to federal regulations also have had little impact. Many activities deemed important at times have not been really productive; they have been temporary trends peripheral to the basic direction of the system.

Minimally Influential. Activities such as increasing voluntary support, lobbying at the state house, and providing good management and internal leadership certainly have been valuable to individual institutions and have most likely contributed to the well-being of higher education in general. It is difficult to make a case, however, that they have significantly influenced American higher education.

Influential. The following leadership activities or characteristics have contributed significantly to the development of the system. First, leaders of existing institutions have been willing to accept new forms of higher education as an alternative to revolutionizing the existing system. Generally speaking, existing public and private institutions did not try to block the development of community colleges. Rather, in most states higher education leaders encouraged their creation and development. Acceptance and encouragement of diversity in higher education has been a hallmark of higher education leadership for most of the post-World War II period. Second, higher education leaders for the most part have strengthened the traditional roles of their institutions. Land-grant universities have become better land-grant institutions within the context of a changing economy and society. Private liberal arts colleges, for the most part, have become better liberal arts colleges. The reinforcing of traditional missions has also been a hallmark of higher education leadership in the postwar period. Third, although societal pressures are most difficult to specify when talking about the impact of leadership, college and university leaders have been very successful in reinforcing the basic American belief in the value of education. They have done this in many ways, including speaking out publicly, pointing out the financial return on a college education, and advocating public support of education. Encouraging public policies favorable to higher education has been a hallmark of leadership.

In attempting to look at future leadership requirements, it is useful to look at some of the forces that college and university leaders may have to respond to in the twenty-first century. First, there will be the challenge of demographics. The baby boom peaked in 1961 at 4.3 million births and then bottomed out in 1973 at 3.1 million for a decline in a twelve-year period of more than 25 percent (American Council on Education, 1982a, p. 34). Thus the high school graduates for the 1980s and for most of the 1990s have been born and can be counted. Since the bulk of college students are eighteen-to-twenty-four years old, the decline in eighteen-year-olds will have a very definite influence on the size and perhaps the character of American higher education in the decades ahead. However, many college and university leaders point to the potential of twenty-five-to-thirty-four year olds, which is certain to grow as the population "bulge" moves through the system. If conventional wisdom is proven to be correct, adults returning to college for vocational and retraining education will more than make up for the loss of younger students. This conventional wisdom is being challenged, however, by some recent data regarding characteristics of student bodies. For example, Chancellor Hinson of the Virginia Community College System was recently reported as telling his board that the average age of community college students in Virginia had dropped for the second consecutive year after rising steadily for more than a decade ("Students Getting Younger . . . ," 1982). This obviously means that a greater proportion of the community college students in Virginia are coming from the eighteen-to-twenty-four-year-old population.

Second, there seems to be a growing negative feeling in America about public institutions. Institutions do not help change this attitude as they proceed to pursue their own self-interests, fight each other over turf, point the finger at other sectors, and attempt to stretch their record of achievement in an effort to get a higher priority in the state budget.

Third, public policies are changing. For example, stimulating demand does not appear to be a part of the national agenda whether one is talking about the economy or education. This means a withdrawal, at least partially, by the national government from the extensive student aid programs which have been mounted over the last decade and a half. At the same time, states are cutting those educational programs designed to meet student demands in favor of programs of greater interest to the states. An extensive article in the *Chronicle of Higher Education* contained many examples of governors and state legislators advocating the use of higher education programs to enhance industrial development. Interestingly enough, it contained virtually no reference to using community colleges to support industrial development ("Falling State Revenues . . . ," 1982).

Fourth, the world is entering an era termed the information age by many and labeled the "third wave" by Alvin Toffler (1981). Optics, microcomputers, cable television, communication satellites, video discs, and hundreds of other developments are beginning to change American society dramatically. This new era will bring about many changes for higher education. Who will be taught, what they will be taught, and how they will be taught is certainly going to change.

Fifth, because of communications, transportation, and a growing population in third world nations, the earth is growing smaller. What does a smaller world mean for American higher education? What does it mean for community colleges? As the developing nations struggle to feed, clothe, and care for their millions, the well-established but often overlooked American infrastructure—food production, transportation facilities, public utilities, and the like—will be looked at with envy and hope around the world. This means that traditional American education will eagerly be sought by citizens of developing nations.

American institutions of higher education will be called on to serve more international students, and community colleges have much to offer in the interchange.

What does all this mean for future generations of higher education leaders? There is much to be learned from the past. Continuing to accept and encourage diversity, to reinforce the traditional role of individual institutions, and to encourage good public policies should be a mark of future higher education leaders.

Encouraging diversity will be difficult. Already, community college leaders are critical of the acceleration of the private sector into job training (a movement now calling itself human resources development), just as over the years they have been openly critical (and perhaps even envious) of adult vocational education in the public schools and adult education and community services in four-year colleges and other institutions such as libraries and museums. A fundamental challenge for community college leaders is to accept diversity of educational institutions, including the forms now developing.

Encouraging traditional roles does not mean going back to teaching Latin and Greek; it means tailoring traditional programs to changing times and technologies. Agriculture has been revolutionized during the past 100 years, but agricultural education is still a dominant feature of land-grant universities; extensive continuing education for medical doctors is an adaptation of medical schools' traditional role and thus is appropriate. As the work force grows older and middle aged and as people need to be trained and retrained in a technological society, job training will become an increasingly important responsibility of the community college. Such training is an extension of its traditional role of vocational and occupational education.

America is being challenged for world economic leadership by corporate Japan and other nations, and this challenge must be met effectively if the nation's economy is to sustain a free society. This challenge extends directly to community college leaders who will need to develop a consensus on the fundamental role of community colleges in America.

Finally, there will be the challenge of encouraging good

public policies. More frequently than in the past higher education leaders will discover that good public policies can be contrary to the perceived best interest of individual institutions. The nation does not need leadership that will be inclined to stall and hope for miracles but leaders who can see and are not afraid to advocate the public interest.

As one contemplates the federal role in higher education in the future, one finds that the issues are unclear. The public continues to view federal involvement with higher education as desirable, especially in the areas of research and student financial aid; yet the present administration seems determined to lessen that involvement. One thing is clear: the federal government will have a role in charting the future of higher education. Community college leaders must understand that role and work to influence the direction federal policy takes in the future.

11

Establishing Alliances with Business and Industry

Harold L. Hodgkinson

There are a number of forces at work increasing the possibility of alliances between higher education and other segments of society. Probably the most important of these is the principle of market disaggregation. Twenty years ago, colleges and universities had the field of postsecondary education pretty much to themselves. It was an aggregated market, if not a monopoly. All during the 1970s, however, many markets in American economic life have become disaggregated. In television broadcasting, for example, domination by three major networks has given way to a multiplicity of cable channels. Similarly, the all-purpose magazine has largely given way to highly specific publications that appeal to specific audiences. Other areas, too, such as food items, leisure time activities, sports and recreation, and clothing have reflected a marked increase in the range of choices available to Americans.

This trend has transformed the nature of postsecondary education in the United States. Twenty years ago, colleges and universities constituted an aggregated market, if not a monopoly, and they have been slow to see the enormous range of other providers of postsecondary education in our country. Presently, only about twelve million American adults are being educated in colleges and universities, compared to the better than forty million being educated in other settings (Moon, 1981).

One of the largest educational alternatives to colleges and universities is that provided by American business and industry. International Business Machines (IBM) is one of the oldest examples of this phenomenon. In 1969 it had a faculty of 3,417 individuals offering eighteen million contact hours of instruction to 40,000 full-time students. American Telephone and Telegraph (AT&T), for example, operates hundreds of educational facilities for employees. Among the thousands of teachers it hires are some 2,000 Ph.D.'s, including several Nobel Prize winners. As of 1982, AT&T had spent $1.7 billion on its own educational and training programs. Other cases include the Xerox training center and the Dana Corporation's Dana University. Having visited these and many other corporation-run training programs, I estimate that there are over 100 buildings on industrial sites that bear the name "college," "university," "institute," "center," or "academy." Increasing employee learning has, therefore, become an important corporate activity, especially in the postindustrial climate of concern for development of human resources. It is likely that corporations will continue to invest in their own internal educational systems. About seven of them are now offering advanced degrees, including Wang and General Motors; approximately fifty offer joint degrees; a number of others have the matter under development. These programs are usually good enough to be accredited by regional and state educational authorities.

In addition to corporate business ventures, increasing numbers of educational programs are being run by federal agencies and by nonprofit corporations. These include the Federal Executive Institute run by the federal government and the U.S. Department of Agriculture Graduate School; the National Society for Training and Development, an independent training agency for municipal administrators; the Management Academy run by the Detroit Public Schools for its own internal management; and the National Academy for Volunteerism run by the United Way of America. Indeed, on weekdays in any hotel in America, one can find numbers of eager adult students attending one-day seminars, weekend conferences, and special institutes—usually sponsored by a noncollegiate educational organization.

One characteristic of markets that become disaggregated is that it is extremely difficult to reaggregate them. Apparently, when educational needs emerged within corporate as well as government and nonprofit organizations, explicit decisions were made: Given the alternatives of hiring programs from colleges and universities or creating them themselves, most organizations chose to create them. The reasons are not yet clear. They may involve a suspicion of the academic beast, an assumption that in-house programs could be offered more cheaply, or a desire to retain control over the instructional process. Whatever the reasons, a fairly historic trend was set. As a result, we now seem to have a second major post-high school educational system—dominated by business and industry. The costs of this system are estimated to range from $20 to $50 billion, as compared to only $50 billion spent on college and university education ("Measuring the Amount of Training . . . ," 1983). Americans have created a shadow system of postsecondary education—one almost as large as that created by colleges and universities.

There is, then, a formidable array of noncollegiate education providers, which is large in number and, in some cases, awesome in terms of educational competence. Consider the abilities of:

- the military in training for adult literacy, task analysis, and relearning skills;
- the professional association in offering highly individualized instruction to its members;
- the industrial education system in using job assessment, programmed learning, and motivational techniques;
- the museum in providing sequencing of instructional events, multimedia simulations in gaming, and enhanced learner involvement;
- the proprietary institution in conducting first-rate marketing, apprenticeship training, linkages with local business and industry, and excellent job placement and vocational counseling.

It is no longer possible to ignore the existence of such alternatives to traditional learning. The choice of colleges and universities is to compete or collaborate.

Making Collaboration Work

Collaboration appears to be in the interest of both collegiate and noncollegiate parties. The decline in the eighteen-to twenty-four-year-old age group has hurt not only higher education but also many American businesses—especially those that either sell products to or are heavily dependent for their work force on this age group. Various community projects brought educators, business, and government leaders together far more often in the 1970s than in earlier eras, and as a result, these groups now do not seem as strange to one another as they once did. The human resource development movement is becoming more established in business, and concern for problem-solving skills and techniques tends to occupy all organizations. There are, then, strong reasons why more alliances are being formed today than a decade ago.

Alliances occur when one party can offer things the other party needs and vice versa. Colleges and universities have what other institutions frequently need: buildings, faculty, courses, libraries; noncollegiate organizations have what colleges frequently need: money, students, management and counseling skills. The most frequent form of collaboration involves a college providing and receiving cash payment for a tailor-made course that meets the specific needs of an outside agency.

However, this indicates just one of many possibilities for mutually agreeable exchange. A great deal of barter goes on in many of these situations—for example, a community college may have a swimming pool that is unused for four hours during the day, while a business needs a physical health program for employees and has unscheduled time available on word processors. Barter becomes a matter of deciding how many hours of pool time make up one hour of word processor time. Once this decision has been made, the economy and Gross National Product can fluctuate as they will: The relationship between swimming pool and word processor remains a constant. Several

sources dealing with the range of collaborative activity between
colleges and universities and other agencies are now available
(Gold, 1981; Hodgkinson, 1981; "Community Colleges–We
Mean Business! . . . ," 1983).

Part of what we learned during the 1970s was that just
raising money is not enough to support higher education institutions. The transition from fund raising to resource raising is an
important step that institutions take when they begin to realize
that their underutilized capacity can be brokered with someone
else's underutilized capacity in order to accomplish the objectives of both organizations. This trend will undoubtedly continue in the 1980s as institutions become less able to attract dollars and need to rely on better utilization of nondollar resources.

Community Colleges and New Alliances

Some universities have engaged in spectacular collaborative programs with industry. Among them are the Massachusetts
Institute of Technology's and Exxon's ten-year, $7 million pro-
gram for studying more effective burning processes; Harvard's
relationship with Monsanto for developing programs on the bio-
chemistry of organ development; California Institute of Technology's cooperative research programs involving many private
companies; and Johns Hopkins' establishment of an institute of
dermatology with Estee Lauder. While such developments have
occurred in only a handful of universities, I would estimate that
half of the community colleges in the country are engaged in
some form of systematic collaboration and sharing with business, government, and nonprofit organizations in their service
area.

Indeed, many characteristics of community colleges are
highly favorable to the development of alliances with other
agencies. Community colleges usually have had good and close
linkages to the communities in which they exist, unlike many
other institutions of higher education. They show a willingness
to consider the demands of the work place within the college
structure and mission. Instructional resources are usually flexible enough so that a single course can be generated that will

meet the needs of a particular business, industry, or government agency wishing to buy it.

The quantity of relationships between community colleges and other agencies has been excellent but the quality of these relationships needs to be improved. Too much attention has been given to the single-course-for-cash model of interchange with other organizations. More attention should be given to shared physical and human resources. Consultant trade-offs often are very useful. For example, a graphics design expert from the community college may give a day to a rapidly growing small business in the community in exchange for a day of consultation by the firm's expert on cash management.

During their slack periods, some commercial printing houses will print community colleges' bulletins and brochures for free or at drastically reduced rates. Equipment donations and partial purchase plans can often be exchanged for specific consulting services from the college and vice versa. Conducting programs on the premises of a local company or agency is another possibility; it is far more economical from the company's point of view than having its employees travel to the community college. Rotational arrangements whereby persons agree to leave their industries for a fixed period of time to teach in the community college, and vice versa, can often increase the flexibility of both institutions. These suggestions support the notion that there is no reason to be dependent on the single-course-for-cash model.

In addition, I am convinced that the average community college does not measure resource utilization very effectively. College budget officers know extremely well what equipment has been purchased in what divisions and departments, but information concerning the relative utilization rates of the equipment is almost impossible to acquire at the central office level. The system of management in many community colleges needs to be altered in such a way that the right to create alliances is delegated to the arms of the institutions that relate most closely to other organizations—usually departmental and divisional structures. Although most good alliances I have studied have occurred through departments, not through the president's office,

in many community colleges, the departmental and divisional
structures are still not trusted enough by the central administration. As a result, many innovative alliances that would be effective if handled by the department or division become ineffective
if handled by the institution's president. Alliances can and
should be initiated at the "work group" level with support from
the central administration.

Another deficiency is the failure to use faculty and student contacts in business, government, and voluntary organizations. In many cases, only contacts known to administrators are
solicited and used in networking, while faculty and students
(whose average age is in the thirties) may have even more valuable and more personal contacts with key leaders in the other
organizations. (In some cases, faculty members have been pun-
ished for using these contacts on the grounds that the faculty's
only responsibility is teaching!)

Some community colleges have been willing to collaborate only with large and well-established businesses, avoiding
alliances with small young firms—firms that may become important community assets in a few years. In at least one case known
to me, a potentially useful collaboration with a minority-owned
business was refused because it involved a small amount of risk.
Community colleges are perhaps preoccupied with the necessity
of having every project turn a dollar profit from its beginning.
Many collaborative tasks generate no new income but may com-
pensate by increasing the knowledge and skills of community
college staff members. It is in the area of staff development that
collaborative programs can have their greatest benefit. I believe
that the next century will see an investment in human resources
comparable to the investment in physical resources seen in this
century. If direct costs can be offset and if staff members return
from a collaboration with enhanced knowledge, skills, and contacts, the venture must be seen as a success.

I know that in a time of fiscal uncertainty such talk may
seem utopian, but it is not. Every seasoned administrator knows
that deferred maintenance is poor economy: The leak in the
roof that isn't fixed in 1982 becomes the new floor that must
be installed in 1983. Considering faculty as an important dollar
resource, like a building, how much money is saved by "de-

ferred maintenance"? A faculty of 100 members, 80 percent tenured with an average age of thirty-five, represents an investment over its "useful life" of about $90 million, excluding inflation. It is now known that the value of this investment can be increased through the development of human resources. As people learn new skills, their value to the college increases. A faculty that does everything the same way for a full year has not been maintained but has deteriorated, while other faculties have been learning and growing.

Occasionally, I hear the comment that instruction on a given campus is "good enough for the students they teach." It seems a great tragedy that such attitudes can hold sway. Fine teachers do not exist only at Harvard and Princeton. (Indeed, those places are probably populated more by great learners than they are by great teachers.) Exceptional teachers can be found at every level from kindergarten to graduate school. They can be found teaching flight engineers, Boy Scouts, secretaries, mechanics, company presidents, and accountants. Although some basic talent is probably needed, it is known that excellent teachers can be developed and good teachers improved. Similar investments need to be made in increasing the number and sophistication of administrative skills in the college.

One of the most useful ways of accomplishing this investment in human resources is to visit a new site and watch others do work similar to one's own. I am constantly amazed at the number of teachers and administrators who have not visited another college for this purpose. It offers a new rationale for alliance-building. The graphic arts teacher who needs some new equipment and gets it by "lending" him- or herself as a consultant to the company that manufactures it is accomplishing two things: getting the needed equipment and learning what it is like to practice the trade in a commercial workplace. Many who feel that human resource development is an expensive frill need to think of some of the simple devices that provide for professional development, such as seeing others do similar work in a different environment, developing teaching teams, providing inbaskets, creating simulations at administrative workshops or retreats, and using teaching skills as consulting skills.

Apart from the direct benefits of collaboration, the community college can gain much by observing the internal operations of other agencies' educational programs. Most of their instruction is highly specific in nature. Although it may emphasize generalizable things like problem solving, it nevertheless is based on specific skills and knowledge that will be useful to the worker, either on the job or in other activities. The units of instruction are short, and the material is specifically targeted to students' needs. Student motivation is probably stronger in these programs than in colleges and universities where students are involved in two- or four-year programs during which they must take courses only indirectly related to their specific needs and interests in order to get a degree. Community college leaders, especially those in community services and continuing education, need to concentrate on programs that offer specific skills. As pointed out in the chapter by McCabe and Skidmore, skills training, to be effective in this age of information, must include communication and computation skills as well as specific job skills. These are areas in which colleges have considerable pools of talent and experience to draw upon.

Conclusion

In the past, many community college leaders have been reticent in dealing with industry and other agencies, in spite of the close ties they have had with them. With assertive leadership, these ties can be parlayed into a true partnership whereby the community college is an equal, rather than a "junior," partner responding to the whims of industry. Community college leaders must work to ensure that institutional integrity is maintained when working with outside agencies. Such agencies must not be permitted to dictate what constitutes the college curriculum; the community college must not barter control of educational matters in return for full-time equivalent students. Enlightened community college leaders can and should work with other institutions to see that their thrust into higher education supplements rather than supplants the work of the community college.

Many community college alliance programs in the 1970s

were low-risk, conservative measures designed for short-term financial gain only. What will be needed in the 1980s and beyond will be a larger range of collaborative activity with a greater variety of types of staff involvement and institutional benefit.

In the future, more expert use can be made of collaborative arrangements given the fact that most community colleges now have almost a ten-year history of interinstitutional development. Alliance building is one of the areas in which the community college of the future can become a leader, setting a standard of quality that other institutions in American higher education may come to emulate. The performance of community colleges in creating and utilizing new alliances with other groups has so far been above average, but there is more to be done.

12

New Concepts for Community Colleges

Robert H. McCabe
Suzanne B. Skidmore

The American community college of the 1980s is a vital and dynamic institution whose mission can and should be more important to our nation than ever before. Since its inception, the fundamental qualities of the community college have been responsiveness and flexibility in meeting the educational needs of our society. For more than thirty years, its primary thrust was to expand access to higher education, and the considerable challenge of providing opportunity to new populations was met with unquestioned success. These institutions were eminently practical and, without the binding traditions of universities, were able to react spontaneously. Because of this adaptive flexibility, the community colleges made enormous contributions to changing American society and became the most important educational institution of the mid-twentieth century.

Social evolution, however, has clearly outpaced advances in education in recent decades; this has resulted in a strong and justified public outcry for reform and revitalization throughout the total educational system. It is now the beginning of a new era in American society. The rapid transition to the information age has begun, and our institutions are faced with a great challenge and a great opportunity to help this nation as never before. The community college must again rely on the major

232

assets that made it so unique and important through the mid-twentieth century—responsiveness and flexibility. It must address societal needs vigorously and directly through strong leadership and must place renewed emphasis on its practical nature and ability to react spontaneously. In the past, enrollment growth and accompanying financial support made it easy to be responsive. New programs were established with additional income and constantly increasing numbers of students. Now, new programs must result from a reconfiguration of existing resources, and this requires more sophisticated planning and management.

Current Environment

In recent years, dramatic and systemic shifts have altered the nature of work in America. Prior to World War II, 80 percent of all jobs in America were unskilled. With industrialization and mechanization escalating during the war, a massive change began, characterized by a significant decline in the number of farm workers, growth in the number of manufacturing occupations, and increases in the number of skilled jobs. By 1980, less than 20 percent of all jobs in America were unskilled (Whited, 1982, p. 2B). We are now entering (or, in fact, have already entered) a similar transition from industrialization and mechanization to computer and robot-aided manufacturing. Significant growth in the use of computers and data utilization in all fields is the basis of "the information society." In *Putting America Back To Work,* the American Association of Community and Junior Colleges and the Association of Community College Trustees (1982) estimate a continuing decline in manufacturing jobs over the next twenty-five years. This work reports that the percentage of the American work force in manufacturing jobs was 41 percent in the 1950s—today it is 27 percent; and it quotes Peter Drucker's prediction of a continuing decrease to less than 5 percent within twenty-five years (p. 6). Just as mechanization eliminated many unskilled jobs in recent years, the communications fields, high technology, and information revolution will certainly eliminate many semiskilled jobs in the future. New jobs will require more skill and involve either technology or information processing. Currently, more than half of all positions in America are in office occupations, and this figure will continue to increase (Zorn, 1981, p. 17A).

Perhaps the major contributor to the change in requirements of the work place has been the impact of the explosion in information technology. Early developments in this field were completely misinterpreted by many in education, who believed that reading would become less important as other means of communication evolved. What has happened, in fact, is exactly the reverse: Communications technology is rapidly becoming a part of everyone's work and home life and is producing enormous amounts of information that must be read and interpreted. It is estimated by William Brazziel (1981, p. 50) that "the volume of scientific and technical information doubles approximately every eight years." In 1950 only 17 percent of all jobs in America involved information processing compared to 54 percent today (Boyer and Hechinger, 1981, p. 27). As a result, the level of communications skills necessary for employment has increased significantly. In the framework of present society, academic skills have become the most important vocational skills. The National Assessment of Educational Progress (1981, p. 5) reports on the need for such skills: "In a world overloaded with information, both a business and a personal advantage will go to those individuals who can sort the wheat from the chaff, the important information from the trivial. Skills in reducing data, interpreting it, packaging it effectively, documenting decisions, explaining complex matter in simple terms and persuading are already highly prized in business, education and the military, and will become more so as the information explosion continues."

Nationwide, newspapers are filled with employment opportunities in accounting, office work, data processing and other computer-related fields, electronics, health care, and virtually all high-technology areas. Unfilled jobs exist in abundance while large segments of our population remain unemployable because of inadequate literacy skills. Employers consistently confirm the lack of good communications skills on the part of those seeking positions. In many areas of the country, industrial and economic development is not being appropriately supported because the skills of high school and college graduates are not adequate to meet current industrial needs. The dearth of capable individuals entering high technology fields is well documented; it results both from a lack of assessment and planning to meet regional educational needs and from the wide-scale problem of students who are inadequately prepared to undertake curricula in science and mathematics. In a report published by the Southern Regional Education Board, Eva Galambos (1980, p. 15) predicted the future in these fields: "The signs in terms of demand are fairly clear: even with a continuation of past trends, the demand for engineers, computer and mathematics specialists, and other high technology manpower will exceed the supply . . . In short, without deliberate action at all educational levels, if present trends are allowed to continue their own apparent course, then a serious shortage of high technology manpower may be in the offing."

At the same time that the need for strong academic skills has increased dramatically, the level of such skills attained by Americans has evidenced substantial decline. The National Assessment of Educational Progress (1981) reports that during the 1970s there was a 20 percent decline in the number of seventeen-year-olds able to satisfactorily interpret reading matter; that scores on college board examinations declined for fourteen consecutive years, bottoming out in 1981; and that there has been a one and a half year grade-level decline in standardized test scores of American high school seniors over the last six years, with a further one year decline in urban areas. At Miami-Dade Community College, two thirds of all entering students tested are deficient in either reading, writing, or mathematics; more than 90 percent of Black students are deficient in one skill, and of these more than two thirds are deficient in all three essential skills. Furthermore, 20 percent of all white Americans and 36 percent of all Black Americans are not completing high school. The standard of communications skills needed to be functionally literate—that is, employable and able to participate effectively in society—is rising rapidly. The level of academic skill that was satisfactory ten years ago is clearly insufficient today.

A majority of high school graduates now go on to post-secondary education, and this further education is essential for most of them to become employable. National data (Dearman and Plisko, 1981, p. 15) show that within seven years of high school graduation, 61.7 percent of graduates have attended college, and when technical and trade schools are added this figure is much higher. Boyer and Hechinger (1981, pp. 28–30) sum up the situation very well: "We are underscoring the fact that the workplace is changing dramatically, that traditional notions about pre-work preparation are becoming obsolete, and that more education will be required to meet the nation's diverse social and economic needs . . . . It is our conclusion that, from now on, almost all young people will, at some time in their lives, need some form of postsecondary education if they are to remain economically productive and socially functional in a world whose tasks and tools are become increasingly complex."

The combined effect of the changing nature of work in America and the severe decline in communications skills of youth has resulted in a societal dilemma of crisis proportions. The increased requirement for academic skills for employability combined with the decline in those skills leaves literally millions of Americans inadequately prepared, unable to gain employment, and thus unable to sustain themselves as productive members of society. This leaves our nation with a labor force ill-prepared to serve in internationally competitive industry. This crisis clearly reflects the academic shortcomings of our current educational system. Indeed, when viewed in the light of present American society, all levels of the educational system have failed significantly to adjust as societal needs changed—the evolutionary process in education has not progressed beyond the practices that evolved during the 1960s.

Important societal changes took place during the late 1960s as the nation struggled to overcome the impact of a history of racial discrimination and to provide equality and civil rights for all Americans. The educational system struggled to offer expanded opportunity to all, and institutions placed emphasis on the removal of barriers and on assisting individuals to get through the system. The focus was on helping students gain certification and achieve a sense of immediate gratification, often without equal focus on the skills or competencies acquired. Individuals within colleges demanded new rights and freedoms and resisted procedures interpreted as constraints to free choice. Institutions often achieved more success in providing access for new populations than in serving them effectively, and many students progressed through the entire system without being required to meet the firm educational standards of earlier years. This rapid evolution in education occurred to correct a system that seemed geared to inhibit minority and disadvantaged students from advancement. In retrospect, it seems that both society and the educational system overreacted somewhat to these valid concerns. Making it easier to gain a diploma or degree is not the answer: Competence, in addition to credentials, is required.

As times continued to change dramatically over the years, our educational system did not. New problems and demands of a changing social structure could not be effectively accommodated by the traditional approaches and models of earlier times. The 1980s are characterized by greater and greater emphasis on personal drive and personal achievement. Broad disillusionment exists, not with the goals, but with the efficacy of some of the social programs of earlier decades; nationally, it is a time of more carefully conceived approaches to such programs. Not surprisingly, over a period of time, the American people have developed a negative attitude toward an unresponsive educational system. Currently, demands for improvement and comprehensive reform of the total system are prevalent; a broad-scale public attitude places emphasis on quality rather than access, the maintenance of strict standards, and higher academic expectations at all levels.

In response to frustration with the efficacy of many social programs and to the failure attributed to the educational system, the open door philosophy of the community college has been seriously questioned. A reemergence of elitism has occurred as many wonder whether it is beneficial to offer postsecondary education to those with poor academic competence, particularly in a time of national economic constraint.

This attitude was well illustrated recently by Derek Bok, president of Harvard University, who suggested that the most effective utilization of federal funds for student grants would be to restrict them to students who are most likely to graduate from college, and "that eligibility for Pell Grants be tied to students' scores on college entrance examinations and high school rankings" ("U.S. Aid Should Go First . . . ," 1982, p. 1). Many individuals, including legislators, take the position that increased standards for higher education should be accomplished through restricted admissions. Unfortunately, this position fails to take into account the impact on large segments of our population who are inadequately prepared to gain employment and therefore economically dependent. Restricting admission to postsecondary education to those who are well prepared would exclude millions of Americans from making any productive contribution, forcing them to become burdens on society. As Roger Yarrington (1982, p. 4) puts it, "there is the unhappy vision of a dependent class of persons who, through lack of literate skills, become a dependent drag on those who are literate and thus more productive in a complex world." Because of the higher level of academic skills necessary to fill new jobs in American industry, maintenance of the community college open door has become essential to a healthy economy. Through the exciting high-growth periods of twentieth-century development, the superior ability of American workers played a key role in maintaining a strong national economy. We have now begun to lose that competitive edge, and it must be regained.

The new growth of elitism has been further evidenced recently by the dramatic increase in public funding for private institutions of higher education. Some years ago, these institutions began to accept increasing amounts of federal dollars through student aid programs and began to work for state aid in the form of tuition vouchers. At that time these institutions began to describe themselves as "independent," rather than "private." They maintain that it is less expensive to give such aid than to pay the full costs of a public institution. While this may still be true for many public colleges and universities, circumstances have been altered by rapidly increasing tuition in independent colleges, recent increases in tuition voucher programs, and both state and federal financial aid that is keyed to relative need (expense) rather than to absolute need. In many cases, it is now more expensive for the public to support a student in an independent institution of higher education than in community colleges. Debates concerning the proposed cuts in federal student financial aid emphasized providing a choice of educational options for students. However, as funds are scarce, and as independent schools of higher education continue to raise tuition fees (recently at a rate exceeding inflation), the first priority should be to provide opportunity while maximizing the return of public funds invested. In many instances, this is best achieved through services provided to the commuting student attending a community college.

The environment of the 1980s is characterized by significant changes in the nature of the services needed in occupational education. There is growing recognition that in virtually all occupations individuals will require continual upgrading and retraining. As a result there is greater participation and involvement in continuing occupational education by agencies other than formal educational institutions. Since schools and colleges are not producing the labor pool required by most industries, companies are creating their own on-site educational programs to meet training needs. Many businesses are providing a full range of educational services in order to keep members updated and upgraded, and some commercial organizations are actually awarding degrees. The Wang Corporation in Massachusetts now gives a master's degree in software engineering, and Brazziel (1981, p. 52) states that "IBM, Xerox, AT&T, and General Electric now grant the bachelor's degree. The Rand Corporation offers the Ph.D. in policy analysis, and Arthur D. Little offers a master's degree."

Community colleges should be organizing to provide customized and responsive in-service occupational education. At Portland Community College in Oregon, for example, the Institute for Community Assistance has been established as an outreach program directed toward business, industry, governmental agencies, and labor unions. Classroom facilities are provided at the work site, credits are awarded for training, and the curriculum is designed to meet specific needs of the agency. In the *Community and Junior College Journal* ("Institute Is Broker to Portland," 1982, p. 51) Don Fiser, director of the institute, describes the cooperative arrangement thusly: "We're really a partnership between the college and business. They have the employees, we have the curriculum and instructors. We can offer college credits and facilitate customers' goals."

Occupational programs should be designed to specifically match industry requirements and should remain unencumbered by bureaucratic regulation and outdated concepts or format. A good illustration of movement in the appropriate direction exists in the Los Angeles Community College District where development of an industry-responsive technical institute has begun to meet the growing local demand for high-technology occupational training. Key goals of the technical institute are flexibility and responsiveness to the training needs of the community. Close cooperation between education and industry is maintained with ongoing curriculum development, utilization of the latest equipment, and innovative instructional techniques and schedules. The technical institute model "responds to the need to regionalize costly equipment, maximize facility utilization, pool specialized expertise, educate individuals of varying backgrounds, develop alternate sources of funding, promote coordination with industry, and adapt quickly to frequently-changing 'state-of-the art' " (Division of Educational Services, 1981, p. 9).

Future Directions

It is time to carefully examine the current environment and to forecast future needs as a basis for redesigning all segments of the educational system. There must be concentrated focus on our literacy crisis and future occupational requirements in order for education to become a positive force in improving society. Boyer and Hechinger (1981, p. 30) define the task: "The conclusion is clear. Higher learning must redouble its efforts to meet more effectively the needs of those who have been inadequately served by education in the past." It is essential that the open door concept of the community college be retained. A policy of restrictive admissions criteria, applied to all of higher education, would have a devastating impact on our country. The American economy needs more, rather than fewer, well-educated individuals.

The community college now stands as the single institution capable of salvaging opportunity for the large numbers of Americans whose academic and occupational skills have prepared them neither to participate in society nor to achieve any measure of success. This critical societal dilemma wastes the lives of millions of Americans and forecasts serious problems for American industry. The *Miami Herald* (1982, p. 7A) described a recent study conducted by Richard Lynn at the University of Ulster, Northern Ireland, which indicates that the intelligence quotient (IQ) scores of Japanese children now average eleven points above those of American children. In addition, "at least 10 percent of the Japanese population has an IQ of 130 or more [while] only about two percent of the American population has an IQ of 130 or more." There is no doubt that an effective educational system and full development of academic skills contribute to higher IQ scores. The introduction of more complex work requirements along with the provision for essential training has helped development of Japanese industry. If America is to remain competitive, not only must future generations be adequately prepared but those who are already past high school must be helped to improve their academic skills. This becomes critically important in light of current occupational shortages and America's declining birthrate; most of the individuals who must find employment in the new, more demanding occupations have already passed their high school years. The seriousness of the situation is described by the American Association of Community and Junior Colleges (1982, p. 4): "Today almost 10 million Americans are on record as unemployed. In addition, many individuals have simply given up in the search for work and have sunk below the statistical level . . . Ironically, at a time when we are experiencing high levels of unemployment, nearly every trade association in this country reports skilled craftsman shortages—shortages that will increase to dangerous levels if solutions are not applied soon." Salvaging opportunity for underprepared adults is of overwhelming importance to this country.

In order to successfully meet the important needs of our society, there must be a complete shift of emphasis away from the 1960s mentality that still dominates much of community college activity. At the same time, there must be a shift from concern with program completion to an emphasis on high achievement and maintenance of standards. The goal should be excellence for everyone. Concern about the negative impact of emphasizing achievement is expressed by staff members in higher education rather than by students, who react positively to greater structure and increased requirements wherever such program changes are instituted. At Miami-Dade Community College, for example, nearly 11,000 students have been suspended since implementation of standards of academic progress in 1978. Although this program represented a drastic change of policy at Miami-Dade, students have been very supportive and have endorsed the imposition of higher expectations. It is clear that they want to take pride in their achievements and to know that they are making significant gains with the time invested.

Another important future focus for community colleges is planning for the increased use of communications technology. Because there is no short-term expectation for substantial increases in funding for community colleges, individualized assistance to students must be achieved within acceptable cost parameters. Without doubt, application of communications technology offers important prospects for attaining this goal. The economic aspects of the use of communications technology continue to improve while the capability and cost of hardware rapidly decline. Higher education is an interactive communications business, and technology should be utilized in its communications to equal the advances being made by other industries. This will not decrease the need for human interaction, but it should provide additional opportunities in teaching, learning,

and provision of specialized assistance to students. As more people become comfortable with the technology that is all around
them, the institution that does not prepare well for integration
of this technology will find itself left behind.

An example of effective planning for use of technology is
currently underway at Maricopa Community College where
Chancellor Paul Elsner has instituted a college-wide program to
introduce computers into every phase of its work. At Miami-
Dade Community College, computerized instructional systems
are used in more than a hundred courses, and all students receive individualized information about their current academic
progress approximately six weeks into each term. Ninety-three
percent of our students have expressed appreciation at receiving
this personal computerized information, and recent studies
show that students improve performance, increase completion
rates, raise grade point averages, and lower suspension rates
when they are informed early of deficiencies and avail themselves of needed special assistance.

As previously stated, forecasts of changing employment
patterns indicate significant increases in high technology, information processing, and office careers—particularly computer-
related, health care, automation, robotics, and other fields requiring high academic and technical skills. The community
college is in a particularly advantageous position to respond to
current societal needs because the greatest percentage of growth
in these fields will be in jobs appropriate for community college preparation. It is estimated that the majority of jobs in
high-technology areas are at the two-year associate degree level,
and this is true as well in many of the other high-demand occupational areas. In addition, studies are now showing that, in
some cases, those with associate degrees can achieve a high level
of success and receive a good rate of pay compared to those with
bachelor's degrees. This was illustrated by a recent study of
graduates from the City University of New York (CUNY) (Kaufman, Murtha, and Warman, 1982, p. 47), which concluded
that "associate's degree graduates were equally as likely as
bachelor's to be employed full time . . . [that] associate's degree graduates were somewhat more likely than were holders of

bachelor's degrees to find jobs 'directly related' to their under-graduate majors . . . [and] as far as initial salary is concerned, those with associate's degrees do as well as those with the bacca-laureate. Many do better." It is clear that community colleges should be preparing for large enrollment increases in high-tech-nology areas, as well as health care, skilled office jobs, data processing, and other fields requiring two years of postsecond-ary education.

In order to serve the growing population of individuals re-turning for additional schooling after employment, the commu-nity colleges must develop programs that tailor curricula in direct response to the needs of industry. Components of these cooperative arrangements will very often include cooperative education programs with classes occurring at the industry site. Developing such custom-designed programs will be a significant challenge for community colleges, particularly in breaking away from traditional concepts of semester hours and two-year pro-grams and moving to contracted arrangements developed for the specific number of hours required. Several programs currently operating at Miami-Dade's Medical Center Campus illustrate this type of arrangement.

The Alliance for Employee Advancement is a newly established program with local hospitals focusing on educational benefits for the hospital employee who wishes to pursue one of the health programs provided by the medical center campus. This model for college/employer cooperation has the advantages of providing on-site, "clustered" educational services to individ-uals currently employed in the health care industry. In addition, opportunities for employee advancement are conveniently avail-able, complete with educational reimbursement benefits pro-vided by the employer. As a result, the turnover rate in service personnel is often significantly reduced and the funds that would have been used for recruitment and training can be used elsewhere within the clinical agency.

The Community Extension Nursing Program is designed to provide seminars, workshops, special events, and a full range of educational services directed toward nurses working in the field. This unit of the college program is responsible for assessing, designing, developing, and implementing continuing education offerings that address the needs and goals of the nursing community. The program objectives are to increase knowledge and skills necessary to utilize and synthesize emergent technologies into the practice and to provide lifelong learning and personal and professional growth.

The Post-Registered Nursing Opportunity (PRO) program represents a coordination of college services designed to assist nurses interested in preparing for the New York Regents External Degree Examinations. Miami-Dade's PRO program is a three-dimensional approach providing upward career mobility for registered nurses. Complete advisement and assessment services are provided to help individuals make decisions about the need for specific course enrollment, to assist in the review of basic nursing skills, and to provide feedback regarding performance and the current level of clinical skill development. Specific nursing courses are available to build on already acquired knowledge, to expand scope of practice, and to prepare for the New York Regents Examinations.

During the last academic year, Miami-Dade's Medical Center campus offered clinics in approximately sixty-five local hospitals, nursing homes, and other county health care agencies. Such programming is an integral part of campus planning, as these external agencies represent a component of curriculum which the college could not provide independently. Planned sharing of health-care facilities and ongoing efforts to establish articulated programming within specialities are central to the philosophy of providing practical service to both the student and the community.

Community colleges have the basic foundation to become a natural partner of industry. For many years community colleges have operated with advisory committees of employers and business leaders for each occupational program. They have thus had extensive experience in building cooperative arrangements and maintaining effective liaison with local businesses. Such experience should form a strong basis for significant program expansion or total program redesign where necessary.

With the current concern for making the best use of public funds, there must be a new analysis of available alternatives in education. In terms of expenditures by the family, the individual, and the public, the conclusion almost certainly will be that the community college offers the best and most cost effective program for the first two years of the baccalaureate track. The individual lives at home, making a second domicile unnecessary, the fees are low, and support per full time equivalent student is far lower than in independent colleges and universities. In addition, the high student financial aid costs and tuition voucher programs in independent institutions reinforce the fact that community colleges often cost the public less. It is in the public's best interest for community colleges to be the principal provider of cost effective lower-division baccalaureate programs.

For many years, community colleges have quietly made their facilities available to their local communities for public recreation, health-related activities, various sports leagues and other athletic activities, as well as performance in theater, music, and the arts. This public facility use has been accomplished at a surprisingly low cost and is of great benefit to communities. Such emphasis should be continued and should certainly draw public support. In many cases, this activity should be separated from formulas based on enrollment and funded as a public service.

Lifelong learning programs provided by the community college present a significant dilemma: The public need for such programs is clearly expressed, and the support is clearly withheld. Our growing elderly population benefits substantially from continuing education; there is much documentation and testimony about the enrichment which results from ongoing educational opportunities. As the world becomes increasingly complex and tension filled, large percentages of Americans look for life-enriching activities outside the work environment. Provision of such services can be of tremendous value to this country. Even so, there is little evidence that state legislatures are willing to make significant effort to fund lifelong learning. Individuals at middle- and higher-income levels seem willing to pay for such services; individuals at lower-income levels certainly need them just as much. Since legislatures continue to shift this cost to individuals, it is very difficult to determine what the future of these programs will be. Considerable change will be required to bring support.

Conclusions

Just as programs designed in the 1940s and before had to be reviewed, revised, and renewed to meet the needs of the 1960s, so too, programs designed in the 1960s will have to be recast to meet the needs of the 1980s. The flexibility that community colleges espouse has typically been the flexibility to add new programs and services, which were funded from the proceeds of growth or from grant funds. Resources will be more limited than in the past; enrollments will no longer increase at the rates of the past; special grant funds will be scarce. Flexibility will have to be accomplished by change rather than growth.

In the 1960s a number of community college leaders were starting fresh. They were a new group who were willing to reject much of traditional education. Now these leaders must reconsider the structure they so carefully built just a few years ago. Will they have the strength and the courage to redesign their own creation as they did the structure developed by their predecessors in higher education?

Current trends clearly indicate that community colleges will become even more essential to the well-being of America in the late twentieth century than they have been during the mid-twentieth century. We have already entered a period in which most individuals will require continuing professional or occupational education in a postsecondary institution. With the current rapid growth of high-technology and computer- and information-related occupations, jobs appropriate to the two-year associate degree are on the threshold of rapid expansion. In addition, at a time when the public is questioning the cost effectiveness of educational as well as social programs, the community college provides the most economical method to attain the first two years of a baccalaureate degree programs. No other institution is as well prepared to offer solutions to our national literacy crisis. Through its continued commitment to the open door, the community college stands as the essential institution to assist such individuals.

It is time once again for community colleges to do what they do best—to design innovative and diversified programs to meet the rapidly changing needs of society. Traditional approaches must be abandoned and basic reform undertaken to permit continuation of the open door. Through such strengthening and growth, this institution will retain its position of central importance in the future evolution of American society.

References

Aberle, D. F., and Naegele, K. D. "Middle-Class Fathers' Occupational Role and Attitudes Towards Children." *American Journal of Orthopsychiatry,* 1952, *22,* 366.

American Association of Community and Junior Colleges. *1982 Community, Junior, and Technical College Directory.* Washington, D.C.: American Association of Community and Junior Colleges, 1982.

American Association of Community and Junior Colleges and the Association of Community College Trustees. *Putting America Back to Work.* Washington, D.C.: American Association of Community and Junior Colleges, 1982.

American Association of Junior Colleges. *Junior College Student Personnel Programs: Appraisal and Development.* Washington, D.C.: American Association for Junior Colleges, 1965.

American College Testing Program. *College Student Profiles: Norms for the ACT Assessment.* Iowa City: Research and Development Division, American College Testing Program, 1966–1981.

American Council on Education. *1981–82 Factbook for Aca-*

demic Administrators. Washington, D.C.: American Council on Education, 1982a.

American Council on Education. *A Fact Book on Higher Education.* Washington, D.C.: American Council on Education, 1982b.

"Applications for Fall Admission Decline at Private and Public Colleges." *Chronicle of Higher Education,* July 28, 1982, p. 8.

Association of American Colleges. *General Education: Issues and Resources.* Washington, D.C.: Association of American Colleges, 1980.

Association Transfer Group. College Transfer: Working papers and recommendations from the Airlie House Conference. December 2-4, 1973.

Astin, A. W. *The College Environment.* Washington, D.C.: American Council on Education, 1968a.

Astin, A. W. "Undergraduate Achievement and Institutional 'Excellence'." *Science,* 1968b, *161,* 661-668.

Astin, A. W. *Preventing Students from Dropping Out.* San Francisco: Jossey-Bass, 1975.

Astin, A. W. *Four Critical Years: Effects of College on Beliefs, Attitudes, and Knowledge.* San Francisco: Jossey-Bass, 1977.

Astin, A. W. *Minorities in American Higher Education: Recent Trends, Current Prospects, and Recommendations.* San Francisco: Jossey-Bass, 1982.

Astin, A. W., King, M. R., and Richardson, G. T. *The American Freshman: National Forms for Fall 1980.* Los Angeles: University of California Press, 1980.

Astin, A. W., and others. *The American Freshman: National Norms for Fall 1979.* Los Angeles: Cooperative Institutional Research Program, Graduate School of Education, University of California, 1979.

Astin, A. W., and others. *The American Freshman: National Norms for Fall 1981.* Los Angeles: Cooperative Institutional Research Program, Graduate School of Education, University of California, 1981.

Astin, H. S., and Cross, P. H. *Student Financial Aid and Persis-*

tence in College. Los Angeles: Higher Education Research Institute, 1979.

Atwell, C. A., Vaughan, G. B., and Sullins, W. R. *Reexamining Community Services in the Community College: Toward Consensus and Commitment.* Topical paper no. 76. Los Angeles: ERIC Clearinghouse for Junior Colleges, 1982.

Baldridge, J. V., Curtiss, D. V., and Riley, G. L. "Diversity in Higher Education." *Journal of Higher Education,* 1977, *XLVIII* (4), 367–388.

Banning, J. H. "The Campus Ecology Manager Role." In U. Delworth, G. Hanson, and Associates, *Student Services: A Handbook for the Profession.* San Francisco: Jossey-Bass, 1980.

Barshis, D. E. "Comprehensive Block Program for Students Reading Below the Seventh Grade." *Center Notebook* (Center for the Improvement of Teaching and Learning, Chicago), 1982, *1* (7).

Beal, P. E., and Noel, L. *What Works in Student Retention: The Report of a Joint Project of the American College Testing Program and the National Center for Higher Education Management Systems.* Iowa City, Iowa and Boulder, Colo.: American College Testing Program and the National Center for Higher Education Management Systems, 1980.

Bers, T. H. "Politics, Programs and Local Governments: The Case of the Community Colleges." *Journal of Politics,* 1980, *42,* 150–164.

Blackburn, R., and others. *Changing Practices in Undergraduate Education.* Berkeley, Calif.: Carnegie Council on Policy Studies in Higher Education, 1976.

Block, J. H. (Ed.). *Mastery Learning: Theory and Practice.* New York: Holt, Rinehart and Winston, 1971.

Block, J. H., and Anderson, L. W. *Mastery Learning in Classroom Instruction.* New York: Macmillan, 1975.

Bloom, B. S. "Learning for Mastery." *Evaluation Comment,* 1968, *2.*

Bloom, B. S. *Human Characteristics in School Learning.* New York: McGraw-Hill, 1976.

Bloom, B. S. "The New Direction in Educational Research:

Alterable Variables." In K. D. Sloane and M. L. O'Brien (Eds.), *The State of Research on Selected Alterable Variables in Education.* Chicago: Department of Education, University of Chicago Press, 1980.

Boyer, E. L. "Quality and the Campus: The High School/College Connection." *Current Issues in Higher Education,* 1980, *2* (4).

Boyer, E. L., and Hechinger, F. *Higher Learning In The Nation's Service.* Washington, D.C.: Carnegie Foundation for the Advancement of Teaching, 1981.

Boyer, E. L., and Levine, A. *A Quest for Common Learning: The Aims of General Education.* Washington, D.C.: Carnegie Foundation for the Advancement of Teaching, n.d.

Brandenburg, J. B. "The Needs of Women Returning to School." *Personnel and Guidance Journal,* 1974, *54* (1), 11–18.

Brazziel, W. F. "College-Corporate Partnerships in Higher Education." *Educational Record,* 1981, *62* (2), 50–53.

Breneman, D. W., and Nelson, S. C. *Financing Community Colleges: An Economic Perspective.* Washington, D.C.: The Brookings Institution, 1981.

Brick, M. *Forum and Focus for the Junior College Movement: The American Association of Junior Colleges.* New York: Teachers College Press, Columbia University, 1964.

Briggs, N. L. *Women and the Skilled Trades.* Columbus, Ohio: ERIC Clearinghouse on Adult, Career, and Vocational Education, 1978.

Brubacher, J. S., and Rudy, W. *Higher Education in Transition.* New York: Harper & Row, 1976.

Buchanan, J. M., and Tullock, G. *The Calculus of Consent: Logical Foundations of Constitutional Democracy.* Ann Arbor: University of Michigan Press, 1962.

Buckley, A., Freeark, K., and O'Barr, J. "Support for Returning Students." *Adult Leadership,* Sept. 1976, *25* (1), 21–23.

Buros, O. K. (Ed.). *Eighth Mental Measurements Yearbook.* Vol. 2. Highland Park, N.J.: Gryphon Press, 1978.

California Community Colleges. *Credit and Noncredit Courses in the California Community Colleges, Part II.* Sacramento: Chancellor's Office, California Community Colleges, July 1980.

California Postsecondary Education Commission. *Missions and Functions of the California Community Colleges.* Sacramento: California Postsecondary Education Commission, 1981a.

California Postsecondary Education Commission. *Remediation Study Campus Survey.* Sacramento: California Postsecondary Education Commission, 1981b.

California Postsecondary Education Commission. *Update of Community College Transfer Student Statistics.* Sacramento: California Postsecondary Education Commission, 1982.

Campbell, C. B. "A Supportive Services Program for Students with Predicted Low Academic Abilities: A Coordinated Approach." *Journal of College Student Personnel,* 1981, *22,* 453–454.

Caponigri, R., and others. *Mastery Learning Workbook.* Chicago: City Colleges of Chicago, 1982.

Carhart, J. I., and Collins, C. C. *Governance: A Community College Model.* Los Medanos, Calif.: Community College Press, 1977.

The Carnegie Foundation for the Advancement of Teaching. *Missions of the College Curriculum: A Contemporary Review with Suggestions.* San Francisco: Jossey-Bass, 1977.

Center for the Study of Community Colleges. "Course Enrollments and Completions in Six Large Urban Community College Districts." Unpublished paper, Los Angeles, Nov. 1982.

Chausow, H. M. "Remedial Education: A Position Paper." Unpublished manuscript, Chicago, 1979. (ED 170 013)

Chickering, A. *Education and Identity.* San Francisco: Jossey-Bass, 1969.

Cohen, A. M. "Assessing College Students' Ability to Write Compositions." *Research in the Teaching of English,* 1973, 7 (3), 356–371.

Cohen, A. M. "Counting the Transfer Students." *Junior College Resource Review.* Los Angeles: ERIC Clearinghouse for Junior Colleges, 1979. (ED 172 864)

Cohen, A. M. "Maintaining Perspective." *Community College Review,* 1981, *8* (4), 5–11.

Cohen, A. M., and Brawer, F. B. *The American Community College.* San Francisco: Jossey-Bass, 1982.

Cohen, E. G., and others. *A Study of Remedial Reading Courses*

(BE-03) Offered During the Fall 1972 Semester: A Baseline for Longitudinal Studies. Bayside, N.Y.: Queensborough Community College, 1973. (ED 144 653)

Collins, C. C., and Drexel, K. O. *General Education: A Community College Model.* Pittsburg, Calif.: Community College Press, 1976.

"Community Colleges—We Mean Business! Cooperative Efforts Between Two-year Institutions and Business/Industry." Proceedings from a conference of the National League for Innovation, Maricopa Community Colleges, Phoenix, Arizona, March 1983.

Corson, J. J. *The Governance of Colleges and Universities.* New York: McGraw-Hill, 1960.

Cowley, W. H. "An Overview of Higher Education in the University in the United States." Unpublished manuscript, Stanford University, 1964.

Creamer, D. G. (Ed.). *Student Development in Higher Education: Theories, Practices and Future Directions.* Cincinnati: American College Personnel Association, 1980.

Cross, K. P. *Accent on Learning: Improving Instruction and Reshaping the Curriculum.* San Francisco: Jossey-Bass, 1976.

Cross, K. P. *Adults as Learners: Increasing Participation and Facilitating Learning.* San Francisco: Jossey-Bass, 1981a.

Cross, K. P. "Community Colleges on the Plateau." *Journal of Higher Education,* 1981b, *52* (2), 113–123.

Dearman, N. B., and Plisko, W. V. *The Condition of Education, 1980 Edition.* Washington, D.C.: National Center for Education Statistics, 1980.

Dearman, N. B., and Plisko, W. V. "Test Scores and Attainment Rates." *American Education.* Washington, D.C.: U.S. Department of Education, 1981.

Division of Educational Services, Los Angeles Community College District. *Meeting Technical Education Needs: An Industry-Responsive Model.* Los Angeles: Division of Educational Services, 1981.

Douvan, D., and Adelson, J. *The Adolescent Experience.* New York: Wiley, 1966.

Edge, D. *Report of the New Jersey Basic Skills Council.* Trenton: New Jersey State Department of Higher Education, 1979. (ED 185 098)

Educational Facilities Laboratory. *The Neglected Majority: Facilities for Commuting Students.* New York: Academy of Educational Development, 1977.

Eliason, N. C. *Neglected Women: The Educational Needs of Displaced Homemakers, Single Mothers, and Older Women.* Washington, D.C.: National Advisory Council on Women's Educational Programs, 1978.

Eliason, N. C. "New Directions for Women's Studies and Support Services." In J. S. Eaton (Ed.), *New Directions for Community Colleges: Women in Community Colleges,* no. 34. San Francisco: Jossey-Bass, 1981.

"Fact-File: Status of Female Faculty Members, 1979-80." *Chronicle of Higher Education,* 1981, *21,* 87.

"Falling State Revenues, Cuts in Payrolls Bring Hard Times to Public Institutions." *Chronicle of Higher Education,* Feb. 10, 1982, p. 1.

Fenske, R. H. "Historical Foundations." In U. Delworth, G. Hanson, and Associates (Eds.), *Student Services: A Handbook for the Profession.* San Francisco: Jossey-Bass, 1980.

French, M. *The Women's Room.* New York: Summit Books, 1977.

Friedlander, J. *Science Education for Women, Minorities, in an Urban Community College.* Topical paper no. 76. Los Angeles: Center for the Study of Community Colleges and ERIC Clearinghouse for Junior Colleges, 1981. (ED 214 578)

Friedlander, J. "Should Remediation Be Mandatory?" *Community College Review,* 1981-1982, *9,* 56-64.

Gaff, J. G. "Avoiding the Potholes: Strategies for Reforming General Education." *Educational Record,* 1980, *61* (4), 50-59.

Galambos, E. C. *Engineering and High Technology Manpower Shortages: The Connection With Mathematics.* Atlanta: Southern Regional Education Board, 1980.

A Gallup Study of the Image of and Attitudes Toward America's Community and Junior Colleges, 1981. Washington, D.C.: American Association of Community and Junior Colleges, 1981. (ED 213 452)

Glass, G. V. "Primary, Secondary, and Meta-Analysis in Social Research." *Educational Researcher,* 1976, *5,* 3–8.

Gleazer, E. J., Jr. *The Community College: Values, Vision, and Vitality.* Washington, D.C.: American Association of Community and Junior Colleges, 1980.

Gold, B. K. *Performance on the Fall 1976 Los Angeles City College Guidance Examination: Research Study #77-7.* Los Angeles: Los Angeles City Colleges, 1977. (ED 140 919)

Gold, G. G. (Ed.). *New Directions for Experiential Learning: Business and Higher Education: Toward New Alliances,* no. 13. San Francisco: Jossey-Bass, 1981.

Gould, J. E. *The Chautauqua Movement: An Episode in the Continuing American Revolution.* Albany: State University of New York Press, 1961.

Griffith, W. S. "Harper's Legacy to the Public Junior College." *Community College Frontiers,* 1976, *4* (3), 14–20.

Guskey, T. R., Barshis, D. E., and Easton, J. *The Center for the Improvement of Teaching and Learning: Exploring New Directions in Community College Research.* Chicago: City Colleges of Chicago, 1982.

Guskey, T. R., and Monsaas, J. A. "Mastery Learning: A Model for Academic Success in Urban Junior Colleges." *Research in Higher Education,* 1979, *11,* 263–274.

Hammons, J., Thomas, W., and Ward, S. "General Education in the Community College." *Community College Frontiers,* 1980, *8* (3), 22–28.

Harlacher, E. L., and Gollattscheck, J. F. (Eds.). *New Directions for Community Colleges: Implementing Community-Based Education,* no. 21. San Francisco: Jossey-Bass, 1978.

Harris, N. C., and Grede, J. F. *Career Education in Colleges: A Guide for Planning Two- and Four-Year Occupational Programs.* San Francisco: Jossey-Bass, 1977.

Hechinger, F. M. "The Losing War Against Literacy." In *The 1977 World Book Year Book.* Chicago: Field Enterprises, 1977, 78–81.

Herrscher, B. R. "Designing Instruction." In J. E. Roueche (Ed.), *New Directions for Higher Education: Increasing Basic Skills by Developmental Studies,* no. 20. San Francisco: Jossey-Bass, 1977.

Heyns, R. W. (Ed.). *Leadership for Higher Education: The Campus View.* Washington, D.C.: American Council on Education, 1977.

Hodgkinson, H. L. "The Art of Barter." *AGB Reports,* 1981, *23* (5), 3-6.

Hudson, J. A., and Smith, R. B. "Does General Education Have a Future?" *Community College Review,* 1976, *4* (2), 57-63.

Hunter, J. O. "General Education and a New World View." *Community College Frontiers,* 1980, *8* (3), 17-20.

Hunter, R., and Sheldon, M. S. *Statewide Longitudinal Study: Report on Academic Year 1979-80, Part 4: Spring Results.* Los Angeles: Los Angeles Pierce College, n.d.

"Institute Is Broker to Portland." *Community and Junior College Journal,* 1982, *52* (8), 51.

Ireland, J. "The Role of Community Services in a Time of Fiscal Constraint: A California Perspective." *Community Services Catalyst,* 1982, *12* (3), 11-15.

"Japanese Widen Lead in I.Q. Scores." *Miami Herald,* May 21, 1982, p. 7A.

Karabel, J. "Community Colleges and Social Stratification: Submerged Class Conflict in American Higher Education." *Harvard Educational Review,* Nov. 1972, 42, 521-562.

Kaufman, B., Murtha, J., and Warman, J. "Will Success Spoil Community College Graduates?" *Community and Junior College Journal,* 1982, *52* (8), 46-47.

Kelly, J. T. *Restructuring the Academic Program: A Systems Approach to Educational Reform at Miami-Dade Community College.* Miami, Fla.: Miami-Dade Community College, 1981. (ED 211 138)

Kemmerer, F. R. "The Clouded Future of Faculty Governance." *The Educational Forum,* Jan. 1978, *XLII* (2), 233-243.

Kintzer, F. C., "Articulation in Perspective." Unpublished manuscript, University of California at Los Angeles.

Kirby, E. B. "Petticoats to Jackhammers: Strategies for Women in Occupational Education." In J. S. Eaton (Ed.), *New Directions for Community Colleges: Women in Community Colleges,* no. 34. San Francisco: Jossey-Bass, 1981.

Knowles, M. *Self-Directed Learning.* New York: Association Press, 1975.

Koch, A., and Peden, W. (Eds.). *The Life and Selected Writings of Thomas Jefferson.* New York: Random House, 1944.

Kraetsch, G. A. "The Role of the Community College in the Basic Skills Movement." *Community College Review,* 1980, *8,* 18–23.

Kulik, C.-L., Kulik, J., and Shwalb, B. "College Programs for High-Risk and Disadvantaged Students: A Meta-Analysis of Findings." Paper presented at the annual meeting of the American Educational Research Association, New York, March 1982.

Lenning, O. T., Sauer, K., and Beal, P. E. *Student Retention Strategies.* AAHE-ERIC/Higher Education Research Report No. 8. Washington, D.C.: American Association of Higher Education, 1980.

Lombardi, J. *Community Education: Threat to College Status?* Topical paper no. 68. Los Angeles: ERIC Clearinghouse for Junior Colleges, 1978.

Lombardi, J. "Developmental Education: A Rapidly Expanding Function." *Community College Review,* 1979, *7,* 65–72.

London, H. B. *The Culture of a Community College.* New York: Praeger, 1978.

Lukenbill, J. D., and McCabe, R. H. *General Education in a Changing Society: General Education Program, Basic Skills Requirements, Standards of Academic Progress at Miami-Dade Community College.* Dubuque, Iowa: Kendall/Hunt, 1978.

Luskin, B. *Personal Communication.* Sept. 7, 1982.

McCabe, R. H. *Now is the Time to Reform the American Community College.* Miami, Fla.: Miami-Dade Community College Press, March 1981.

McCabe, R. H. "Excellence is for Everyone: Quality and the Open Door Community College." Paper presented at the national conference of the American Association for Higher Education, Washington, D.C., March 1982.

McCabe, R. H., and Skidmore, S. "The Literacy Crisis and American Education." *ERIC Junior College Resource Review,* Spring 1982, 2–6.

Maccoby, E. E., and Jacklin, C. N. *Psychology of Sex Differences.* Stanford, Calif.: Stanford University Press, 1974.

Maccoby, M. "Leadership Needs of the 1980s." Paper presented at the national conference of the American Association for Higher Education, 1979.

Magarrell, J. "Swing from Private to Public Colleges Noted in Applications for Fall." *Chronicle of Higher Education,* May 5, 1982, pp. 1, 8.

March, J. G., and Simon, H. A. *Organizations.* New York: Wiley, 1958.

Martorana, S. V., and Smutz, W. "State Legislation: The Transition to the 80s." *Community and Junior College Journal,* 1981, *51* (6), 32–36.

"Measuring the Amount of Training in American Business." National conference of the American Society for Training and Development, Washington, D.C., Feb. 1983.

Medsker, L. L., and Tillery, D. *Breaking the Access Barrier: A Profile of Two-Year Colleges.* New York: McGraw-Hill, 1971.

Miami-Dade Community College. "An Individualized Learning System at Miami-Dade Community College." Paper presented at a meeting of the League for Innovation in the Community College, Dallas, Tex., 1982.

Miami Herald. "Japanese Widen Lead in I.Q. Scores." May 21, 1982, p. 7A.

Miller, T. K., and Prince, J. S. *The Future of Student Affairs: A Guide to Student Development for Tomorrow's Higher Education.* San Francisco: Jossey-Bass, 1976.

Millett, J. D. *Management, Governance and Leadership.* New York: AMACOM, 1980.

Mink, O. G. "A Composite Counseling Strategy." In J. E. Roueche and O. G. Mink (Eds.), *Improving Student Motivation.* Manchaca, Tex.: Sterling Swift, 1976.

Monroe, C. R. *Profile of the Community College: A Handbook.* San Francisco: Jossey-Bass, 1972.

Moon, R. (Ed.). *New Directions for a Learning Society.* New York: College Entrance Examination Board, 1981.

Morrison, J. R., and Ferrante, R. "The Public Two-Year College and the Culturally Different." Paper presented at the annual meeting of the American Educational Research Association, New Orleans, Feb. 1973. (ED 073 765)

Mortimer, K. P., and McConnell, T. R. *Sharing Authority Effectively: Participation, Interaction, and Discretion.* San Francisco: Jossey-Bass, 1978.

National Assessment of Educational Progress. *Reading, Thinking and Writing: Results from the 1979–80 National Assessment of Reading and Literature.* Denver: National Assessment of Educational Progress, Education Commission of the States, 1981.

National Commission on Allied Health Education. *The Future of Allied Health Education: New Alliances for the 1980s.* San Francisco: Jossey-Bass, 1980.

Parnell, D. "Will Belly Dancing Be Our Nemesis?" *Community Services Catalyst,* 1982, *3,* 4–5.

Perrow, C. "Disintegrating Social Sciences." *Phi Delta Kappan,* June 1982, *63* (10), 684–688.

Pincus, F. "The False Promises of Community Colleges: Class Conflict and Vocational Education." *Harvard Educational Review,* 1980, *50* (3), 332–361.

Redmon, T. "Preparation for College: A National Approach." *Journal of Remedial and Developmental Education,* 1982, *5* (2), 3–5.

Richardson, R. C., Jr. (Ed.). *New Directions for Community Colleges: Reforming College Governance,* no. 10. San Francisco: Jossey-Bass, 1975.

Richardson, R. C., Jr., Blocker, E. E., and Bender, L. W. *Governance in the Two-Year College.* Englewood Cliffs, N.J.: Prentice-Hall, 1972.

Richardson, R. C., Jr., Fisk, E. C., and Okun, M. A. *Literacy in the Open-Access College.* San Francisco: Jossey-Bass, 1983.

Richardson, R. C., Jr., and Leslie, L. L. *The Impossible Dream? Financing Community College's Evolving Mission.* Horizons Issue Monograph Series. Washington, D.C. and Los Angeles: American Association of Community and Junior Colleges and ERIC Clearinghouse for Junior Colleges, 1980.

Richardson, R. C., Jr., and others. *Literacy Development in Community Colleges.* Technical Report for Project NIE–400–78-0061. Tempe: Arizona State University, May 1982.

Rio Salado Community College. "Intensive In-Plant Technician Training Model." Unpublished proposal submitted to the

Fund for the Improvement of Post-Secondary Education, Phoenix, Ariz., Nov. 1981.

Rogers, C. R. *On Becoming a Person: A Therapist's View of Psychotherapy.* Boston: Houghton Mifflin, 1961.

Rogers, R. F. "Theories Underlying Student Development." In D. G. Creamer (Ed.), *Student Development in Higher Education.* Cincinnati: American College Personnel Association, 1980.

Romine, L. "Quality Circles That Enhance Productivity." *Community and Junior College Journal,* Nov. 1981, *52* (3), 30–31.

Romoser, R. C. *Results of the Second Assessment Study of Developmental Education Programs in Ohio.* Prepared for the Ohio Statewide Advisory Committee on Developmental Education, 1978. (ED 157 587)

Ross, E. D. *Democracy's College: The Land-Grant Movement in the Formative Stages.* Ames: Iowa State University Press, 1942.

Ross, R. A. *The Reverse Transfer Phenomenon at Piedmont Virginia Community College* (Research report no. 3–82). Charlottesville: Piedmont Virginia Community College, 1982.

Roueche, J. E. "Let's Get Serious About the High-Risk Student." *Community and Junior College Journal,* Sept. 1978, 28–32.

Roueche, J. E. *Holistic Literacy in College Teaching.* New York: Media Systems, 1980.

Roueche, J. E. "Don't Close the Door." *Community and Junior College Journal,* Dec.-Jan. 1981–1982, 17–23.

Roueche, J. E. Closing address delivered at the 9th Annual Developmental Education Conference, Chicago, April 1982.

Roueche, J. E., and Snow, J. J. *Overcoming Learning Problems: A Guide to Developmental Education in College.* San Francisco: Jossey-Bass, 1977.

Roueche, J. E., and Wheeler, C. L. "Instructional Procedures for the Disadvantaged." *Improving College and University Teaching,* 1973, *21,* 222–225.

Rudolph, F. *Curriculum: A History of the American Undergraduate Course of Study Since 1636.* San Francisco: Jossey-Bass, 1977.

Salancik, G. R. "Commitment is Too Easy!" *Organizational Dynamics,* 1977, *6* (1), 62-80.

Salancik, G. R. "Commitment and the Control of Organizational Behavior and Belief." In R. M. Steens and L. W. Porter (Eds.), *Motivation and Work Behavior.* New York: McGraw-Hill, 1979.

Sayers, D. L. *Are Women Human?* Grand Rapids, Mich.: William B. Eerdmans, 1971.

Shaffer, R. H. "Analyzing Institutional Constraints upon Student Development Activities." In D. G. Creamer (Ed.), *Student Development in Higher Education.* Cincinnati: American College Personnel Association, 1980.

Sharon, A. T. "Assessing the Effectiveness of Remedial College Courses." *Journal of Experimental Education,* 1972, *41,* 60–62.

Shearon, R. W., and others. *Putting Learning to Work: A Profile of Students in North Carolina's Community Colleges, Technical Institutes, and Technical Colleges.* Raleigh: North Carolina State University Press, 1980.

Spann, M. G., Jr. "Building a Developmental Education Program." In J. E. Roueche (Ed.), *New Directions for Higher Education: Increasing Basic Skills by Developmental Studies,* no. 20. San Francisco: Jossey-Bass, 1977.

Staff of the Office of Research. *The American Freshman: National Norms for Fall 1971.* Washington, D.C.: American Council on Education, 1971.

Steers, R. M. "Antecedents and Outcomes of Organizational Commitment." *Administrative Science Quarterly,* 1977, *22,* 46–56.

"Students Getting Younger at Community Colleges." *Roanoke Times,* Roanoke, Va., June 25, 1982, p. 1.

Toffler, A. *The Third Wave.* New York: Bantam Books, 1981.

"U.S. Aid Should Go First to Students Likely to Graduate, Bok Suggests." *Chronicle of Higher Education,* May 5, 1982, p. 1.

U.S. Bureau of the Census. *Historical Statistics of the United States, Colonial Times to 1970. Bicentennial Edition,* Part 1. Washington, D.C.: U.S. Bureau of the Census, 1975.

U.S. Department of Labor, Bureau of Labor Statistics. *Eco-*

nomic Report of the President, 1980 and the Annual Report of the Council of Economic Advisors. Washington, D.C.: U.S. Government Printing Office, 1981.

U.S. National Center for Education Statistics. The Condition of Education, 1980. Washington, D.C.: U.S. Government Printing Office, 1980a.

U.S. National Center for Education Statistics. Participation in Adult Education, 1978. Washington, D.C.: U.S. Department of Education, 1980b.

U.S. National Center for Education Statistics. Digest of Education Statistics, 1981. Washington, D.C.: U.S. Government Printing Office, 1982a.

U.S. National Center for Education Statistics. The Condition of Education, 1982. Washington, D.C.: U.S. Government Printing Office, 1982b.

U.S. National Center for Education Statistics. Unpublished data from "Opening Fall Enrollment in Higher Education, 1978 and 1980." Washington, D.C.: U.S. Department of Education, 1982c.

Vaughan, G. B. "Thomas Jefferson, the Community College, and the Pursuit of Education." Community College Frontiers, 1980, 8 (4), 4–10.

Vaughan, G. B. The Community College in America: A Pocket History. American Association of Community and Junior Colleges Pocket Reader no. 4. Washington, D.C.: American Association of Community and Junior Colleges, 1982a.

Vaughan, G. B. "Burnout: Threat to Presidential Effectiveness." Community and Junior College Journal, 1982b, 52 (5), 10–13.

Vitalo, R. L. "A Course in Life Skills." Journal of College Student Personnel, 1974, 15, 34–39.

Wagoner, J. L., Jr. Thomas Jefferson and the Education of a New Nation. Bloomington, Ind.: Phi Delta Kappa Educational Foundation, 1976.

Watkins, B. T. "21 Million Adults Found Taking Part in Continuing Education Programs." Chronicle of Higher Education, May 5, 1982, p. 8.

Whited, C. "There's a Lesson for Educators in 3 R's Crisis." Miami Herald, Jan. 29, 1982, p. 2B.

Wilms, W. W. *Public and Proprietary Vocational Training: A Study of Effectiveness.* Lexington, Mass.: Lexington Books, 1975.

Wilms, W. W. *Vocational Education and Social Mobility: A Study of Public and Proprietary School Dropouts and Graduates.* Los Angeles: Graduate School of Education, University of California Press, June 1980.

Wohlers, R. *Statistics on Community College Faculty, Administrators, and Presidents.* Washington, D.C.: American Association of Community and Junior Colleges, 1982.

Yarrington, R. "Issues in Literacy." Unpublished manuscript, American Association of Community and Junior Colleges, Washington, D.C., 1982.

Zorn, E. "Why Can't Johnny Log On?" *St. Petersburg Independent,* Aug. 18, 1981, p. 17A.

Index

125, 130-131; and residency,
126, 132-133
Drucker, P., 233
Dziech, B. W., 55-75

E

Easton, J., 80, 256
Economic forces: enrollments related to, 208-210; impact of,
206-207
Edge, D., 165, 254-255
Educational Facilities Laboratory,
133, 255
Educational programs: analysis of,
159-185; background on, 159-
162; and collegiate education,
175-182; and community educa-
tion, 168-174; and compensa-
tory education, 162-168; leadership for, 182-185; trends in, responses to, 159-161
Educational Resources Information
Center (ERIC), 10, 95; Clearinghouse for Junior Colleges, 200
Educational Testing Service, 156
Eells, W. C., 4, 18
Eliason, N. C., 57, 70, 255
Eliot, C. W., 140
Elitism, growth of, 237-239
Elsner, P. A., 139-158, 243
English as a Second Language
(ESL), concept of, 24-25
Enrollments: and demographics,
208; and economics, 208-210;
and finances, 209-210; and fi-
nancial aid, 213-214; and popu-
lation trends, 205, 213-214;
shifting patterns of, 41; and so-
cietal factors, 208-209; and un-
employment, 214-215
Estee Lauder, collaboration by, 226
Evaluation, program, for develop-
mental education, 95-96
Exxon: collaboration by, 226;
grant from, 150

F

Faculty: and collaboration, 228-
229; and commitment building,
186-187, 192-193, 196, 199-

200, 202-203; and community
education, 171-172; and compensatory education, 164-166;
development of, and collaboration, 228-229; for developmental
education, 89-91; and general
education, 113, 118, 120; num-
ber of women as, 59-61; salaries
of, 58-60; union of, and commit-
ment, 193, 202; women as, 58-66
Faure report, 56
Federal Executive Institute, 223
Federal government, policies of,
206-208
Federal Reserve Board, 206
Fenske, R. H., 139, 255
Ferrante, R., 77, 259
Finances, and enrollments, 209-210,
213-214
Fiser, D., 240
Fisk, E. C., 160
Florida, transfer information in,
156
Folwell, W. W., 3
Freeark, K., 70, 252
French, M., 55-56, 61, 255
Friedlander, J., 78, 168, 255
Functions: developmental educa-
tion as, 76-99; general education
as, 100-121; student services as,
139-158; transfer as, 122-138
Fund for the Improvement of Post-
secondary Education, 153
Funding: community college, 13;
and community education, 169-
170, 172-173; and community
services, 15-16; and developmental education, 82, 97; and leadership, 183; and mission, 14-16;
and transfer function, 34-35

G

Gaff, J. G., 116, 255
Galambos, E. C., 235, 255
Gallup Poll, 177, 255
Gardner, J., 9
General education: analysis of, 100-
121; approach of, 109; and as-
sessment for reformulation, 114-
115; background on, 100-101;